ALSO BY DEBORAH RUDACILLE

The Scalpel and the Butterfly

The Riddle of Gender

ROOTS OF STEEL

ROOTS OF STEEL

Boom and Bust
in an American Mill Town

DEBORAH RUDACILLE

PANTHEON BOOKS   NEW YORK

Published in the United States by Pantheon Books,

a division of Random House, Inc., New York,

and in Canada by Random House of Canada Limited, Toronto.

Pantheon Books and colophon are registered trademarks of Random House, Inc.

Library of Congress Cataloging-in-Publication Data

Rudacille, Deborah.

Roots of steel : boom and bust in an American mill town / Deborah Rudacille.

p.   cm.

Includes bibliographical references and index.

ISBN 978-0-375-42368-0

1. Steel industry and trade—Maryland—Sparrows Point—History.   2. Sparrows Point (Md.)—

Economic conditions.   3. Sparrows Point (Md.)—History.   I. Title.

HD9518.S6R83 2010

338.4'76691420975271—dc22   2009020962

www.pantheonbooks.com

Printed in the United States of America

First Edition

2 4 6 8 9 7 5 3 1

For Amelia, Jake, and Sofia

Two are better than one: they get a good wage for their labor. . . .

Where a lone man may be overcome, two together can resist.

A three-ply cord is not easily broken.

—ECCLESIASTES 4:9, 12

CONTENTS

ROOTS OF STEEL

HOURS OF STAR

◆ PATRIOTS ◆

In Dundalk, Independence Day is a sacred celebration—its holy feast beer and hard-shell crabs, and its central ritual the biggest parade in the state. Stars-and-stripes bunting or a flag drapes from every house, and families set out their lawn chairs the night before to secure a spot along the parade route. At nine in the morning, earsplitting sirens from the fire trucks open the parade, followed by the thrumming of drums from marching bands and the steady shuffling of veterans' groups. Hand-painted banners proclaiming LET FREEDOM RING flap above local residents in colonial costumes riding on the floats of civic and church groups.

"Whenever the governor or members of Congress come to Dundalk for the parade, they always talk about the American pride," said John Olszewski Jr., a twenty-six-year-old state delegate, who, like me, grew up in this blue-collar community just outside Baltimore. I once marched in the Independence Day parade myself as a clumsy eleven-year-old majorette prone to dropping her baton, but I still remember my pride and excitement as I high-stepped up and down the leafy streets in my green-and-white uniform, for once a participant rather than an observer.

After the parade, everyone follows the charred aroma of pit beef and the sweet scent of fried dough to nearby Heritage Park, where a three-day festival provides an opportunity to run into old friends, classmates, and neighbors. People who grew up in Dundalk tend to come home for the holiday in the same way that others return for Thanksgiving, Passover, or Christmas. It is, as Olszewski pointed out, "the first day of the year."

Dundalk's flamboyant celebration of the Fourth is rooted in its history. A few miles east of the parade route, a band of citizen soldiers fought off British troops headed for Baltimore during the War of 1812. The invaders were repulsed by land and by sea in the battle memorialized in our national anthem. In the twentieth century, tens of thousands of Americans poured into the community from Pennsylvania, New York, New Jersey, the Carolinas, the Midwest, and Appalachia to work in industries critical to national defense—shipbuilding, steelmaking, and aviation—during World War II.

Many of those war workers remained, joining the European immigrants and Southern migrants drawn to town by the manufacturing jobs that gave Baltimore its iconic image as the hardworking, hard-drinking working-class oasis lovingly parodied by its native son filmmaker John Waters. "You can look far and wide, but you'll never discover a stranger city with such extreme style," Waters once said. "It's as if every eccentric in the South decided to move North, ran out of gas in Baltimore, and decided to stay."

Waters's description of the city goes double for the working-class district below its southeastern border, whose residents have long been the butt of local jokes for their extreme accents, hard dirty jobs, and retro tastes in music, fashion, and home décor. Growing up there gave me an enduring appreciation for Lynyrd Skynyrd that is hard to explain to those with more sophisticated musical tastes, and I loved Pabst Blue Ribbon beer long before urban hipsters wearing trucker hats adopted it as their brew of choice a few years ago. My father always had a six-pack of Pabst in our avocado-green refrigerator in the seventies.

The mullet, stonewashed jeans, and dark wood paneling never went out of style in Dundalk. But it was there that I learned the virtues of hard work, community, and family. My paternal forebears arrived in the 1920s, and my maternal grandparents—first-generation Italian Americans—during World War II. Most of them worked at one time or another at the colossal Sparrows Point steelworks or its shipyards rimming Baltimore harbor, just a few nautical miles from the broad waters of the Chesapeake Bay.

Grover Cleveland was president when the Pennsylvania Steel Company broke ground at Sparrows Point in 1887. The works and company town grew slowly, surviving recessions and market downturns until shortly before the United States entered World War I. Flush with money from arms sales to the warring nations of Europe, Bethlehem Steel Corporation, Pennsylvania Steel's rival, bought the Point in 1916, inheriting its Chesapeake works and company town. From its earliest days Sparrows Point was the most racially diverse steel mill in the country—but in those days diversity meant native-born whites on top, immigrants and blacks on the bottom.

The company long recruited African American men from Virginia, the Carolinas, and farther south. "It provided a great foundation for folks who were making that transition from farmland to big-city life," said Deidra Bishop, the director of community affairs for East Baltimore for the Johns Hopkins Institutions. Bishop's grandfather, born in 1905, and various uncles worked at the Point. "For my family it provided a very good life—one that was not fraught with economic uncertainty. And it provided a circle of friendship for the men as well."

That was true for white men like my Virginia-born grandfather too. Born in the shadows of the Shenandoah Mountains, he came to Sparrows Point looking for work in 1927, roomed with my great-grandparents, and married their daughter. They had five sons together, and the first three, including my father, were born in "the bungalows"—tiny workers' cottages on the edge of the company town.

Southern roots were shared by many in the town, yet barely a generation after the Civil War, the sons of rebels and the sons of slaves were toiling together on Sparrows Point, a workingman's utopia conjured by a former Union major. "Blacks and whites got along good," in the mills and town, eighty-year-old Lee Douglas Jr., who followed his father and uncles from South Carolina to the Point, told me in 2006. "Only thing was, whites didn't want anybody promoting to their jobs."

Work, family, and community were tightly braided together on Sparrows Point, where an employee needed a letter from his foreman to rent a house and where three generations of some families lived surrounded by coke ovens, open hearth furnaces, rolling mills, and enormous piles of limestone and coal. During the Great Depression, Bethlehem let laid-off workers and their families stay in their company houses and charge groceries at the company store. The United Steelworkers of America—voted into the plant in 1941—also "really helped carry people" during the steel strikes of the fifties and sixties, Ed Gorman, a retired steelworker and union vice president, told me, by giving rent money to those in danger of losing their homes in nearby Dundalk and Baltimore and groceries to those who couldn't afford to feed their families. That commitment bred a fierce loyalty to the company and the union.

Year after year, the ovens, furnaces, and finishing mills of the great works on the Chesapeake belched fire and smoke, crafting the ships and armaments that helped win World Wars I and II and churning out the raw steel and finished products that were the backbone of postwar America. In 1959 Sparrows Point claimed the title of the largest steelworks in the world. By then, Bethlehem (known locally as "Bethlem") employed over forty thousand Maryland residents at its steelworks and shipyards, and the fortunes of thousands of small businesses throughout the state were tied to Sparrows Point.

Steelworkers were among the best paid of all Baltimore's industrial workers in the postwar boom, and their union wages sent many children of steel like me to college. But by 1985 the American steel industry was on the ropes, and on the Point, as elsewhere, jobs were cut, layoffs were made permanent, and mills were closed. There is still a steelworks on Sparrows Point today, but it employs fewer than three thousand people, compared with the thirty-six thousand who worked on-site at its peak. Employees endured four changes of ownership from 2003 to 2008, as globalization and consolidation reshaped the industry.

Still, those who survived the upheaval were luckier than most. Until the recent recession, the wages of some hourly workers were topping $100,000 a year. "They are making more money than we ever made," LeRoy McLelland Sr., a Bethlehem retiree, told me in the run-up to the 2008 presidential election. "But there are less people making it."

McLelland labored for forty-two years in the tin mill at Sparrows Point. Like a lot of Bethlehem retirees, he is "bitter, very bitter" about the company's 2001 bankruptcy and subsequent sale of assets to the private-equity-funded International Steel Group. That deal stripped retirees of health and life insurance, liquidated their company stock, and cut deeply into many pensions, which were taken over by the federally backed Pension Benefit Guaranty Corporation. Shorn of fiscal responsibility for Bethlehem's retirees, ISG became hugely profitable, netting its investors billions when ISG was folded into the global steel goliath ArcelorMittal two years later. The retirees have neither forgiven nor forgotten the Bethlehem and ISG executives and bankruptcy judge who sealed the deal.

"We looked forward to retirement as something we would enjoy," McLelland said, "not worry from month to month about whether the PBGC could afford our pensions, whether Social Security is still gonna be there kicking in a dollar or two, whether Medicare is still going to be available. It's a daily fear that each and every one of us has."

It's a refrain I heard often as I researched this book. Like similar communities around the country, Dundalk has been hard-hit by deindustrialization, and its people haven't totally adjusted to the fact that the manufacturing jobs that were the basis of the community's prosperity are gone for good. Older folks mourn the passing of not only prosperity but the strong sense of pride and self-sufficiency that once defined Dundalk.

"We had Lever Brothers, General Motors, Crown Cork and Seal, Eastern Stainless Steel, Sparrows Point, the shipyard. We had all those big companies down here, and people were working," Judy Martin, a lifelong Dundalk resident, reminisced when I met her at the Independence Day celebrations in 2006. Judy had tinted one side of her white hair red and the other side blue and had sprinkled it with silver stars in honor of the day. But she wasn't in a very celebratory mood when we spoke at her home a few days later.

Throughout most of her life, Judy said, she knew all of her neighbors. "You used to hang over the fence. You used to say, 'Oh, we've got too much of this. Let's take it over to Patsy and see if she wants it.' Or knock on the door and say, 'Hey, Miz Minnehan, we're out of ice. Got any?' We'd all come together to help, to contribute to church baskets. Everybody looked out for everybody else." Those days are gone, she said. "Now everyone is so afraid of opening doors."

As the manufacturing jobs that once sustained the community have disappeared and older people have died off, newcomers who don't share the town's traditional values of hard work, family, and community service have moved in, and crime has gone up. Still, she won't leave. "I grew up here. All of my memories are here. I guess I'm just one of those people who sits back and prays and hopes that things won't get too bad."

I could see for myself that beneath the red-white-and-blue bravado, my hometown had grown rougher around the edges. "We have a lot of homeless now," Judy pointed out. "You never saw homeless people here before the nineties. At St. Rita's and the Methodist church, the soup kitchens are almost standing room only." Olszewski pointed out that gentrification of neighborhoods on the east side of the city pushed poorer people over the county line to Dundalk, where "housing is very affordable. So you see a proliferation of challenges like Section 8 and concentrations of low-income housing, which tend to attract additional crime activities and also can attract the need for additional social services."

Hearing about the community's troubles, I feel a great sadness. Though I haven't lived there in decades, some part of me has always remained a Dundalk girl. In recent years I've realized how much growing up there shaped me. The people I was raised among are extraordinarily generous—you can't enter someone's home without being offered food or drink—unpretentious, direct, and brutally honest. They tend to wear their hearts (and opinions) on their sleeves. If they like you, you'll know it, and if they don't—well, you won't be in any doubt about that either. As a child, I was often teased for always having my nose in a book, and formal education isn't especially prized in Dundalk. But that doesn't mean that its people aren't intensely interested in politics and current events or that they aren't great story-tellers.

The community wasn't a utopia. Like many teens and young adults, I was often frustrated by the narrowness and insularity of my hometown, summed up in a bumper sticker popular in the 1970s: LIVE, WORK, SHOP . . . DUNDALK. A stubborn self-sufficiency and suspicion of outsiders have always defined the community, for better or worse. Still, when my parents decided to move to a new suburban subdivision when I was in college, my brother and I both protested. Our new neighborhood seemed boring in comparison to Dundalk.

The racial attitudes of some community residents, including members of my own family, also bothered me growing up. My parents didn't raise my brother and me to be "prejudiced," as we called it back then, but we had very limited contact with people of other races. "You lived here and they lived there," as one of my sources phrased it. I can't remember any real discussions of civil rights as a child, but I do recall getting into violent arguments as a teenager with some of my brother's friends who had been raised in homes where the word "nigger" was in common use. I'm not saying that I never heard that word in my own extended family, because I did. But it was not used in our house nor in the homes of any of my friends.

Personal prejudice was, I believe, less in evidence than the systemic racism that long privileged white men on the job at Sparrows Point. Blacks and whites worked closely together in the mills, and many became friends. But a 1976 Department of Justice ruling altering union seniority rules in steel mills to promote black advancement shocked and angered many whites. "I lost a lot of good white friends when the consent decree came down," said Eddie Bartee Sr., the first African American president of USW Local 2609.

In 1977, the white steelworker LeRoy McLelland filed a lawsuit joined by about three hundred Sparrows Point employees (about 10 percent of whom were black, he said) to protest the ruling, which he still maintains was not about race but about seniority. "I got really irked that they could bring someone in from another part of the mill to take my seniority in the unit," he told me, recalling the frustration of those days. The U.S. Supreme Court's refusal to hear the case after a series of appeals was, he said, "a bitter pill to swallow."

Time has not so much changed his mind as given him a broader perspective. "If you were really to reach into your heart and look back, you would say to yourself that it was a case where they denied blacks the right to be on the mills on productive jobs other than the jobs no one else wanted," he said. "What makes it easier to identify is that it is so far back. But when you are sitting right in the middle of things, you don't see what's going on."

Younger steelworkers say that job elimination, not civil rights, defined their years on the Point. "For my father's generation, the battles were all about race," said Eddie Bartee Jr., who followed his grandfather, father, and uncles into the mill. "For us, it was about fighting to hold on to our jobs." Drastically reduced employment at Sparrows Point and the shutdown of the General Motors plant and other local factories have had a devastating effect on the black working class in Baltimore, said former circuit court judge Kenneth L. Johnson: "It has been the economic downfall of Baltimore blacks." Discriminatory hiring practices notwithstanding, those old dirty jobs at the Point put food on the table for a lot of black families, as well as white ones. "When those jobs moved away, it had a tremendous impact on the whites, but it had double that impact on blacks," Johnson said. "When there is an economic shift, those at the bottom rung take the greatest hit."

In little more than a generation, an industrial economy that enabled people without much formal education to create stable families and communities has become a technocratic one in which most of the nation's wealth—in the form of both wages and investment—flows inexorably to the best-educated, most affluent Americans. "A lot of workers feel like they've been betrayed," said Bill Barry, who teaches labor studies at the Community College of Baltimore County (CCBC), Dundalk campus. "They don't know who betrayed them, but they are trying to personalize it. Some blame the unions, some blame the companies, some blame the government." That frustration has fueled a populist rage stoked by right-wing talk radio hosts and cable news anchors who offer few solutions but a long list of enemies—liberals, immigrants, "elites," and, the best target of all these days, the president and members of his administration.

Barack Obama was criticized when he pointed out during his presidential campaign that many people in blue-collar communities are bitter and angry about their losses. But he was only saying what anyone who comes from a place like Dundalk knows full well is true. Over the past thirty years, its residents have watched a hard-won prosperity and security slip away. Though they don't know for sure who is to blame, they do know what they want: a return to the old days, when the jobs that could support a family were plentiful, streets were safe, and workers could take pride in their contributions to the nation's wealth and power.

Still, few who make a living catering to populist rage are willing to point out that the economic pain of many formerly prosperous working-class neighborhoods has been worsened by a lack of family and community emphasis on education. "For young kids today, it's really stacked against them," Bill Knoerlein, a Dundalk resident and retired steelworker, told me. "The better-paying jobs are based on technological knowledge, but you need basic skills, and a lot of kids coming out of high school aren't prepared." In fact, according to the 2000 census, a little more than 30 percent of Dundalk residents 25 and older did not complete high school. Another 20 percent had earned a high school diploma, but only 4.8 percent of Dundalk residents had graduated from community college, and 4.4 percent had earned a bachelor's degree. A tiny 1.8 percent of Dundalk residents had earned a graduate or professional degree in 2000, the year before the Bethlehem bankruptcy.

"Decades ago you could leave high school and make more money than people who went to college" at local factories and mills, Olszewski pointed out. That is no longer true, but many still view higher education as a luxury, not a necessity. His parents, who were high school graduates, "instilled in me at a very early age the importance of an education," he said. "I imagine that part of that was seeing those other options fade away." Aris Melissaratos, former secretary for the Maryland Department of Economic and Business Development, said that "the Point provided great jobs to a lot of people that never finished high school. But that's over. Today all of our population needs to focus on finishing high school and getting skills."

Even blue-collar distribution jobs at the port are automated, Melissaratos said. "So distribution workers will need to be knowledge workers as well—and the knowledge economy will demand much better education." He told me that the largest private employer in the state is now Johns Hopkins. With 46,000 employees, the university and its health system and affiliates now provide more jobs in Maryland than Bethlehem did at its peak.

Health care comprises a big chunk of the state's economy, and at CCBC Bill Barry sees a number of people heading for hospital jobs. "There are a lot of workers here, not necessarily from Sparrows Point, who are coming out of manufacturing and being retrained at age forty-five to be nurses, physical therapists, stuff like that," he said. "It's interesting because nursing has traditionally been a woman's job. But [displaced industrial workers] look at what is the high-paying industry in the Baltimore area and it's nursing." Younger students enrolling just after high school are looking for job security, he said. "They are thinking nursing or dental hygiene or police officer because these are the growth industries. And so instead of going to Sparrows Point they'll come here to get into a certain line of work."

Putting on a uniform seems the best alternative to some young high school graduates. "For my class [1997], the military was the new Bethlehem Steel," Andrew Layman, a thirty-year-old Iraqi war veteran, told me. "Easily ten percent of my graduating class went into the various services. It offers the same thing Beth Steel once offered—a steady paycheck." Given the community's strong roots in defense work and proud history of service, this is not surprising. But military service alone will not arrest the community's downward economic slide. Layman, an air force officer who served as an analyst for the U.S. Army in Baghdad, took a job with a government contractor in Saudi Arabia after leaving the service and worked there for two years. "For other vets I imagine that things are tough right now," he said. "Enlisted guys returning without degrees are probably forced to reenlist with outside firms not hiring." Officers and enlisted men and women with college degrees are likely faring better, he pointed out. He has taken advantage of the GI Bill to return to school.

Olszewski succinctly summed up the challenges facing Dundalk and communities like it around the country today: "How do we retool and equip people who are still in those working areas as industrial jobs are failing—and what do we do when industry abandons people who gave their entire lives to it?"

There are no easy answers to these questions. But as President Obama noted in his inaugural address, "It has been the risk-takers, the doers, the makers of things—some celebrated, but more often men and women obscure in their labor—who have carried us up the long, rugged path towards prosperity and freedom." The struggles and sacrifices of such men and women inspired me to write this book. The community where I was raised has responded to times of enormous challenge in the past with courage, fortitude, and resolve. I believe that if they are given the help they need to retool, retrain, and rebuild the community, those qualities will once again carry them through to a new day and provide a fitting tribute to their (and my) roots of steel.

• ROOTS •

On a sultry August day in 2006, I spent an afternoon driving around what remains of the old company town of Sparrows Point with a family friend named Willy Cohill. I have known Willy all my life. His wife, Betty, is my mother's best friend and my brother's godmother, and they lived one street over in the neighborhood where I grew up. I spent a lot of time in their house as a kid, and I greatly admired their 1960s silver Christmas tree, which had a spinning wheel that cast a mesmerizing rainbow of colors. My mother has always said that my father would never have been able to go to college in his forties while working full-time as a steelworker if it hadn't been for Willy, who took all of his three-to-eleven shifts for him.

Though he is over eighty and almost died of congestive heart failure in 2005, when I called to ask him to share his memories of growing up in the company town, Willy agreed right away but said that we couldn't do it on Friday. An old-school Catholic, he attends mass on the first Friday of every month and then goes out for a few beers with his retired steelworker buddies. He has known most of them since he was a kid because, like him, they grew up in Sparrows Point and began working for Bethlehem Steel as teenagers.

"I started when I was fourteen," he told me, "making tags in the wire mill for my dad." In the early years of World War II, Bethlehem hired the teenage sons of employees for summer jobs because they needed all the workers they could get. After graduating from high school, most of those young men entered the service, returning to the mills as full-time employees once the war was over. "Your seniority continued when you went into the service, and when you came home, you went right back to the Point," he said. "Some of the old people down there, by the time they were sixty-five, had fifty years of service."

I asked Willy what the most dangerous job on the Point was, and without hesitation he replied, "The open hearths. You could get burned real bad there, or you could fall in those ladles, which some-times happened." Feeling smothered by the heat that dropped on us like a soggy blanket when we stepped out of the car, I said that the Point must have been a terribly hot place to work in the summer, and Willy laughed. "Aw, it was nothing *but* hot. It was hot!"

Though I've known him all of my life, I learned many new things about Willy that day, like how he had helped liberate concentration camps in Germany in 1945, just after he was shipped overseas in the final days of the war. "Those poor kids had legs on them not bigger than my finger," he said. "What they did to them poor Jews, nobody should have done to them. It was sickening." I asked him if the things he had seen had given him nightmares. He said no, but "one of my brothers was in Korea and Vietnam. He has nightmares."

After he was discharged in 1946, Willy scored an easy job in the chemical lab at Sparrows Point analyzing the steel that came out of the furnaces. "The heaviest thing I had to lift was ten grams," he said. "But I had $3,800 mustering-out pay, and I didn't like working Satur-days and Sundays, so I started tending bar and hacking cabs." After knocking around for two years, he finally took a job at Signode, a steel strapping company down the road from Sparrows Point, where he remained until retirement. Unlike Bethlehem, Signode wasn't a union shop. "But every time the Bethlem boys got a raise, so did we," he said.

One thing I already knew about Willy but didn't ask him about was how, after he retired but before he got so sick, he used to fix breakfast for the mostly African American county sanitation workers when they came by to pick up his trash twice a week. He would get up early, make the men bacon, eggs, and toast, and set out the meal with orange juice, coffee, and beer on folding tables in the basement because Betty wouldn't let him entertain in her kitchen men who spent their days driving around on the back of garbage trucks.

"You know Willy feeds the garbagemen," Ed Gorman said when Willy's name came up during our talk, and I nodded. The two men have known each other since they were children growing up on the Point, where Willy's family occupied a unique position in the segregated company town.

"We were from what you might call the other side of the tracks," Willy told me. "People on the other streets looked down on people who lived on H Street and in the bungalows." Former residents of the Point like Willy are sensitive to these things. Your family's address told the whole world what kind of job your father had and where your family stood on the social ladder. If you lived on B or C Street, your father was a manager or a foreman and you were a member of the town's elite. E and F streets were reserved for the families of skilled workers.

An address on I or J Street was a marker of a different kind. In the town's early decades, I and J were cut off from the rest of the town by a wide creek spanned by a bridge. Hundreds of men walked over the bridge each day to work in the mills on the other side of the town. All the residents of the North Side were black, save for the Cohills and another white family who lived on H Street, the only "white" street across the creek.

When he was a child on Sparrows Point, "colored people couldn't walk on H Street," Willy said. "They couldn't walk in the white neighborhoods at all back in those days. Cops would run 'em off." That didn't change until the fifties, he said, but even before then, there was some mixing between the residents of H Street and I and J.

"My family had a little newsstand down there, and most of our clientele was colored," he recalled. He and his four brothers organized a private athletic league—"all H Street and the bungalow boys and the colored boys." The Cohills preferred organizing their own teams to playing for the YMCA ones in town, he said, because the townsfolk "were snooty. We stayed with the people from the bungalows and I and J streets."

Despite his affection for the community in which he was raised, Willy was willing to discuss the underside of life and work at Sparrows Point in those days. "In the mills, if you were a Catholic, you were low man on the totem pole," he told me. "Masons had all the power back then—Lutherans, Presbyterians. If you had a Mason ring, you were a big shot." But if Catholics like the Cohills had a tough time advancing, black men had it worse. "They always give them the hot jobs, the dirty jobs," he said.

He saw the color system at work in the wire mill. "I was the weighmaster in the wire mill. When that wire would come out, it was red-hot. And the colored folk used to have to go in and put tags on the wire." Willy didn't question this arrangement, but it's clear that he felt a much greater degree of kinship with his neighbors on I and J streets than was typical for whites of his generation. He may still say "colored" rather than "black" or "African American," but his affection and respect for his former neighbors are genuine. The families from I and J streets "were good people, very good people," he told me.

Willy's sister, Helen, the only girl in a family of five boys, agreed that her family had good relationships with their African American neighbors. "We respected them," she said. "And that's all they wanted, really."

I wondered if that was true, so I asked Eddie Bartee Sr. what it was like to grow up on the North Side. Tall and powerfully built, Bartee became the first African American vice president (and later president) of United Steelworkers of America Local 2609 in 1963. He was two years old when his father brought his family to Sparrows Point in 1936. Some white kids played with black kids, he told me.

"We used to shoot marbles together. The Costello boys from the bungalows, we used to play football against them. Some of the white boys used to come to the black poolroom to shoot pool. The Cohill boys would shoot pool in the black poolroom."

When I informed him that most of the white people I had spoken with told me that in the town blacks and whites "got along good," he laughed and said the reason for that was simple: "Everyone knew their place, and they more or less stayed in their place." Black residents of Sparrows Point could not eat in the restaurants in town, though they could get carryout. Lunchrooms, locker rooms, and other public facilities in the mills were also segregated. When the black men of his father's generation went hunting, he told me, they brought their white bosses back squirrel and deer meat. They also brought them cakes baked by their wives, some of whom worked as cooks or domestics in the big houses on B and C streets. Bartee recalled that some of his father's friends did handyman work at their foremen's homes on their days off.

"Let's put it this way," he said. "My father put up with a lot that I wouldn't put up with, just like I put up with a lot that my son wouldn't put up with."

Still, North Side families stuck together, he told me, and the values he absorbed in the community—hard work, mutual courtesy and respect, churchgoing, and education—remain with him today, as does the feeling of neighborly solidarity and support during good times and bad. There were eight children in his family, Bartee said, including two sets of twins, and when his father, who had respiratory problems, got sick, "people would take money up at the church or in the mill. There was a lot of that in the steel mill. If somebody was off sick for a long time, they would take up a collection. In those days people helped each other."

Just about everyone I've spoken to who grew up in the town of Sparrows Point—black or white—has said that they feel lucky to have grown up there, even though by contemporary standards, their living conditions were far from ideal. My father's cousin Donald Lindemann was born in 1933 in one of the tiny 550-square-foot bungalows on the outskirts of the company town. Donald said that his family "never went hungry," but he also admitted that as a child he was usually forced to put cardboard in his shoes near the end of winter. "You'd only get one pair of shoes a year. For Easter every year you'd get a shirt, a pair of trousers, and a new pair of shoes"—which had to last until the next spring.

He slept in the same bed as his older brother until he was fourteen and his brother went into the navy. "My sister Anna slept on a little twin bed, all three of us in the same room. The house was heated by a little potbellied stove, and in winter my mother would wake me up in the middle of the night to go out and get a bucket of coal from out in the shed." He did it without complaining. Children on the Point were raised to respect their elders. "I don't care if they are one hour older than you, you'd better say, 'Yes, sir' and 'No, sir,' 'Yes, ma'am' and 'No, ma'am.' Blacks too," he recalled his father saying. "And that's the way I grew up."

> *I hear the distant thunder-hum,*
> *Maryland!*
> *The Old Line's bugle, fife, and drum,*
> *Maryland!*
> *She is not dead, nor deaf, nor dumb—*
> *Huzza! she spurns the Northern scum!*
>
> —"MARYLAND, MY MARYLAND" (STATE SONG)

Long before the town of Sparrows Point was founded, Baltimore was known for its iron. In 1773 there were eight forges and furnaces in the city and surrounding counties. To make iron, you needed iron ore—and there were ore banks aplenty snaking through the rich soil in the Baltimore area—wood that could be converted to charcoal to fuel the fires, and lime (calcium carbonate) to "flux" the mix. Oyster shells, abundant in the Chesapeake Bay watershed, were the first source of lime. Later, limestone deposits were discovered nearby.

The process of making iron changed hardly at all for a hundred and fifty years. Dig the ore, fell the trees, use the timber for charcoal to fuel the furnace, mix the ore and the lime, and "blast" the mix to separate out the impurities, leaving a liquid waste product, slag, floating on top. Then drain the slag and cool the iron, shaping it into bars (pig iron) to sell to other industries or to immediately transform into commercial products (kettles, pots, farm equipment) in your own forge.

Some of the region's most prosperous and esteemed citizens were investors in the colonial ironworks. Charles Carroll, the only Marylander (and the only Catholic) to sign the Declaration of Independence, was part owner of the Baltimore Iron Works, one of the largest and most successful companies in eighteenth-century America and the first iron firm financed exclusively by colonists. The father and brother of George Washington were shareholders in the Principio Company, a big British conglomerate that owned and operated three furnaces in the Baltimore area.

Planters like Carroll and the Washingtons were particularly welcome as investors because they contributed a commodity that greatly reduced production costs: slave labor. In 1773, Charles Carroll wrote to a fellow investor that the Baltimore Iron Works should consider completely replacing their paid workers with convicts and slaves. Purchasing "35 or 40 young, healthy and stout country-born Negroes" would, he said, save two-thirds of what the company spent on wages. By the time of the American Revolution, industrial slavery in the ironworks was common practice.

Early on, owners tried to lure skilled ironworkers from England and Germany to the colonies, planning to use forced labor (convicts and slaves) only for the brute tasks of cutting down trees, mining ore, and feeding the forges. But they soon found that free men were nearly impossible to control and that ironworkers were a particularly unruly bunch. If they didn't like the work or had a problem with the foreman, free men would simply walk off the job. Slaves were not only "cheaper, more reliable and pliable," but some were skilled at making iron, either because they had brought the knowledge from Africa or had been owned by someone who taught them the trade.

Iron making was a very lucrative business, but profits were heavily
dependent on the skill and cooperation of workers. Negligence or outright sabotage by hostile workers could seriously disrupt business and
result in inferior products. Consequently, colonial ironmasters used
both the carrot and the stick to manage workers. Some literally
worked their slaves to death, using the whip and the threat of worse
punishment to push them to the limit of human endurance. But others
set up incentive systems, awarding extra food, alcohol, and in some
cases cash to industrious workers, including "hired-out" slaves, who
exceeded production quotas.

By the Civil War, Baltimore had the highest free black population
of any city in the nation. Despite the Southern sympathies memorialized in its state song, a call for Maryland to join its sister-state Virginia
in rebelling against the "despot" Lincoln, Maryland remained in the
union. Throughout the mid-nineteenth century, skilled black ironworkers continued to labor together with immigrants, mostly German
and British, and native-born whites to operate furnaces and forges in
the region. The ongoing challenge of maintaining a stable workforce
led to the creation of small workers' villages clustered around the
forges. At the Ashland and Locust Grove furnaces outside the city,
workers rented lodgings from the company. Families lived in narrow
row houses, with one family occupying an upstairs room and one a
downstairs room, sharing a kitchen. Single men lived in company-
owned boardinghouses. Household supplies and groceries were purchased at a company store.

Churches provided the only opportunities for socializing and
entertainment—not that there was much time for those activities
when workers toiled twelve hours a day. Company owners were happy
to encourage the growth of congregations, particularly evangelical
ones, as religious workers tended to be sober workers, in more ways
than one. Each of these elements would later be re-created on Sparrows Point, an isolated peninsula at the southeasternmost point of Baltimore, where the broad waters of the Patapsco River reach out to the
Chesapeake Bay.

We had water all around us. We had creeks, fish.
It was beautiful.

—DONALD LINDEMANN

In 1886, the Pennsylvania Steel Company sent surveyors to Maryland
to locate a site on tidewater where iron ore imported from its mines in
Cuba could be mixed with coke and limestone in a blast furnace to
produce pig iron. The company planned to ship the iron by rail to the
big Bessemer ovens at its mill in Steelton, Pennsylvania, ninety miles
north, where it would be transformed into steel.

Pennsylvania Steel began manufacturing steel rails soon after an
Englishman named Henry Bessemer discovered in 1856 that blasting
cold air through molten iron superheats the mix to a temperature of
three thousand degrees Fahrenheit. At that temperature, most of the
carbon and other impurities evaporate, producing steel, far stronger
and more resilient than iron due to its lower carbon content. By the
time Sparrows Point was founded, the age of iron was over; the new
century would be forged in steel.

Pennsylvania Steel's president, Luther Bent, chose a young engineer named Frederick Wood to supervise construction of the Sparrows Point works. Wood, Bent's cousin by marriage, had graduated
from the Massachusetts Institute of Technology with a degree in mining engineering. In 1882, at the age of twenty-five, he located a source
of high-quality iron ore in the highlands of Cuba. Because developing
a mine and constructing a rail line connecting the mine to the harbor
at Santiago was an expensive venture, Pennsylvania Steel brought in
another player to help share the costs: Bethlehem Iron Works. A few
years later that company would begin to make a reputation for itself as
an arms merchant, but in 1882, Bethlehem, like Pennsylvania Steel,
manufactured steel rails. Together, the two companies began stripping
the Cuban soil, using its rich ore to feed their ovens in the United
States.

When Frederick Wood and the Pennsylvania Steel surveyors set

up camp on Sparrows Point in the summer of 1887, the land was
mostly Chesapeake Bay marsh—"wetlands," in contemporary language. Construction workers used windmill-powered sump pumps to
drain the marshes and built both a pier for unloading supplies arriving
by sea and a rail line for those arriving by land. By the fall they had
broken ground for two blast furnaces.

Wood imported materials and men from the former Ashland Iron
Works outside Baltimore (Pennsylvania Steel had acquired the Ashland works and its limestone quarry the year before). Men who had
tended the blast furnaces at Ashland dismantled them and rebuilt
them, with improvements planned by Wood, at Sparrows Point.
Meanwhile, African American men recruited from the South began
laying the railroad track that would transport goods and workers to
and from the peninsula.

In the new works on the Chesapeake, the offspring of former
slaves and former Union and Confederate soldiers were soon sweating
together in the furnaces. European immigrants pouring into Baltimore's Locust Point, later called the other Ellis Island for the sheer
number of foreign arrivals processed there, also found their way to the
Point.

Margaret E. Lindemon, who arrived as an infant soon after the
first houses were built, recalled in a memoir that "my father and
grandfather, along with a dozen or more men, came to Sparrows Point
from Ashland. There were no houses in which to live, so my father and
his father set up 'Batchelor [sic] Quarters' in one of the shanties which
bordered the River, just about at the site where the furnace was being
erected." Her mother stayed in Ashland with their young son, "anx-
iously awaiting a house in Sparrows Point." The family was not
reunited until early in 1890, when her father secured a newly built
house on the Point. "Although it was not fully completed, he brought
my mother and brother to the new home. They were happy to be
together again."

From Lindemon's account, it's clear that Sparrows Point was created to house women and children as well as the men who would work
in the mills. Not only was there a precedent for this arrangement in

the old Baltimore ironworks like Ashland, but the superintendent, Frederick Wood, himself had been raised in Lowell, Massachusetts, the Zion of company towns. Frederick brought in his brother Rufus, an accountant, to plan the town of Sparrows Point. Because he too had been raised in Lowell, Rufus knew exactly what sort of town—and what sort of workers—his brother wanted on the Point: sturdy, industrious, and God-fearing men who could be counted on to show up to work sober and on time, to carry out their duties responsibly, and to spend their spare time, what little they had of it, in wholesome pursuits.

As the colonial ironmasters had already discovered, the kind of man willing to risk life and limb to make iron, and later steel, was not easily controlled. In order to keep these men anchored in place, willing slaves to industry, the brothers tried to create a model steel town—safe, clean (as clean as a steel town could be), orderly, and full of happy, contented workers and their families.

The brothers, particularly Rufus, aimed to build a community, not just to cobble together a workforce. An anonymous eulogizer at the company had this to say about Rufus after his death: "A part of the life-work of the late Rufus K. Wood, brother of the president, was the conception of plans for making the working people see the brighter side of life by giving them homes fit to live in, educating their children, furnishing public amusements and carrying out other ideas for their social betterment. Mr. Wood lived among his men. His leisure time was practically devoted to a work which has given Sparrows Point a reputation throughout the country for its success as a model industrial center, and a center where the workman is treated like a man, not a human machine."

Rufus Wood brooded over Sparrows Point like Jehovah fashioning Eden. The town that he created was similar in some ways to its predecessors in Baltimore. Just as in Ashland and Locust Grove, workers lived in houses owned by the company and shopped at the company store. But Sparrows Point was constructed on a much larger scale and was meant to be almost entirely self-sufficient. In addition to providing low-rent housing for employees, the company ran a dairy, bakery, and slaughterhouse. Meat from cattle, sheep, hogs, and chickens raised on the Point was sold in the company store, whose aisles were stocked with not only groceries but also furniture, shoes, hats, books, stationery, carpets, glassware, and china. The town produced its own ice, canned fruits and vegetables, paint, and, later, gasoline.

The company also provided land for various congregations to build churches and maintained the buildings free of charge. They built an elementary school for white children and, two years later, one for black children. Soon the town had its own movie theater, bowling alley, and pool hall. Residents of Sparrows Point had little need to travel to Baltimore—twelve miles away by rail and, later, trolley—for either supplies or entertainment. They lived in an entirely self-contained community, one in which everything they needed was provided by the company. The downside of the arrangement, of course, was that employees were completely dependent on the company—a crafty strategy that worked very well to rein in the notorious independence of ironworkers and steelworkers for nearly half a century.

The town itself was laid out half a mile upwind from the blast furnaces so that most of the smoke and fumes would be blown away from the houses. Residents learned to adapt to the dirt just as they learned to adapt to the noise of round-the-clock production. "I remember my mother coming out and looking up at the sky and trees, and that would determine whether or not she was going to hang her clothes," said Eddie Bartee Sr. "You couldn't wash clothes because all of the sudden they would dump slag or tap a heat and you'd have to take the clothes off the line and put them back in the wash because they'd be covered with black or red dust," Willy Cohill recalled.

Houses ranged from grand multistory residences with porches running the length of them for the town's elite, to narrow brick-and-frame row houses for white workers and pine-planked duplexes for black workers. The company boasted of the "artesian wells" that provided fresh drinking water—though at first only the homes of managers had indoor plumbing and electricity (powered by an on-site generator). The tiny bungalows a half mile from the town proper, built in 1922, also initially lacked indoor plumbing. My paternal great-grandparents, George and Anna Lindemann, moved into one of those houses soon after arriving on the Point in 1923.

George, a small, agile man whom I remember only as a frail figure in a sickbed, had been a circus tumbler. After he married Anna, they scratched out a living farming in Virginia and Delaware before moving to Maryland. They lived in the self-contained little village on the edge of the company town for the rest of their lives. My great-grandmother Anna became midwife to the community. After he retired from steel-making, my great-grandfather operated a newsstand there. The community had a rustic feel, and its residents kept to themselves. "We called the people who lived in town the rich people because they had three-story houses," Donald Lindemann recalled.

Unlike smoky urban steel towns in Pennsylvania and Ohio, Sparrows Point was geographically blessed. Before decades of steelmaking fouled the waters surrounding the town, they were full of fish, crabs, and oysters. "My mother would say, 'Go get a bushel of crabs for dinner,'" Willy Cohill remembered. "We'd go down under the bridge and get a bushel of crabs you could hardly carry home, they were so big and heavy." Donald Lindemann told me that he used to fish for his breakfast. "My big thing when I was eight or nine years old was to get up at five-thirty in the morning and go fishing, bring back one or two fish, and my mother would fry them for my breakfast with home fries. Then I would walk to school."

The school was in the town proper, half a mile from the bungalows. In the town, lettered streets ran east to west, beginning at the water, and numbered streets ran north to south. A Street, fronting the water, had a bathing beach and, close by, an athletic field. The managers' big houses with wide yards filled B and C streets. D Street was the shopping district, and narrow row houses for skilled white workers lined E and F streets. Initially, all those "streets" were boardwalks— Sparrows Point was still somewhat wet underfoot when the first workers and their families began arriving.

Alice Kelly remembered that when her family reached the Point in 1891, "what struck us more than anything were all the boardwalks. It was very swampy down there; they had bridges made over all the marshes with a railing around them so you wouldn't fall off. When the blast furnaces started to put out slag, they did away with the boardwalks and made the sidewalks out of slag."

Kelly, interviewed by the local historical society in 1973 at the age of ninety-one, recalled that tropical illnesses were a big problem for the town's early inhabitants. "We had a terrible lot of malaria," she said, "on account of the marsh and the mosquitoes in the swamp. It was all full of cat-o'-nine tails and spongy and awful-looking." Erestus Gladfelter, who was born on the Point in 1892, told the historical society that you could "cut the malaria with a knife, it was so thick. Everyone took quinine."

Apart from making early residents sick, the town's geography helped its planners deal with a pressing social problem: On such a small strip of land, how could they possibly keep separate the various ethnic groups that composed the workforce? As in the colonial ironworks, the plan was to use native-born whites of Anglo-Saxon heritage (English, Scottish, German) as managers, foremen, and skilled workers. The heavy labor of shoveling coal, feeding the furnaces, lifting, and hauling would be done by the people who usually did that kind of work: poor whites, immigrants, and blacks. "Colored and foreign labor constitute each one-third of the whole number of employees at Sparrows Point; the other third is of mixed character," the president of Pennsylvania Steel told inspectors in 1892, describing the Point's workforce.

Though the various groups might work together in the mills, they certainly couldn't live together. Geography solved the housing problem. Native-born whites lived in the town, on the lettered streets, where in the early days it was exceedingly doubtful that you would find a Catholic or anyone speaking broken English from A Street all the way down to the banks of Humphrey's Creek. There, Hungarian, Romanian, Italian, Polish, and other immigrant families lived "in shacks along the banks of the creek," where they raised their own chickens, ducks, and other small animals in old country style.

Across the creek—which, from an aerial photograph of the town, looks as if it were as broad as a small river—the streets of the North

Side, I and J, ran close by the dairy. A school, two churches, and a satellite of the company store, later supplemented by other small businesses, served the needs of North Side residents. Not until 1967 were black families permitted to move "across the creek"—which by that time had been filled in with slag to the point where it was little more than a narrow stream—into the "white" sections of town. A few years later the town, which had been steadily shrinking for years as houses were torn down for mill expansion, was completely demolished.

Throughout the history of Sparrows Point, management chose carefully which families they allowed to rent houses in the community—and everyone from the plant superintendent to the lowliest laborer rented. You could not buy a house on Sparrows Point. The company's real estate department took care of all maintenance and repairs on the houses, which rented for substantially less than comparable homes in Baltimore and its surrounding suburbs. "My mother paid $19 a month to live in a three-story house," Eddie Bartee Sr. told me. "When I left the Point, I was paying $64 a month, when the same house would rent for $300 or $400 a month in Baltimore City. Plus, [the company] did everything for that house."

By providing low-cost housing, management was able to populate the town with particularly loyal and industrious employees. "The applicants were carefully screened, and [the real estate department] tried to be very careful as to who got the houses," Raymond Witmyer, a longtime resident, told the local historical society in 1972. If a family proved undesirable in any way, they were told to vacate their home. "If your kids were bad, they made you go," Eddie Bartee Sr. recalled.

Company police had full authority to discipline those who stepped out of line. "The police on Sparrows Point knew every kid," Donald Lindemann said. "They walked through [the bungalows] twice a day. In the summertime, when it would get dark at nine, the policeman would say, 'Donald, get on home.' If I give them a look, they'd take that stick with rawhide on it and put it across your back. And you went home, but you didn't tell your parents, because you'd get a second one for embarrassing them. On Halloween you never heard of scratching cars, none of that. The worst thing we ever did—when I was about fourteen or fifteen, we took a trash can and put it in front of a door and knocked it down, and we had to run and hide in the woods because the police were out with searchlights looking for us."

Most families on the Point took in at least one boarder and often-times many more. In her study of the women of the town, *Wives of Steel*, the sociologist Karen Olson notes that many housewives on the Point were actually running small boardinghouses, feeding and doing laundry for anywhere from one to ten resident steelworkers who were not members of the immediate family. The boarding arrangements produced many marriages, as it did in my own family. My paternal grandfather, Elmer Rudacille, boarded with my Lindemann great-grandparents when he came up from Virginia in 1927 looking for a job in the works. He married their seventeen-year-old daughter, Eliza-beth, a year later. Even after they moved from the company town to a big white frame house on North Point Road, a short walk from the mill, my Rudacille grandparents always took in boarders.

How Sparrows Point families managed to cram boarders into the tiny 550-square-foot bungalows is a mystery to me, but my uncle explained that "they would just finagle people around." With the men on shift work, beds were shared and mealtimes staggered. "The board-ers had dibs on the beds," Bob Butler, born on the Point in 1923, told me. As Olson points out in her book, the income from boarders helped supplement steelworkers' wages, which were, in the pre-union days, quite meager.

The boarding arrangement also promoted ethnic loyalty in the town and in the works, where people from the same background helped each other advance. "Irish tended to board with the Irish, Poles with Poles, and so on," Ed Gorman said, recalling his own family's his-tory on the Point. Ed's Irish father, who had trained as a machinist in Liverpool, England, before arriving on the Point in 1929, boarded with an Irish family named Durkin and married their daughter Mary. Her grandparents had immigrated to Baltimore during the potato famine of the 1840s. "I heard my mother, when I was small, say that they dumped their mattresses off in Locust Point because they came here through steerage," Ed said. "They didn't have enough money for a berth, so they slept on the deck."

As we chatted in the study of his Dundalk home, Ed pulled out a 1930 census form listing the name, place of birth, mother tongue, citizenship, and occupation of all the residents on his grandparents' block in Sparrows Point. "They lived here at 325 E Street," Ed said, pointing to the household on the list. "Here's my grandfather, grandmother, my uncle John, my mother, and my younger uncle Pat. And this is my mother's cousin Patrick McGrath. And there's my dad, who was a boarder."

Ed's copy of the census shows that the residents of E Street were mostly native-born Americans. Save for three Swedes and one German, those not born in the United States were either English or Irish, like the Durkins. Their occupations—carpenter, blacksmith, painter, roller, checker, heater, teacher, chief of the fire department—reinforce E Street's reputation as the home of the town's working-class elite.

Ed shared with me a story about his father that says a lot about the character and outlook of folks raised on Sparrows Point, whether in the town itself, on the North Side, or in the bungalows. When Ed graduated from high school, he was just sixteen and thought he might enjoy his summer before looking for work. But his father soon made it clear that slacking off would not be tolerated.

"About two weeks after I graduated, my father came home from work—he worked all daylight, and when he came home quarter after four, he'd have his shot and put his slippers on—and he said to me, 'You found a job?' I said, 'No, sir.' And he said to me, 'If I see your ass sitting in that chair Monday and you don't have a job, you're out of here.'"

• DIRT •

In 1892, a delegation from the Maryland Bureau of Statistics and Information journeyed to the Sparrows Point peninsula to inspect the five-year-old company town and works. They were greeted by Rufus and Frederick Wood and Pennsylvania Steel president Luther Bent, who had come down from Steelton expressly for the visit. The three men showed off the beautiful gardens of plants grown in the company hothouse that were beginning to bloom in the workers' backyards, the savings bank, and the company store. They poked their heads into scrupulously clean houses and the two segregated elementary schools, where Rufus Wood had set up the first kindergartens south of the Mason-Dixon Line.

They also visited the works, where four eighty-five-foot blast furnaces churned out iron to fuel the two eighteen-ton Bessemer converters that turned iron into steel. The Bessemers hadn't been part of the original plan for Sparrows Point, but Frederick Wood had convinced his bosses at Steelton that it would be cheaper and more efficient to manufacture steel and rails on-site, and supervised construction of what were then the largest Bessemer furnaces in the world. The steel produced in the furnaces in turn fed operations at the rail mill and shipyard.

Though Wood incorporated both men and equipment from the Ashland Iron Works into the new operation at Sparrows Point, he wasn't just recycling old technology. He and his fellow engineers created a new kind of works, one where each stage of production flowed smoothly into the next without the stop-and-start bottlenecks that had slowed down operations in other American steel mills. At Sparrows Point, liquid iron produced in the blast furnaces was poured into 22-ton open top ladles mounted on railroad cars, which were then poured into one of two 120-ton hot metal mixers—giant blenders. The molten steel produced in the Bessemers was then poured into ingot molds mounted on railroad cars—each ingot weighing thirty-six hundred to four thousand pounds—and transported to the soaking pits, where a pulley lifted the molds up and away from the cooling ingots, which were transferred by cable to the rolling mill.

These innovations significantly enhanced speed and efficiency, while the enormous scale of the equipment ensured high volume. In November 1891, the blast furnaces produced a record 16,332 tons of hot metal. To reward Wood's labors, Pennsylvania Steel made Sparrows Point a semi-independent subsidiary of their operation—Maryland Steel—and named him president of the company.

Nonetheless, it was the peaceful town of thirty-five hundred inhabitants, not the clanging works, that most impressed the state inspectors at the turn of the century. Compared with the steel towns of western Pennsylvania—or the industrial neighborhoods just across the harbor in Baltimore—where workers lived in squalid conditions, Sparrows Point was clean, orderly, and seemingly without vice. The Pennsylvania Steel executives explained why. In 1888, they had lobbied the Maryland legislature to pass a law that banned the granting of licenses for the sale of liquor or beer on Sparrows Point. "We allow no liquor to be sold within two miles," Bent boasted to the inspectors. "If a man wants a glass of beer, he must go to Baltimore to get it."

Bent, who lived in Steelton, may have been convinced that Sparrows Point was as dry as a Baptist college, but by then the Wood brothers must have been crossing their fingers behind their backs as he touted the town's sobriety. Though liquor sales were indeed banned in the town, saloons sprang up just outside its borders and at every stop on the rail route to Baltimore to service Maryland Steel employees. Every Saturday night, carousing Sparrows Point workers returned from Baltimore "on the last train loaded to the guards and with their pockets bulging out with bottles of intoxicants," according to an 1893 editorial in *The Baltimore Sunday Herald* deploring the weekend revelry.

Shantytown, where single men lived packed in filthy dormitories behind the blast furnaces, "turned into a veritable bedlam, and these orgies last fair into the morning," the editorialist complained. Drinking, gambling, and knife fights were common in the shanties, judging by the arrest records of the Sparrows Point Police Department. I found the thick ledgers for the years 1905, 1906, and 1914 at the Historical Society of Baltimore County, and the old books, with their red-and-yellow-marbled pages and flaking covers, provide a colorful account of town residents' misdeeds. Indecent exposure, attempted rape, larceny, shooting craps, and domestic assault are listed in a flowing script (alongside daily weather reports), but the most common crime by far was public drunkenness. Hardly a day passes without a note on some worker being locked up overnight and fined a dollar for being "drunk and disorderly," "on the verge of delirium," or "found wandering about the town drunk" or for "committing a public nuisance."

The workingmen of the town had little free time. Two shifts made steel rails round the clock in the Maryland Steel era on Sparrows Point. The daylight shift worked ten to eleven hours a day, for a total of sixty-four hours per week. The midnight shift worked thirteen to fourteen hours a day and twenty-four hours straight on alternate weekends—a grueling hundred and four hours every other week—to give the alternate shift a day off. Employees had two (unpaid) holidays a year: Christmas and the Fourth of July. Their lives were a brutal treadmill of hard labor punctuated for many by hard drinking. Management tolerated the drinking so long as it didn't interfere with the work.

Though the ban on alcohol sales endured on Sparrows Point until the town's final days, people who grew up there say that it was always enforced with a wink and a nod. "Everyone brewed their own beer at home," eighty-year-old Bob Strasbaugh told me on a hot day in the summer of 2006, laughing as he remembered the time his father's supply of overly yeasted home brew stored in bottles in the kitchen cupboards exploded during a family dinner.

Willy Cohill said his father made "bathtub stuff" and that the town's policemen not only turned a blind eye to the illegal production and consumption of liquor but partook of it themselves. "The policemen never said nothing because they would stop in for a drink now and then too. One was at my house every Christmas. He made sure he worked midnight so he could stop in." Cohill also recalled his parents making a tidy profit from the credit coupon books the company provided for the purchase of food and other household necessities at the company store. "We would buy a $5 book of coupons from the colored folks at the newsstand for $3 a book so they could buy liquor with the cash."

The Narutowicz family built a commercial empire on the thirst of Sparrows Point steelworkers. The family patriarch, Mickey, started the business during Prohibition, brewing moonshine in the woods and selling it out of his basement. "He even had clientele who wore blue uniforms," his son Tony told me. When Prohibition ended in 1933, he opened a saloon and restaurant, Mickey's, just outside the company town. "At lunchtime guys from the Point would come over for a bowl of crab soup and a couple of beers," Tony Narutowicz said. He showed me an original menu from the restaurant—crab cakes were ten cents; an oyster platter, thirty-five cents. When I asked him if men often got drunk on their lunch breaks at Mickey's, he shrugged. "If they wanted to get drunk, they could always get drunk at the plant." Steelworkers, he pointed out, "worked hard and they drank hard"—and he was in a position to know. In later years, the Mickey's empire expanded to include a bar and package goods store, a gas station, a car wash, and a Laundromat on North Point Road, a mile or so from the factory gates and two doors down from my grandparents' house. Mickey's was always a hub for Sparrows Point steelworkers, who would cash their checks, and then hang out in the parking lot to socialize before and after shifts.

A number of saloons just outside the company town profited from the alcohol ban on the Point throughout its long history: the First and Last (because it was the first place you could get a drink coming out of work and the last place before going in), the Jolly Post, Mayby's, the M&M. "They were all crowded," Willy Cohill recalled on our tour of the town. "We produced more steel in the local bars than we did in the mills," LeRoy McLelland boasted. On the job, workers competed as crews, he pointed out, and afterward stopped by the taverns to drink, play pool, throw darts, and shoot the breeze. Drinking together helped create camaraderie, harmony, and solidarity, he said. "It was like a family—you had your family at home and your family down there."

> Those were the kinds of jobs that people were always getting
> killed on. But I never saw anything about anyone getting
> killed in the newspaper.

—AUSTIN McLELLAND

A parade of government officials visiting Sparrows Point during its first decades echoed the praise of the Maryland inspectors who had visited in 1892, one of them going so far as to note that the North Side could serve as a model for other communities of African American workers. None seem to have noticed or cared that the pleasant life of the town was built on a foundation of exploitative labor practices or that the long hours of labor in hazardous conditions fueled the constant threat of serious injury and death.

The accident statistics for the works in the Wood/Maryland Steel era are shocking. During one six-month period—January to June 30, 1910—there were ten fatal accidents at the plant. During the same six-month period, there were three accidents in which workers were partially disabled, 304 "severe" accidents, and 1,421 "minor" accidents. A full 44 percent of those incidents were attributed to negligence on the part of the victim.

The ledgers of the Sparrows Point Police Department contain

accounts of some of those deaths and the inquests that determined that they were accidents. For example, in January 1906, a watchman at the ore pier reported the possible drowning of Matzas Balosic, a laborer at the open hearth furnace, whose cap was found under the pier at about 12:30 a.m. He had last been seen working on a car on the pier, and it was assumed that he had somehow fallen into the water. His body was recovered five days later. In July, twenty-six-year-old Ernest Pickett was killed at the coke ovens when he was run down by a railcar. Pickett, like Mike Cavanaugh, a laborer killed less than a month earlier when he was run over by a railroad car (whose crew was exonerated of all blame), was buried by the company when no family members could be found to take charge of his body.

In order to receive a (puny) settlement, relatives of men killed on the job were obligated to prove that the company's negligence had been responsible for the accident. They were not usually successful. When a workers' compensation bill was introduced in the Maryland legislature in 1914, a company accountant estimated how much Maryland Steel would have been compelled to pay out to victims and their families from 1910 to 1914 if the compensation law had been in effect. Over that four-year period, thirty-nine men were killed on the job and fifteen were disabled. Class 3 accidents, described as severe, numbered 1,329. Only a small number of those accidents would have been covered under the terms of the proposed law, and the calculations show that the company would have paid out only $12,336.52 in claims. It's a ridiculously low number, but Maryland Steel still lobbied against the bill, which passed despite its opposition.

"You wouldn't believe how many people were killed down there," Tom Capecci, the president of a union retirees' group, told me in 2007. The United Steelworkers of America, voted into the plant in 1941, vastly improved safety, he pointed out. An average of five deaths per year from 1947 to 1952 dropped to three throughout the late fifties and early sixties, with occasional spikes (six in 1962). Late in that decade, the mortality rate dropped further, to only one or two deaths per year. In 1978, there was another spike (six deaths), which leveled out again to one or two per year through 1996.

Still, capsule descriptions of these fatal accidents in a company file slipped to me by one of my sources show how little the dangers of steelmaking changed over the decades, and how suddenly and gruesomely a worker could meet his end.

In October 1948, a thirty-year-old laborer was unloading flue dust from railroad cars when an updraft of dust caused him to back away and fall into the dust of a second car, "which was loaded the day before and was quite hot." He suffered first- and second-degree burns on his face, neck, trunk, arms, legs, and extremities.

That same year, a twenty-seven-year-old coke ovens worker was mudding up a door in the ovens when he was caught between two cars; the right side of his head was crushed, and his right clavicle and ribs were fractured.

In July 1950, a sixty-year-old pipe fitter was enveloped in burning oil and either fell or jumped to the ground. He suffered extensive first-, second-, and third-degree burns on his head, body, and extremities, as well as sustaining multiple facial contusions in the fall. Three months later, a forty-eight-year-old blower in the blast furnace was scalded by slag that overflowed the runner and engulfed him as he sat in the control booth. He was burned over his entire body.

In April 1951, a thirty-four-year-old ladle line leader in the blast furnace was asphyxiated by carbon monoxide when a pipe leaked. Four months later, an agitator operator in the coke oven chemical plant was overcome by fumes and died of benzene poisoning. In December of that year, a twenty-four-year-old sheet metal man fell thirty-two feet from a roof truss to the floor. Later that month, a sixty-year-old electrician fell forty-two feet. Six months later, a larry car operator in the blast furnace lost his balance and fell fifty-six feet from a platform.

In July 1953, a sixty-three-year-old carpenter was struck by an ore car and dragged approximately one hundred feet, completely crushing and tearing apart his entire body. In October 1954, an idler car ran over a fifty-two-year-old foreman, fracturing his skull and eviscerating his abdomen.

In January 1956, a forty-five-year-old packer was struck by a magnet and coil suspended by a crane and suffered a compound fracture of his skull. That spring, a forty-five-year-old field engineer was struck by the top part of a boring rig and knocked to the ground. The rig landed on him, fracturing his pelvis, his right leg, and the right side of his face, lacerating his bladder, and abrading his arms. That same month, a twenty-eight-year-old crane follower was struck by a bundle of conduit that fell off the side of a buggy and landed on top of him. He suffered a compound fracture of the skull.

Behind every statistic was a grieving family. At every union meeting I've attended, I've talked with people who had lost fathers, husbands, brothers, and uncles to accidents at Sparrows Point. Gresham Hertt Somerville told me that her father had just bought her class ring and was looking forward to seeing her graduate from high school when he was killed in the summer of 1945.

"He was rolling up some kind of coil," she said, "and instead of this machine picking up the coil, it took him up, about thirty feet in the air, and dropped him. He was broken into pieces." Her father survived the accident for a few hours, long enough to say goodbye. "He said, 'Hunky'—that was his nickname for me—'I want you and your brother to take good care of your mother and pray for me.' That was his last words to me."

Even in the modern era, "it never made the papers how many died or got hurt," Capecci told me. "In the 1990s we had an average of fifty people a month going to the dispensary—and that was really good! People don't realize how much danger we were in just to go in and do our jobs every day."

WHAT IT TAKES TO MAKE 1 INGOT-TON OF STEEL

1 1/5 tons of Iron Ore
3/4 ton of Coal
1/3 ton of limestone
1/3 ton of Scrap Steel
8 tons of air
157 tons of water

—BETHLEHEM STEEL BROCHURE

Anyone who has ever visited a steel mill and seen the red glow of the furnaces, felt their blazing heat, gazed at the massive machinery, smelled the noxious fumes, and watched the hot molten metal being poured knows that a steel mill resembles hell much more than it resembles heaven. And surely many a man who sweated in the ovens must have felt that he was working for Satan and his minions. "You can't be a white hat [foreman] and a Christian too," a man told my uncle soon after he was promoted.

In the early days of steelmaking on the Point, the only finished products besides ships manufactured on-site were rails. That would change over the years as the "finishing side" of the works grew to rival the "steel side" in size and stature, with a rod mill, wire mill, plate mill, pipe mill, and sheet, strip, and tin plate mill. But no matter how prestigious the jobs or high the salaries that operators ultimately commanded on the finishing side, the fiery red heart of the Sparrows Point works always remained the ovens and furnaces.

As more than one steelworker has reminded me, steel is made from dirt. Stuff dug out of the ground—coal, iron ore, limestone, and other alloys—is mixed, melted, and shaped into steel, then shipped back out the way it came in to customers inland and overseas. The raw materials that fed the steelmaking process were brought to the Point by ship and by rail. In the Maryland Steel years, ships were independent of the company; Bethlehem later owned and operated its own ore-shipping line.

My children's paternal grandfather, Manuel Alvarez, a former tugboat engineer, ran ore between South America and Sparrows Point for Bethlehem Steel when he was still in high school. I've known Manny for thirty years, but it wasn't until we sat down in the kitchen where I had eaten many a family meal in the old days that I learned he too had once worked for Bethlehem. A friend of his father, "an old Spanish gentleman named Mr. Sanchez," was the shipping master, and when he was looking for a summer job one year, the older man offered him a place on a Bethlehem ore ship.

"He said, 'I'ma gonna put you inna place where you gonna see the world. You'll see everything!'" Alvarez recalled. "Well, he put me on a ship, thirty days' cruise to Chile. The only thing I saw was a lot of water, flies, fish, and the [Panama] Canal. And if I wasn't on watch, I didn't see the canal. You get there and take the ship into this mountain, and these big slides come down, and within eighteen or twenty hours, twenty-five thousand tons of ore goes into the ship. You back it out and you come back to Baltimore—thirty-three days."

The ore was unloaded into railroad cars on the pier and transported to bins near the furnaces. In 2007, I spoke with two men, childhood friends hired together in 1955 to work on the ore docks. Eugene "Tank" Levy is a big man, bluff and hearty, while Roosevelt Caldwell is slighter, neat and precise in appearance and manner. Back in the day, Tank was seventy pounds heavier than his friend, but both were assigned to the docks, where they shoveled ore out of ships. "The laborers would have to go down into the hold of the ship and trim," said Levy, describing how they worked the ore out of nooks and crannies so that it could be lifted to the surface in twenty-five-ton buckets by cranes. The ladder leading up from the hold "was straight up, about two stories," Levy pointed out. "It was a dangerous job. Some of those ships coming in we would call a bucket of rust. You'd go down that ladder into the hold and those rungs would pull away. Later on they made you wear a safety harness, but during that time you didn't have anything."

The two friends narrowly escaped a horrific accident one day when a crane toppled into the hole. "What happened was this crane comes out, getting ready to lower its bucket into the hole," said Caldwell. Cranes had "twelve wheels, about three hundred pounds apiece, and the whole thing fell right into the hole. Right into the hole. I just stood there. I couldn't believe it. What happened was that the rails tipped to one side for about two or three seconds." The crane operator was pitched into the belly of the ship, Levy said. "When we went in the hole, the back of his head was crushed. They got him out, but he died."

The coke ovens were even more hazardous. At first, coke to fuel the furnaces was brought in by rail from Pennsylvania; then, in 1901, Frederick Wood built a coke works, where coal from West Virginia was baked in giant ovens, producing coke—thirty thousand tons per month when the batteries were fired up in 1903. As it is baked, coal releases numerous gases, which can be captured, distilled, and sold to manufacturers to make plastics, dyes, synthetics, and even drugs. The coke works at Sparrows Point was profitable from the start and eventually became a big moneymaker.

Melvin Schmeiser worked in the coke oven chemical plant for twenty-four years. Mel was wonderfully sarcastic as we sat in the dining room of his bungalow in northeast Baltimore in the winter of 2006 chatting as his wife, Alice, listened in. He had saved the pocket calendars from his thirty-five years at Bethlehem, listing his turns and days off. He also showed me some of his old work clothes, the fireproof suits finally provided by the company in his last years in the coke ovens.

People on the Point called the coke chemical plant the bomb factory, he told me, because of the high-pressure, high-volume conditions. During his time there, two employees were killed on the job in two separate explosions. He himself was burned by hot oil and spent twenty-eight days in the city hospital's burn unit. Schmeiser worked in the area that produced benzene. Some of the old-timers used to actually wash their faces and hands in benzene, he said, but his generation just rinsed their oily work clothes in the stuff because it was such a good degreaser. "You'd wash them in a bucket of benzene, and in the shop we had steam radiators, these steam pipes that went back and forth, back and forth, and that's how we heated our shop. And it had an expanded metal grille over it so that you couldn't actually touch the pipes. We would dip the clothes in benzene, wring them out, and put them over the steam radiator and sit around in our underwear. They'd be dry in ten minutes."

He and the other men would sometimes find themselves "giggling," he said, not because they were in their underwear but because they were getting a benzene high. "I remember one night on the three-to-eleven shift, we had a bad leak in the building and this benzene was all over the floor. Another guy and I had to go in there and make repairs, and we were like, 'We got to get out of here,' because we started getting a little giddy. Me and the other man were sitting outside, and we're looking at each other and we couldn't stop laughing. We knew that we were overexposed to the fumes. You could see 'em. If you looked in the sunlight, you could see the fumes rolling off of this stuff."

He told me about a co-worker who developed leukemia years after retirement. Testing revealed that "he still had high amounts of benzene is his blood," he said. "He probably started in the fifties." I asked Mel if he and his co-workers knew that benzene was a carcinogen. "Did we know or did the company know? Near the end it was acknowledged by the company." Even so, he said, "I thought this was one of the better places to work in the coke ovens." A few months after our conversation, I learned that Mel had been diagnosed with pancreatic cancer at the age of fifty-nine.

Them black guys before me was almost under the whip.

— BLAINE DeWITT

From the time the first coke ovens were installed on the Point in 1901 until they were shut down in 1989, coke oven jobs were among the hardest and dirtiest on the Point. On the coke oven batteries, laborers shoved coal into the furnaces in the midst of choking fumes, mudded up the doors, fired up the ovens, and then discharged the incandescent coke onto railcars to zip to the blast furnaces. They scrubbed out the ovens between batches with long poles furred at the ends, a job made even more arduous when a "sticker," or bad mix, created a tar that adhered to the sides of the ovens.

It was, in words used by many of my sources, "hot bull work," and throughout the Point's history, it was done mostly by African American men. A former neighbor of mine, Pete Selhorst, became one of the few whites on the coke oven labor crews when he requested a transfer to avoid a layoff in 1974. Pete had been hired the year before to work in the tandem mill, an elite, all-white, high-paying unit where finished steel was rolled. It was a clean mill. The coke ovens, he said, were another world entirely.

"I always described it as the plantation in the steel mill," he told me. "We had an overseer with his arms folded, and we would be shoveling. It was all black, except for us new guys. Blacks were always given the dirtiest, most difficult jobs. And they were only hired if they had recently come up from the South because they wanted the guys with the strong backs who had been working since they were kids. People told me where they were from, and there weren't any from the city. They were all from North Carolina, Virginia, and South Carolina, used to hard work and expecting hard work."

Knowing that he had been in his twenties then, I asked him if he found working in the coke ovens challenging, and he laughed. "Oh yeah," he said. "You'd be in fire, literally. You'd be in the middle of flames. Your clothes would disintegrate and stuff. We wore so many layers of clothes. In the summer, you'd wear thermals, just like in winter, to insulate yourself from the heat. Back then they took salt tablets. I remember in summertime in the coke ovens, I'd probably take twelve salt tablets a day. And drink as much fluid as I could. When I got home and would try to sleep—because we worked swing shifts and might be sleeping in the daytime—your bed would be soaked because you couldn't stop sweating."

The difficulty of working in the ovens created "a lot of camaraderie" among the workers there, he said. "We were like a family. Even after you left the coke ovens, if you ran into a coke oven person, it was like a reunion. It was a respect that you had for each other because you were like foxhole buddies."

Pete's account echoes that of another white steelworker, also hired in the mid-seventies, whom I talked to at a union meeting. Blaine DeWitt started working in the coalfields adjacent to the coke ovens in 1972. At that time "the whole coke ovens was less than 25 percent white," he said, and of the approximately 120 people assigned to the coalfields, "there wasn't more than 20 or 30 white guys, and most of them were crane operators or foremen."

DeWitt once emptied out a crane bucket to estimate just how much coal he shoveled in a day. "A crane had a ten-ton bucket. I spread out one of those buckets just to see how much coal it was, and I definitely shoveled a whole bucket in a day. You didn't do it all the time, of course. After shoveling for a while, you'd sit up on your shovel, but don't let the man catch you doing it. If they catch you leaning on a shovel, they'd want to send you right home and write you up."

DeWitt worked with a few old-timers, and from them he learned that being written up was nothing. "Them black guys before me was almost under the whip. I worked with a guy, a black crane operator, that I thought was the laziest man I ever seen. One day I gave him a hard time about it, and he said, 'Look, boy, I'm gonna tell you something. For years I done worked myself to death out here. Don't let the man find you loafing.'"

Southern blacks always did much of the heavy work at the Point. At a time when steelmaking was an extremely labor-intensive process, requiring hundreds to put in twelve- to fourteen-hour days feeding the ovens and furnaces, steelmakers looked for men accustomed to hard physical labor. Sitting smack on the border between the industrial North and the agrarian South, in a state with a long tradition of black ironworkers, Sparrows Point looked south to find those men, whereas steelmakers farther north used mostly immigrants for unskilled jobs in their mills.

Lee Douglas, whose father came to the Point in the thirties from South Carolina and whose two uncles worked for the Patapsco and Back River Neck Railroad on Sparrows Point, said that management recruited black men from the South not only because they were hard workers but also because they were less independent than blacks in Baltimore. "City blacks might say straight out, 'I'm not going to do this job.' But not if you from down south," he pointed out. African American men in Baltimore were well aware of the company's preference for workers from Virginia and the Carolinas, Douglas said. "People who lived down in Baltimore would give their daddy's name from down south to get hired."

Segregation and discrimination were just as pervasive on the Point as in the rest of the United States at the time. "One of the things that we have to acknowledge," Douglas noted, "is that back in those times, the nation itself was under segregation. It was the law of the land. And therefore I was able to adjust myself to it." And Len Shindel, a white steelworker, pointed out that "someone who came from some hamlet in North Carolina where people were being lynched and who was making good money on the Point and able to send his kids to college might compare this horrendous world he left with the imperfect world he came into and feel that this was progress."

For many, it was. Even before the civil rights era, there were a few African American men supervising black units. George Eggleston Sr., hired on March 20, 1890, was foreman of a labor gang in the blast furnaces and worked at Sparrows Point for fifty-two years—"the longest term of service of all the Negro employees," according to a booklet produced by North Side residents for a 1973 reunion.

Gresham Hertt Somerville told me that her father, William Samuel Hertt, who moved to Baltimore from Virginia and started working at the Point in 1905, at the age of twelve, "was really in love with Sparrows Point. He loved his job—the workers and the work." She believes that one of the reasons her father loved his job so much is because it enabled him to provide for her mother, her younger brother, and her. "He took good care of us," she said. "We didn't know we was poor because he would take us to the company store and let us buy whatever we wanted. The men weren't making that much money, but you could get things on credit, and my father always wanted us to have the best. So we had clothes for school and clothes for Sunday. We would meet him down there at the store and get whatever we needed."

> I worked all over. I worked at the blast furnaces. I worked at the open hearths. I worked at the Bessemers. I worked in the pits, the soaking pit, in the blooming mills. The pipe mill, the plant mill, and the sheet mill. Anywhere there was brick and furnaces.
>
> —RAY RUDACILLE

In 1910, Frederick Wood installed five fifty-ton open hearth furnaces to supplement the original Bessemer ovens in the Sparrows Point works. Then novel and innovative, open hearth technology would serve as the linchpin of steelmaking at Sparrows Point for well over sixty years. In an open hearth furnace, molten iron poured from blast furnaces is "charged" with steel scrap, and the mix is scored by flames that sweep across a shallow bowl (the hearth) at the bottom. Test samples of the mix are analyzed at regular intervals to adjust the carbon content, which is responsible for different grades of steel. Steel is produced more quickly and efficiently in the open hearth, without the bubbles that sometimes flawed Bessemer steel, but the high temperatures wear down the bricks lining the furnaces quickly. For that reason, bricklayers became critical craftsmen in steel mills.

Two of my father's brothers, Benjamin and Raymond, were Sparrows Point bricklayers. Benjamin, the eldest, started working at the Point just after completing his service in World War II. He passed away in 1994. Strangely enough, I remember him not as a steelworker but as a farmer. In the seventies, he bought land in rural Harford County, an hour and a half north of Sparrows Point, where he and his wife and three children kept goats, cows, and horses and grew all kinds of vegetables while he continued to work full-time at the Point. Though born and raised in the noisy steel town, he and his brothers had spent summers on their uncle's farm in Virginia, idyllic country summers far from the smoke and grit of Sparrows Point.

Most of the things I know about making steel, I learned from my father's younger brother Raymond, who, as a bricklayer and mechanical foreman, worked all over the plant. Raymond was, in the words of all who knew him, "a true gentleman." Unlike his brothers, he didn't smoke or drink, and I never heard a swearword cross his lips. He had a beautiful voice and sang in a barbershop quartet and the Chorus of the Chesapeake, a local men's choir. When I was thinking of writing this book, he wasn't feeling well, but still he talked to me for hours about his work.

"My father loved that job," his son Ray Junior told me at his funeral in 2005—which is somewhat ironic, as it is indisputable that the job killed him. He died of mesothelioma, a lung cancer caused by exposure to asbestos. "Bricklayer was the worst job down there for asbestos," his cousin Donald Lindemann told me, "because they relined the furnaces, and to reline the furnaces, they put the asbestos between the bricks." In the 1980s, Sparrows Point bricklayers filed and won the first asbestos lawsuits against the company.

When Ray and I talked in the fall of 2004, he was eager to tell me about the work he did at the Point and why bricklayers played such an important role there. "An open hearth furnace could run for about three months before it needed to be completely rebuilt," he explained. When he started doing the job in the mid-fifties, rebuilding a furnace took a huge amount of manpower. "To pull a roof down," he said, "you need maybe a hundred and fifty laborers." In between teardowns, bricklayers would be sent in to do "hot jobs," repairing individual walls that had weakened, and plugging holes. "You'd put in a twenty-seven-inch wall, and after three or four weeks, that wall was burned back to two inches."

Before he became a bricklayer, my uncle always wondered why the men working on the open hearths wore sweatpants and heavy dunga-rees in Baltimore's steamy summers. The first time he went out on a hot job, he found out. "I'm wearing dungarees, and I leaned into the furnace—boom, boom—to knock the hole in, and I stepped back, and those pants came against my legs. I thought I had burned my legs off! People wore all those layers of clothes so as not to get burned. When you started bricking the bulkhead, it was twenty-five hundred degrees, maybe." One time his jacket caught fire while he was working. Another time he was plugging a hole in the arched roof of a furnace, he said, and "my head was so hot, I couldn't understand it. After I got down, I found out that my safety hat had buckled onto my head."

Navigating in the furnaces could also be tricky. "In the open hearth, you've got the hot metal car," he said, "and there was a little room between it and the panel board. But when the hot metal car come by, you had to be pretty close to the panel board. And from here to here were the buggies and the furnace. If you were caught between the buggies and the furnace, you were in trouble. And if you were caught between the hot metal car and the charging machine, you were in trouble."

Still, he was never scared while working on the steel side, he said, because "whenever anything was moving, they blew a siren. So even with all the confusion in the open hearth, you always had some idea of what was going on." The thing that really got to him was walking through the cold rolling mill on the finishing side. "It was a real high mill, and they had a crane up near the ceiling, and the crane had a magnet. Well, you'd be walking through, and it would be real quiet. Then you'd look up and see this [thousand-pound] coil hanging over your head. That scared me to death! I was more scared walking through that mill than any place I ever worked. They didn't blow a siren or shout to you or anything. You'd just look up and it would be there."

When he started working at the Point in the mid-fifties, all the men in his family worked there, he told me, listing ten relatives, including my father, uncles, grandfather, and distant cousins. They are all gone now, save for Donald Lindemann. When I visited Donald in the Dundalk row house where I had spent so many Sunday afternoons as a child, he told me that he had seven cousins who had lived and worked on Sparrows Point who had succumbed to lung cancer, some of them in their forties. Donald is tart-tongued, a trait he attributes to his German-Dutch heritage. "I don't beat around the bush. I don't have to please nobody," he said.

The thing that bothered him most about the job was the heat, he said. "It would get so damn hot that you couldn't stand it sometimes. In summertime it was terrible. We wanted to get a fan one time on the back of our unit, where the doors were. OSHA came in, and the temperature there was 127 degrees. So we got a fan. Of course it was blowing hot air, but it was better than nothing."

Donald worked on the Point for forty-one years, following his father, who had worked there forty-seven years. His dad, who started working in the hot strip mill in 1928 at the age of sixteen, was burned on the chest so badly that he was transferred out of the unit. Donald himself was burned by acid a few months before he retired from the tin mill in 1992. "We used a lot of caustic for cleaning the steel, and I had a line that was clogged up. So I was down on my knees trying to get the line unclogged. Another guy that was filling in as foreman was a goof-ball, and he turned on the air pressure on the line that I had cut off, and [the acid] all blew in my face. Luckily there was a shower about eight feet away, and I jumped in the shower to wash off the acid. I got some new skin out of it. If that shower had been another twenty or thirty feet away, I'd've really got burned up. I've got gashes and scars all over the place, but I don't worry about it."

In four decades on the job, he personally witnessed three deaths. "We'd fill these tanks up on repair days, boiling water, thirty feet down in the floor. A strip run through there, and one guy opened the hatch on there and the water come out, thousands of gallons, and popped him against the wall. He was only thirty-eight years old. Chisholm. Another guy got hit by a tractor. I seen his guts coming out. I went over and took my handkerchief to try to cover his bowels or whatever. He died right away."

Like long hours, layoffs, and race-based job assignments, the pos-sibility of getting killed at work was long considered part of the job by the men who worked at Sparrows Point and their families. "Our wives put up with a lot," a man named John Hardity told me at a union retirees' meeting, "not knowing if you were going to come home in one piece or not."

• GUNS •

On a hot August morning in 1915, a group of union men met in Baltimore to discuss the labor situation at Sparrows Point. Their names were Hayes, Costello, Henderson, Christ, and Griese. I imagine them lounging around the stuffy office, with Hayes sitting behind the desk puffing on a cigar and Costello balanced on its edge, a toothpick in his mouth. Henderson stands looking out the window. Christ is leaning against the wall, and Griese and a couple of other guys are lounging on a ratty sofa. They are a rough-looking bunch in their mid-forties and fifties, accustomed to hard labor. The room smells of sweat and tobacco.

But that's all imagination. The truth is I don't know what the men looked like, how old they were, or how they smelled. I do know what they said, though, because one of them was a spy and submitted a report of the meeting to Frederick Wood:

> This morning I went to Hayes' Office about 11 o'clock and met Costello, Henry Christ, Hayes, Henderson, Griese and others. Christ stated that he had been to Sparrows Point, saw

Jerry Harris and asked him for a job, but that he only want to pay him 27½ cents an hour. Christ told him he would start in at 30 cents an hour and if he proved worth it he wanted more, but Harris told him he could get all the men he wanted for 25 and 27½ cents an hour and he would not pay 30 cents until he had to. Costello told Hayes that he ought to try and get busy with our men and keep them away from the Point and show Harris that he must pay better money or else he will not get men, but Hayes stated that the best thing to do is to let the men go down and when there are enough to make a showing, then pull the men out and let them see that the organization can give them some trouble. Costello said he has been watching that place for a number of years and nothing can be done with it. Hayes claims he could if he could get about twenty or twenty-five good union men to work there for two or three months he will be able to do something with the Point. Costello said, you can try, but if you do it will be something no one else has been able to get away with.

I came across this report, together with expense statements and invoices from the Pinkerton National Detective Agency, in Frederick Wood's files, which are archived at the Hagley Museum and Library in Wilmington, Delaware. Wood's papers reveal his brilliance as an engineer; his notebooks are filled with page after page of meticulous line drawings laying out his plans for the works, and they are impressive. But his papers also show that, like other steel company executives, he was willing to use any means necessary to keep his workers from joining or forming a union. Andrew Carnegie had shown them all that ruthlessness would be rewarded.

In 1892, Carnegie had broken the back of the Amalgamated Association of Iron and Steel Workers by instigating a labor uprising at the Homestead works near Pittsburgh. The Amalgamated, founded in 1876, represented craftsmen whose knowledge, skill, and experience were critical to steel mill operations. Those workers—predominantly from English, Scottish, and German backgrounds—wielded a surprising amount of power because management couldn't just hire men off the street to replace them. They also shared in the profits earned by their labor. Under the contract system then in effect, skilled steelworkers were paid a certain sum for each ton of steel they produced. This sum was called the tonnage rate, and it fluctuated according to the market price of steel.

But by the time Sparrows Point was founded in 1887, the power of the craftsmen was waning. By replacing men with machines—speeding up production and increasing volume through greater mechanization—steel bosses could slash labor costs by using fewer skilled craftsmen, and many more "semiskilled" employees paid a flat rate to run the machines.

Frederick Wood had set up this kind of system from the start at Sparrows Point—one reason why the company rented homes to workers and sold merchandise in the company store at cost. As Luther Bent had explained to the inspectors visiting the works in 1892, when the company's Steelton plant had been founded in 1867, skilled steelworkers were earning from $4 to $10 a day. But at Sparrows Point, the average was $1.75 a day. Those depressed wages were balanced by the Point's low-cost housing and goods at the company store. Employees could not have supported a comparable lifestyle outside the company town.

On the other hand, at mills like the Carnegie-owned Homestead, where skilled employees enjoyed both high wages and independence from the company, the Amalgamated fought any attempt to cut the number of skilled jobs or to elevate unskilled laborers into semiskilled jobs tending the new machines. "Every detail of working the great plant was subject to the interference of some busybody representing the Amalgamated Association," a Carnegie historian wrote of Homestead, where a strong contract negotiated in 1889 gave skilled workers effective control over production and wages.

To break the union, Carnegie turned over operations to Henry Clay Frick, an experienced strikebreaker. When in June 1892 workers refused to accept a 22 percent decrease in pay and elimination of bargaining positions, Frick locked them out of Homestead. By then, he

had turned Homestead into a fortress, surrounding the works with
a three-mile-long, twelve-foot-high fence topped with barbed wire
and ringed by sniper towers, with every entrance guarded by a high-
pressure cannon rigged to spray boiling-hot water. But if the union
men couldn't get into Homestead, neither could the scabs Frick had
hired to take their place. The unionists patrolled the Monogahela
River and drove off anyone who attempted to enter the works.

Frick's muscle, detectives from the Pinkerton National Detective
Agency armed with Winchester rifles, tried to land in the middle of
the night on July 5. The strikers were waiting, and a gun battle followed in which two men on each side were killed and thirty-three
wounded. Four more strikers and one more Pinkerton were killed
early the next day. When the Pinkertons finally surrendered, they
were beaten by strikers. At that the governor called out the state mili-
tia; the furnaces were relit and the mill reopened, but the Amalgamated was broken.

"Our victory is now complete and most gratifying," Frick reported
to Carnegie. Even more gratifying to some, Frick was shot and
stabbed during the strike by the anarchist Alexander Berkman. Frick
survived, but the Amalgamated didn't. Within a few years, the union
had been effectively driven out of every steel mill in America.

The Pinkerton invoices in Frederick Wood's files are evidence that
trade unionists tried to organize Sparrows Point shortly after Homestead. The first bills are dated 1899, and they continue into the new
century. In 1909, Wood paid the Pinkertons $870 to tail suspected
unionists; six years later he was paying $1,948.53 for just six months of
detective work. Based on the expenses listed in the reports, the agents
spent a great deal of time traveling back and forth between Baltimore
and Philadelphia, following organizers into saloons and barbershops,
and paying off informants. The information provided by the spies no
doubt helped keep union men from being hired in the first place,
much less from attempting to organize fellow workers.

Evidence suggests that even when they tried, organizers found
Sparrows Point a tough nut to crack. Many in the town didn't see any
benefit to unionization. The Strasbaughs, for example, were experi-

enced steel men from the day they stepped onto the Point. Bob Strasbaugh, born in 1923, told me that his grandfather was transferred from Steelton to Sparrows Point in 1892, the very year of the great Homestead lockout. Bob's father rolled steel—then, as now, the top job on the line. When Bob was hired in 1940, "there were eleven Strasbaughs working in that plant," he told me proudly, and he worked in the same department as his father, his uncles, and his cousins. Unlike many others who, he said, "jumped at the opportunity to join a union" when they got the chance, his family declined. "Why should we join a union," he asked, quoting his father, "when the company always treated us right?"

Attitudes were different in Baltimore, where the Baltimore Federation of Labor, founded in 1883, included seventy-one unions representing all manner of workers, from brewers, carpenters, and can makers to stonecutters and metalworkers. Even foremen and supervisors in city factories were union members; the rank and file insisted on it. Industrial workers in Baltimore differed from residents of Sparrows Point in yet another respect: most were immigrants or the children of immigrants. When the North German Lloyd Line began offering tickets permitting an individual or a family to board a ship in Bremen, Germany, sail to Baltimore, and immediately board Baltimore and Ohio Railroad trains heading west, the number of immigrants landing in Baltimore skyrocketed. In 1907 alone, sixty thousand people— Germans, Czechs, Poles, Hungarians, Swedes, Norwegians, Russians, Bohemians, Russian Jews, and Irish—disembarked at piers on Locust Point, just across the harbor from Sparrows Point.

A lot of new arrivals took those trains heading west, but a good many others fanned out across the city to neighborhoods that soon became tight-knit ethnic enclaves. People tended to live and work among their own kind in Baltimore. Polish immigrants in Canton worked in the canneries, Jews in Oldtown worked in the garment industry, native-born whites in Hampden worked in the cotton mills. Germans made beer in a city neighborhood that is today being marketed in real estate ads as Brewers Hill.

Economic survival for those new immigrants was often a struggle.

For example, a Johns Hopkins Hospital psychologist noted in a report on the children of Locust Point, where many immigrants from central and eastern Europe first settled, that "life is largely colored by industrial conditions. The industries for the most part employ cheap unskilled labor, a fact that keeps the majority of families below the poverty level, and too often far below it." Like many native-born Americans then (and today), Dr. C. Macfie Campbell of the Henry Phipps Psychiatric Clinic at Johns Hopkins didn't expect much from immigrants of "the non–English speaking races." After administering an intelligence test to 1,281 children of immigrants living in the Locust Point school district, he concluded that only 620 of them were of normal intelligence. The rest he judged more or less mentally defective. Charts accompanying the text list the vices and failings of both the children and their parents and make it clear where Dr. Campbell and his associates felt much of the blame for the "subnormal" children lay. The words "alcoholic," "syphilitic," and "immoral" are used to describe quite a few of the parents.

Dr. Campbell was hardly an unbiased observer, but the poverty and misery in which many of the families lived come through quite clearly in his descriptions of the households he visited. Life was a bit more secure across the harbor in the company town, which might explain as much as anything why the residents of Sparrows Point resisted the pleas of union organizers for so long.

> The battlefield of the Somme was drawn in steel: mountains
> of shells trained against underground fortresses of steel, the
> machines of Bethlehem versus the machines of Krupp.
>
> — MARK REUTTER

World War I brought the Pennsylvania Steel era to a close at Sparrows Point. With the start of war in Europe, overseas rail orders dried up, and Frederick Wood was compelled to lay off half the workforce. Shortly afterward, Pennsylvania Steel sold the Point to its biggest rival and erstwhile partner in Cuban mining operations, Bethlehem Steel.

Bethlehem had been founded as an old-fashioned ironworks in 1857. As at Pennsylvania Steel, its primary product was rail. Unlike Pennsylvania Steel and its subsidiary, Maryland Steel, however, Bethlehem began diversifying its product line early on, producing armor plating for the U.S. Navy and steel for ships and bridges as well as railroads. By 1895, the company was becoming famous as an international leader in the production of munitions. A British ordnance expert visiting the company's Pennsylvania headquarters that year said, "I consider the Bethlehem Gun Plant to be superior to any gun plant in the world."

Fueled by its arms dealing, Bethlehem saw its fortunes rise as those of Pennsylvania Steel fell. When war broke out in 1914, business exploded. "Bethlehem Steel was the first U.S. firm to receive war materials orders from the allied powers of Britain and France," wrote the historian Lance Metz. "By December of 1914, it had received over $50 million in ordnance orders from these nations in addition to a total order of $135 million for items such as shells and submarines."

In 1916, Bethlehem took over Sparrows Point. "I got sold right along with the plant," William Dennis, a seventy-seven-year-old steelworker told a *Baltimore Sun* reporter in 1951, describing the nearly seamless transition from Maryland Steel to Bethlehem. Dennis had been at the Point since 1886. "I went to work at the age of twelve for five cents an hour," he said proudly.

Soon after the deal was consummated, Bethlehem's president, Charles M. Schwab, a former U.S. Steel executive involved in the bloody events at Homestead, admitted to a reporter that he had coveted the great steelworks on the Chesapeake for over twenty years. Schwab picked a particularly good time to snatch up Sparrows Point. Hoping to emulate Bethlehem's success, other steelmakers had gotten into the munitions trade too, violating America's officially neutral stance in the conflict. The Germans retaliated by resuming U-boat warfare on American ships. By April 1917, the United States and Ger-

many were at war, and all of Bethlehem's plants, including the newly
purchased Sparrows Point, were directed to defense work, a very
profitable enterprise for the company—and a moral mission that the
patriotic citizens of Sparrows Point took deeply to heart.

Employees in the furnaces and shipyard—even clerical ones—
labored round the clock. "I worked nights and many Sundays (with no
overtime allowance in those days) and was happy to do so," wrote
Margaret Lindemon, by then a purchasing clerk for the sheet and tin
mill. "I thought I was fulfilling an ideal in my life, when we were all
doing what we could to win the war to end all wars."

On May 17, 1918, the residents of the town and the chief inspector of the U.S. Shipping Board gathered to witness a feat that made
North Siders in particular proud: the African American riveter
Charles Knight set a new world record by driving 541 rivets per hour
into the hull of a steel-bodied ship being built in the yard. "Whistles
blew and foremen and employees alike cheered," the *Baltimore American* reported, as Knight, assisted by an all-black crew—three passer
boys and two heater boys—"wielded two 90 Beyer pneumatic ham-
mers, each weighing 25 pounds, alternating as soon as one became too
hot for handling." Knight drove 4,875 rivets in nine hours. Lest read-
ers miss the military significance of this feat, the reporter pointed out
that "statistics show that one rivet equals seven shots fired at the
enemy. That being the case, Knight fired 34,125 bullets yesterday."

As production ramped up during the war, thousands of new workers were hired in 1917 and 1918. Only four thousand or so of the
twelve thousand employees who filed into and out of the gates of the
mill each day lived in the town. Most of the others lived in Baltimore
and commuted by trolley or rail. But Bethlehem, like Pennsylvania Steel
before it, understood how the bonds of loyalty could be tightened—
and worker independence reduced—when the company was not just
employer but also landlord.

Soon after taking control of the Point, Bethlehem purchased a
thousand acres of farmland across Bear Creek, one stop away from the
works on the rail line to Baltimore. William McShane, an Irish immigrant, had started a foundry there in 1894 and, asked to provide a

name for the stop on the Baltimore and Ohio Railroad, he suggested Dundalk, after his father's hometown in Ireland. The community had fewer than five hundred residents when Bethlehem hired the Baltimore architect Edward L. Palmer Jr. to plan a new company town on what was then mostly farmland owned by families who had lived in the area as far back as the War of 1812.

Like the Wood brothers, Palmer was a bit of a visionary, and he sketched out a blueprint for "sturdy homes, gracefully curving streets and a town center with parks and a shopping district," very much like what his company had created a few years earlier in an affluent north Baltimore neighborhood called Roland Park. Palmer boasted that the new town he was helping to create would be "a Roland Park for the working man," and he brought in the same team to draw up the plat for the new steel town, ensuring that his vision would be realized.

Water and sewer lines had already been laid according to Palmer's plan when Bethlehem's president, Charles Schwab, was appointed director of the Emergency Fleet Corporation (EFC), created in 1917 by the U.S. Shipping Board to put together a merchant marine fleet for the war. Never a man to miss an opportunity to feed at the federal trough, Schwab directed one of his subordinates to prepare a report pointing out that lack of housing was severely hampering the war effort in Baltimore. Sparrows Point defense workers were being forced to spend hours commuting from Baltimore by trolley and rail each day, the report said, when they could be building ships.

In April 1918, the EFC's Liberty Housing Company began building houses according to Palmer's blueprint, on one hundred of the one thousand acres purchased by Bethlehem. "What was a bare field two weeks ago now has the unmistakable marks of a town in the making," *The Baltimore Evening Sun* reported breathlessly on July 11, 1918. Within a few months, the "mushroom" town was filled with Bethlehem employees and their families. Like Sparrows Point before it, Dundalk was a town where workers had the company to thank for their homes. But in Dundalk, employees were encouraged to buy the newly constructed houses, with the company as mortgage holder. For $4,135—or a $34 monthly mortgage payment—workers got three large bedrooms with closets, a full tile bath with a shower and linen closet, hardwood floors, "inlaid linoleum" in the kitchen, hot-water heat, window screens, and a concrete porch with iron railings.

After the war, when the services of defense workers were no longer needed, Congress complained that the EFC had created housing too ambitious and expensive for practical dwellings for the general run of workmen. They had Palmer to thank for that. The 531 solidly built houses of brick and stucco he designed "in a simple picturesque period revival motif" still stand today, which is more than can be said for most World War I–era worker housing. The area was granted National Historic District status in 1984.

Constructed as housing for defense workers, Dundalk was surrounded until the end of the war by a barbed wire fence, with sentries posted at the gates. Residents had to show their credentials to be admitted, and friends needed permission to visit.

Dundalk was also at the start a restricted community in another sense, as I learned when I came across the deed to the land in the archives of the Dundalk–Patapsco Neck Historical Society. Right up till Bethlehem Steel turned over the deed to the community to Baltimore County in 1940, every transfer agreement for each parcel of land included the following clause: "At no time shall the land included in said tract, or any part thereof, or any building erected thereon, be occupied by any other than a person or persons of the white race."

Bethlehem may not have wanted people of color living in its new upscale company town, but it still hired Southern black men to do the bulk of the heavy labor on the Point and wanted them close at hand. So the company built two small subdivisions called Carnegie and Steelton for African American steelworkers in a hamlet called Turner Station, sandwiched between Dundalk and Bear Creek. Turner's had been home to a few black families since the late nineteenth century, but soon after the first steelworkers and shipyard workers moved in, it became a virtual extension of the North Side, though economically far more independent.

"Residents not only built their own homes, they built all kinds of businesses . . . from corner grocery stores, to amusement parks, to their own air-conditioned theaters, to taxi cabs, gasoline stations, doctors, undertakers, and to just about every other commodity needed," the Baltimore historian Louis Diggs wrote in his introduction to an oral history of Turner's and the North Side, *From the Meadows to the Point*. "It was as though these hard-working men and women understood the economics in developing their own community because I found that once a dollar was spent in Turner Station, it stayed and circulated within the community numerous times before it left."

Gresham Hertt Somerville grew up in Turner Station and has fond memories of the place. "They had grocery stores, a pharmacy, and stores where you could buy supplies. Just about a little town," she recalled. Most of the men "relied on Bethlehem Steel for their livelihood," she said, "and they thought that Bethlehem Steel would take care of them forever." One of the few who didn't was her next-door neighbor Mr. Adams. "He had worked down there and didn't like it. He said it was too-hard work for him, so he built the Adams Bar and Lounge." The bar hosted many famous black singers and comedians of the day. Once a year on Easter Monday, Somerville's wife recalled, her family would take the trolley to Baltimore to go to the movies on Pennsylvania Avenue, the central hub for shopping and entertainment for black Baltimoreans. "We wasn't used to all that excitement," she told me, because Turner Station was "a really quiet town back then."

A creek had separated black from white in the old company town. The dividing line between black Turner Station and white Dundalk was a wall of green. Harry Young, a 1947 graduate of Sparrows Point High School who went to work for Baltimore County after he returned from the Korean War and who processed right-of-way applications for the Bureau of Land Acquisition, told me that Bethlehem Steel planted a tall hedge to separate the two communities. Throughout his decades in the bureau, Young said, "Bethlehem wouldn't sign any right-of-ways for anything that was going to knock that hedge down."

But in Dundalk, just as on Sparrows Point, there was a kind of border territory where segregation was slightly relaxed. Roy Walker, born in 1924, was raised in "white Turner's," which was divided from "black

Turner's" by a railroad track. "I had a black doctor," Walker told me. "He treated my whole family"—an unusual state of affairs in the 1930s and '40s. "And until I turned eighteen and went in the army, I had black barbers too."

Like the Cohills of H Street, the citizens of white Turner's had friendlier dealings with black neighbors than was common for the time. "We lived on one side of the tracks, and the whites lived on the other. But if we wanted to go over to their stores, we could," Somerville recalled. She and her family and friends used to patronize the market and shoe repair shop across the tracks, and the owner of the latter "even bought my father's Packard," she said. "After that they became good friends. He was a foreigner—an Italian, I imagine. He talked with an accent. He was very nice."

Valuable as those sorts of contacts might have been for the individuals involved, they could not change the overall pattern of segregation and discrimination in the mills and in the community at large. Even happy, well-cared-for children like Gresham Hertt knew that the promises and rewards of American life were not equally distributed. "In school when we said the Pledge of Allegiance, I couldn't say that last part about freedom and justice for all," she told me. "When I did, it hurt me."

> I became a union man at my father's knee, and I'll be one till
> they put me in a box.
>
> —MANUEL ALVAREZ

In October 1916, munitions workers at a Baltimore factory walked off the job when their employer, the Poole Engineering Company, began giving bonuses to gun shop and toolroom workers whom bosses considered particularly loyal or industrious. The strikers milled about in front of the plant for the rest of the day, urging new shifts of workers to stay out. Militant workers in the city fought piecework and bonus pay systems, which they viewed as "twin evils—schemes to lower pay and rush work," according to the historian Roderick Ryon. By the end of the first day, management at the munitions factory was negotiating with a strike committee. "Eleven days later," Ryan noted in his account of the strike, "the company abolished bonus work, and the strikers won a five percent wage hike."

No such thing happened at Sparrows Point when Charlie Schwab instituted a similar incentive plan in Bethlehem's mills. Skilled and semiskilled workers were given the opportunity to augment their wages by boosting production on the line or, in the case of craft workers, by finishing up assigned work ahead of schedule and taking on other tasks. Workers earning bonuses for ramping up production thus had a great incentive to push not only themselves but also their "unskilled" helpers to the limit. Those at the bottom of the job hierarchy weren't paid any more for their stepped-up labor, however. As it did in his other mills, Schwab's bonus scheme worked well on the Point to keep different classes of workers divided and to diminish the potential for any sort of collective action.

The bonus system on Sparrows Point was even more toxic because there the best-paying and most prestigious jobs were long passed down from family member to family member or ethnic group to ethnic group. "The company was very successful in segregating the workforce into ethnic and racial groups," Tom Capecci wrote in a history of Steelworkers Local 2610. "Ethnic and racial groups were kept in separate jobs and were pitted against each other to prevent their uniting."

Still, enough workers were dissatisfied with the bonus pay system that Bethlehem employees filed a petition with the National War Labor Board, the first government agency in U.S. history to provide material support to workers. That this unprecedented step was taken during wartime was no accident. The major objective of the War Labor Board, created by President Woodrow Wilson in the spring of 1918, was to dampen any labor unrest that might interfere with war industries. And there was a great deal to smooth over as newly empowered industrial workers throughout the country began to fight for safe workplaces, fair wages, and the right to organize as production increased during the war. In 1919 over four million workers—21 percent of the labor force—went out on strike.

President Wilson pledged his support for working people, whose labor was critical to the war effort, at the 1917 national convention of the American Federation of Labor. "I am with you if you are with me," Wilson promised the delegates. A string of labor victories followed, including a ruling against Bethlehem Steel in the matter of the bonus pay system, which the War Labor Board called "an unacceptable substitute for overtime and Sunday pay mandated for companies holding war contracts." The feds ordered the company to eliminate the plan and to begin collective bargaining with elected representatives of Bethlehem steelworkers—the first-ever acknowledgment by the U.S. government of the right of workers to organize, to negotiate, and to help set the terms of their employment.

Cornered, Bethlehem president Charlie Schwab proposed a sneaky compromise, one that had been tried by other companies hoping to stave off the threat of unionization. The company announced that Bethlehem steelworkers had formed their own Employee Representation Plan (ERP) and that it met the terms of the War Labor Board's decision.

Reading through a year's worth of handwritten minutes of the Sparrows Point ERP that I stumbled upon at the Baltimore Museum of Industry, I was reminded of my high school days serving on student council, organizing social events and bake sales. As a seventeen-year-old, I learned that student councils exist for one reason: to provide an illusion of student representation while carrying out the will of the administration. The minutes make devastatingly clear that Bethlehem's ERP carried out much the same function. Meetings were mostly devoted to a discussion of burning issues like the planning of oyster roasts, timing of mill restaurant openings, and "grant[ing] the use of the old service store building to the colored boy scouts."

Occasionally, the committee did get around to discussing issues of substance, as when it met to determine whether Frank Brandt, an open hearth employee discharged, purportedly for being drunk on the job, should be rehired. It's clear that Brandt didn't have a chance. Harvey Stiteler, the open hearth foreman, testified that he had warned Brandt on several occasions "to straighten himself out and correct his habits."

But the minutes suggest another reason that Brandt may have been let go: "[Stiteler] stated he had never made any remark concerning Brandt's affiliation with a labor organization, as his only concern is the work under his supervision."

The committee was deadlocked, without a majority in favor either of giving Brandt another chance or of keeping him laid off. Finally, after management's "special representative," J. A. Northwood, exited the meeting, two employee representatives proposed a solution: How about the committee recommend that Frank Brandt be given a fresh start in some other department? The motion was put to a vote—and was defeated, 4 to 5. One employee rep declined to vote at all. The meeting adjourned at five, having met for four hours to discuss a matter of great importance—a family man losing his job, possibly due to his support of union organizing—without reaching a decision.

Ed Gorman told me that neither his father nor any of the other men of his generation at Sparrows Point "talked union" at home. "Remember, they lived in a company town," he said. "You don't talk union in a company town. You'd lose your house, and then what would you have? I didn't know any union organizers who lived on the Point."

Consequently, few Sparrows Point steelworkers joined in the great organizing drive that swept through steel towns in the immediate aftermath of World War I, when the Amalgamated, hoping to rebound from its 1892 defeat, developed an ambitious plan to organize all four hundred thousand steelworkers in the nation, including the unskilled black and immigrant laborers the union had previously shut out.

The Amalgamated's demands seem reasonable today: an eight-hour day, one day's rest in seven, abolition of the twenty-four-hour swing shift, increase in wages, double pay for overtime, advancement based on seniority, elimination of company unions, reinstatement of men discharged for union activity. But steel company executives saw them as radical concessions and refused to recognize or even negotiate with the Amalgamated. In response, 367,000 steelworkers across the country walked off the job on September 22, 1919.

Union leaders and steelworkers themselves were confident that the strike would succeed. After all, the president had pledged his support to workers only two years earlier. But the Wilson administration, which had previously backed steelworkers' grievances through the National War Labor Board, suddenly went limp and, in a repeat of past practice, sided with the steel companies when they brought in scabs to replace striking workers. Federal troops were sent into the mills to protect these strikebreakers, and the four-month walkout ended in complete defeat for the union.

The failure of the organizing drive was partly linked to past practices. African American steelworkers had long been excluded from the Amalgamated, which, like most AFL unions, focused exclusively on protecting the workplace rights of native-born white craftsmen. As a result, black steelworkers did not trust the strike's organizers and did not support the 1919 strike in great numbers. The strike itself sparked violent interracial clashes in some steel towns because many of the workers who kept the mills running were impoverished black men from the South lured north by the promise of high wages. Sparrows Point escaped the turmoil, with fewer than five hundred workers of any race walking out. It's doubtful that a single one of the strikers was a resident of the town, where fear or loyalty (or some combination of the two) prevented a mass uprising.

The poststrike backlash was vicious. Steel manufacturers and the government accused striking laborers and their unions of being in league with the communists and Bolsheviks plotting worldwide revolution. American steelworkers went from being patriotic heroes laboring night and day to turn out the munitions required to win the war against the kaiser to being painted as Reds and revolutionaries plotting to destroy America. After the war, President Wilson had no further use for his former union allies. Deprived of federal support, steelworkers saw the gains they had achieved during the war vanish like smoke from a discharged gun.

The steel strike was called off on January 8, 1920, but even before then, many steelworkers had returned to work, beaten into submission by the charges of disloyalty to their country, the need to provide for their families, and the fear of the consequences should they continue to strike. As punishment, many were busted back to lower-paying jobs or fired outright. It was 1892 all over again.

The anti-union backlash overlapped with a postwar depression that crushed Bethlehem employees in Baltimore. The defense workers whose labor had been so critical for the war effort that (relatively) luxurious housing was built to lure them to the steel mill and shipyard became expendable. Postwar layoffs and cutbacks hit the residents of the new community of Dundalk particularly hard. Wages dropped to as low as $15 and $20 per week, and hundreds of new Dundalk homeowners were unable to pay their mortgages.

Facing eviction, they banded together and sent a delegation to Washington to ask for help. A Baltimore newspaper article published in 1921 poignantly stated their case, noting that "the community is practically bankrupt; . . . householders cannot keep up the payments on the houses at the present rate; . . . most of them are behind in their payments and many are out of work." The struggling workers were, the article noted, "brought from all parts of the country to help build ships which the government urgently needed." Now that the war was over and the company was laying them off or cutting their hours, "there will be wholesale evictions at Dundalk and the community will be destroyed."

With the U.S. government looking at a loss of nearly $1 million on its investment, the mortgages on the properties built by the Emergency Fleet Corporation were taken over by Bethlehem's real estate division, the Dundalk Company, which cut the monthly payments by 22 percent. Even so, some workers did lose their homes, while others managed to hang on until work in the shipyard picked up again.

Edward Palmer's grand plans of creating a workingman's Roland Park in Dundalk had stumbled on the painful reality of working-class life. A steelworker or shipyard worker could be making big money one year and be out of work or cut back to a few days a week the next. How could such a man take out a thirty-year mortgage on a house when he had no job security nor wage security? When he could not predict how much money he would make from one year to the next? When he could be fired at a moment's notice?

In 1920, Bethlehem's war workers in Dundalk learned that loyalty had limits. It would not put food in the mouths of their hungry children nor pay their mortgages. A seed of rebellion had been planted; fertilized by an even greater catastrophe, it would bloom into outright revolt.

• UNITY •

Mildred Stelfax was a public health nurse during the Great Depression. In 1972 she sat down with Ben Womer, president of the Dundalk–Patapsco Neck Historical Society, and recalled the suffering she saw as she visited the families of southeastern Baltimore County during those dark days. "I worked for the Baltimore County Health Department and my headquarters was located at Sparrows Point, Fourth and D Streets," she told Womer. "The hours were 9:00 to 4:30 in the winter, but sometimes I didn't get off until 10:00 or 10:30. I didn't feel like leaving the territory when the deprivation was so great. . . . Every thing you saw was some kind of trouble."

Some of her patients didn't have shoes, she said, so she arranged for the members of a private charity committee who visited Sparrows Point once a week to distribute food and clothing to call on them in their homes. She helped set up clinics for tuberculosis and venereal disease in the Health Center building on the Point, examined all the children in school, and provided pre- and postnatal care for mothers. "In a way [the job] was depressing," she admitted, so depressing that she took a leave of absence for a year, "with the understanding I would come back if I wanted. I never went back."

The Great Depression hit steel towns hard. Average weekly earnings for steelworkers nationally dropped from $32.60 per week in 1929 to $13.20 a week in 1932. Things were no different at Sparrows Point, where hourly wages were cut by 10 percent in 1931 and another 15 percent in 1932. By March 1933, Bethlehem had discharged twelve hundred workers on the peninsula; those who hadn't been laid off were cut back to a few days a month. The noisy, smoky steel town became eerily quiet and clean as the number of people working on-site each day shriveled from eighteen thousand to thirty-five hundred.

"People used to look down their noses and say, 'How can you live in that dirty place?'" recalled Nonnie Strasbaugh. "We used to tell them, 'When that place is dirty, our husbands and fathers are working.'" But during the Depression, "the silence of the mills and the cleanness of the smoke stacks were reflected in the silence and emptiness of the employees' pockets," the Sparrows Point resident Lois S. Myers wrote in a memoir archived at the local historical society.

"I remember my dad coming home at Christmastime with a check of $9," Bob Strasbaugh told me, recalling those hard times. To my surprise, he laughed. "We had a hell of a good Christmas." Those who lived in the company town were somewhat better off than many unemployed or underemployed workers around the country. Bethlehem Steel did not evict laid-off employees and their families from the company houses, and farmers in nearby Edgemere "would let people come out in the fields and pick crops so long as they didn't destroy them," said Strasbaugh. "All the women knew how to can," he added. "That's how they survived."

Sparrows Point employees could also buy groceries on credit at the company store. "During the Depression, the company kept many families in necessities," Myers wrote. "When the company store went out of business in the forties, tens of thousands of dollars in debt were ignored. It may have been a monopolistic business in the first quarter of the century, but it helped many thousands to survive."

Residents of the town stuck together, pooling their meager resources. I recall my paternal grandmother saying more than once that during the Depression, she kept a pot of soup on the stove and would feed anyone, black or white, who came to the door—a startling admission from a woman who casually used the word "nigger" to describe African Americans. But my grandmother was also what my Catholic mother called a Holy Roller—an evangelical Christian who attended a small white-frame church where people spoke in tongues. She was always taking people in, and she raised an orphaned girl who somehow wound up on Sparrows Point. So maybe it's not so surprising that though she shared the prejudices of her time, she also practiced a color-neutral charity.

There were soup lines on the North Side during the Depression, but whites in the bungalows struggled too. "My mother said that when I was born, she had to borrow a blanket to bring me home in because they didn't have money to buy one," said Donald Lindemann. Both Nonnie Strasbaugh and a man named Daniel Fisher, whom I interviewed at a bungalows reunion, remembered different families pitching in ingredients to make a cake. The close-knit nature of the community, with generations of the same families living nearby, combined with the company's willingness to extend credit, may have helped insulate the residents of Sparrows Point from the worst ravages of the Great Depression.

In the city, the situation was more dire. The historian Jo Ann E. Argersinger reports that by 1933, over 20 percent of Baltimoreans were unemployed and 10 percent of the population of 804,874 was on relief. Within six months, another 42,425 cases were added to the rolls, and local charities struggled to meet the enormous need. The desperation of some city residents was nakedly revealed (in a story related by Argersinger) when one family kidnapped their relief worker to protest bureaucratic delays in getting food. "We've been nearly starving for the past three weeks, and if we are going to starve, you are going to starve with us," the distraught mother told the official.

Your president wants you to join a union.

—CIO ORGANIZING SLOGAN

Both of my parents were born at the height of the Depression—my father in Sparrows Point and my mother in Vandergrift, Pennsylvania, a company town founded by the Apollo Iron and Steel Company in 1895. All four of my mother's grandparents emigrated from Italy in the late 1890s, arriving in Philadelphia and making their way to the steel mills and coal mines of western Pennsylvania. Her grandfathers, Vincenzo Milito and Martino Carricato, and most of their sons worked at the former Apollo works, then Carnegie-Illinois (later U.S. Steel), though Milito was a miner for a time.

My mother's father, Alphonse, the youngest child of four, was born in Salida, Colorado, not too far from the site of the great Ludlow massacre, where the Colorado National Guard burned down a tent colony of striking miners in April 1914, killing twenty, including eleven children. The Ludlow victims were mostly Greek, but the mines of Colorado were also full of Italians and Mexicans. (As on Sparrows Point, mixing ethnic groups helped suppress union organizing.)

By the time of the Ludlow incident, my grandfather, then three, was in Pennsylvania, where his family rented a house from the slightly more prosperous Carricato family. In 1929, at seventeen, he eloped with their sixteen-year-old daughter, Amelia, and he too went to work for Carnegie-Illinois. My mother, the middle child of three, was born four years later. Though she doesn't really remember the Great Depression, my mother still maintains that Franklin Delano Roosevelt "was the greatest president of my lifetime," a perspective she shares with many working-class people of her generation, no matter how many Republicans they may have voted for in the second half of their lives.

Roosevelt swept Baltimore's working-class precincts in the 1932 election, even those like Sparrows Point that had gone strong for Herbert Hoover four years earlier. Roosevelt pledged a new deal for working Americans, and he kept his campaign promises, initiating a whirlwind of programs and signing fourteen major acts of legislation in his first one hundred days in office, all directed at providing immediate practical relief. The ones that would bear the most fruit for families like mine were the labor laws and reforms that radically shifted the balance of power between capital and labor.

The National Industrial Recovery Act, passed on June 16, 1933, was the first of these bombshells. The goals of the act were to increase employment, raise the wages of low-paid workers, and permit industries to eliminate unfair competition. But the heart of the act, which was to begin the process of overturning half a century of paternalism, union-busting, and the outright murder of workers and union organizers, was Section 7(a); it guaranteed the right of employees to organize and bargain collectively with their employers and to be "free from the interference, restraint, or coercion of employers." Moreover, no employee was to be forced to join a company union or to be prevented from "joining, organizing, or assisting a labor organization of his own choosing."

When Roosevelt's secretary of labor, Frances Perkins (the first woman to serve in the cabinet), visited Sparrows Point in July 1933, she didn't meet only with plant managers. She insisted on speaking to workers too, questioning them about wages, working conditions, and safety. She wanted to hear what they had to say about the Bethlehem Employee Representation Plan—or, as she termed it, "the company union." Speaking to some of the men privately, she asked if they wanted an independent union. One of them told her, "I think we ought to have a union, but the company doesn't want a union, and so none of us are going to kill ourselves to have one."

When a *Baltimore Sun* reporter asked her to comment on the difficulties the Roosevelt administration might have in "disciplining industry throughout the country," the quick-witted Perkins tartly replied, "The Government is not disciplining industry. Industry is disciplining itself."

Unlike some of the militants fighting to form unions in the midst of the Great Depression, steelworkers tended to be a cautious bunch who knew better than most the power of the companies they were fighting. Many lived in company towns like Sparrows Point or Vandergrift, where union organizers had literally been run out of town in an earlier organizing drive. So when a group of Bethlehem steelworkers began to discuss starting a real union at Sparrows Point, they held their secret meetings not in Sparrows Point but in Highlandtown, a Baltimore neighborhood bordering Dundalk that was home to immigrants of every nationality. "Italian, Spanish, Hungarian, Germans, a lot of Polish," said Manuel Alvarez, who grew up there. "Everyone around us was an immigrant, except for the Smiths from Virginia and one family across the street named Baker. They all worked for Bethlem."

His father's first job at the Point, Alvarez told me, was picking up the pieces of slag that littered the ground around the blast furnaces—a typical "immigrant" job for which he was paid $1 per bucket. By the time he became a husband and father, the elder Alvarez had graduated to a labor gang—but outside the company town, a laborer's wages didn't support a very comfortable lifestyle.

"Before World War II, we were living hand to mouth," Alvarez told me, describing those lean times. The family—parents and three children—lived in three rooms on the first floor of their rented row house. In turn, they rented rooms on the top floor (three small bedrooms) to boarders, an arrangement common in the neighborhood, where working poverty bred the kind of radical thought suppressed in the company town.

"When I was a kid, I overheard a lot of conversations about workers' rights. It was a little more than socialism, almost communism," he recalled. "A lot of it was in Italian. They thought they would have more rights in this country, and that was why they left. But it turns out that they didn't. So there was a lot of left-wing talk, and these were people who were more easily able to organize."

It's not hard to see why socialism appealed to working-class Americans during the 1930s. A flyer distributed by the Socialist Labor Party of Maryland succinctly summarized their problem:

> In this Machine Age, when industrial methods are revolutionized over night, NO MAN IS SECURE IN HIS JOB. This will continue to be as long as the FEW, enriched by taking for their own use what the Working class produces . . . keep the WORKERS IN SUBJECTION AND SERVITUDE. Hence the WAGE SLAVERY that prevails. WORKERS WILL CONTINUE TO BE A SUBJECT CLASS exploited to the bone, in which the constantly increasing number of jobless unfortunates will be left to the tender mercies of Capitalist Charity or become criminals, or make away with their miserable selves. ALL THIS CAN BE CHANGED IF THE WORKERS WANT IT CHANGED.

As the Depression ground on and hours were cut and cut again, steelworkers accepted the Socialist Party's diagnosis, though not its cure: "If the Workers shall be free, the existing form of Government, the Political State (the State of the Owning Class), must be ABOLISHED and a new form of government take its place." The steelworkers weren't interested in revolution. Instead, they were inspired by what autoworkers had accomplished in Flint, Michigan.

In December 1936, the United Automobile Workers (UAW)—which at that time had signed up less than 10 percent of the workforce—managed to shut down six General Motors plants throughout the city. For six weeks, striking workers occupied the plants in what labor historians call "one of the epic confrontations in American labor history." In February, the Flint strikers declared victory when GM agreed to recognize the UAW as the exclusive bargaining agent for its workers.

United Mine Workers (UMW) president John L. Lewis negotiated the one-page agreement between the company and the striking workers. When it looked like the steelworkers might be next, Myron Taylor, the president of U.S. Steel, appealed to Lewis for help. Lewis, who had helped draft the labor provisions of the NIRA, had long dreamed of organizing steelworkers. After he and a group of dissident labor leaders founded the Committee for Industrial Organization (CIO) in November 1935, he arm-wrestled the leaders of the moribund Amalgamated into affiliating with the Steel Workers Organizing Committee (SWOC), formed in Pittsburgh in June 1936.

Philip Murray, vice president of the UMW, became director, controlling an organizing budget of half a million dollars. Murray understood very well the psychological, as well as the systemic, obstacles confronted by organizers. "Our first task was to banish fear from steelworkers' minds," he recalled years later.

SWOC's first victory came in March 1937 when Lewis and Taylor hammered out a compromise in which Taylor agreed to recognize SWOC as a bargaining agent for U.S. Steel employees and Lewis agreed to accept the continued existence of the company union so long as the company stopped intimidating men trying to join SWOC. Employees of U.S. Steel gained seniority rights and improved wages and hours of employment as well as a grievance procedure administered by SWOC.

With the nation's largest steel producer accepting the CIO, many thought that the struggle to unionize steel was over. Not quite. The smaller independent companies like Bethlehem, Republic Steel, and Youngstown Sheet and Tube Company—known collectively as Little Steel—refused to follow U.S. Steel's lead. As those companies together produced 38 percent of the nation's steel, their continued resistance was no minor setback.

The form their resistance took was squarely in line with their past behavior. "Company police at Sparrows Point and other plants were supplied in early 1937 with several boxcars' worth of guns and ammunition," Mark Reutter points out in *Making Steel*. "The munitions included army-type machine guns, submachine guns, army rifles, shotguns of the regular, repeating, and sawed-off variety, as well as pistols and revolvers of all makes and calibers. Bethlehem also purchased more tear gas equipment than any law enforcement agency in the 1936–37 period."

Clearly Bethlehem, like the other Little Steel companies, was spoiling for a fight. When the fight actually broke out, however, it wasn't Bethlehem but Republic Steel that began shooting. On May 26, 1937, Murray called for a strike against Republic, Inland, and Youngstown Steel. A few days later, police shot and killed ten strikers near the South Chicago plant of Republic Steel; another seventy-five were wounded. A week later, three strikers were killed by police in Youngstown. On June 11, workers at Bethlehem Steel's plant in Johnstown walked out.

As the strike, and the potential for violence, showed every indication of escalating, Franklin Roosevelt intervened, creating a mediation board that recommended calling off the strike and letting the National Labor Relations Board conduct elections at the various plants. The union men agreed; the companies did not. Labor and Little Steel were at a stalemate.

It would take an outsider to settle their dispute, forcing Bethlehem and the other independent steel companies to recognize SWOC, dismantle the company unions, and begin the process by which American steelworkers would at last achieve the power to bargain collectively with their employers. Few could have guessed that the catalyst would be Adolf Hitler. But it was war that finally ended the Depression and compelled stubbornly anti-union companies like Bethlehem to recognize the CIO unions formed in the gathering storm.

The greatest enemy of our nation is the poverty and insecurity of American life.

—FATHER JOHN F. CRONIN, 1941

When the SWOC organizers came to Baltimore in 1936, they joined up with the Highlandtown group. Most of the out-of-town organizers came out of Lewis's UMW, and some were radicals—communists, socialists, and anarchists. Unlike the AFL, the CIO and SWOC welcomed leftists because they recognized the organizing skills of those who were schooled in the struggle for workers' rights.

"A lot of so-called radicals helped organize the place," recalled Joe Kotelchuck, who began working at Sparrows Point in 1947 and joined the Steelworkers union in its first decade, later becoming president of Local 2610. "In fact, under John L. Lewis there were a lot of communists in the organization," he told me. "After the steelworkers and coal miners got organized, they threw out the so-called radicals. But they used them in the beginning because they were good organizers."

Unsurprisingly, the steel companies and even rival labor leaders tried to dissuade workers from joining the CIO unions by painting these organizations and their members as anti-American revolutionaries intent on overthrowing the system. Lewis and Murray outwitted them by officially denouncing "foreign 'isms'"—communism, fascism, Nazism—at the CIO's 1940 convention in Atlantic City.

A flyer distributed by SWOC to steelworkers during the organizing drive there turned the conservative argument against unions on its head, equating trade unionism with patriotism: UNION STEEL WORKERS ARE THE BULWARK OF DEMOCRACY read the banner headline. The text of the flyer pointed out "the many benefits a signed union contract means to you and your family—time and one-half for work on holidays; vacations with pay; job security and promotions." Just as important, by supporting SWOC, steelworkers could be part of something much bigger, the union's leaders and supporters argued: "a union dedicated to the building of a better America, under the American form of government."

In Baltimore and other cities with large Roman Catholic populations, that argument was supported by an influential ally—the Catholic Church. SWOC's president, Philip Murray, was himself a devout Catholic who anchored his fight for economic justice in Catholic teachings on social justice. Labor priests like Baltimore's Father John F. Cronin—backed by their bishops—talked up trade unionism and spoke out in the community in support of CIO organizing efforts.

"You need a labor union if you are going to get any kind of decent working conditions, wages and security," Cronin urged steelworkers in *Steel Labor,* SWOC's newsletter. "Even a man who works for a good corporation—a corporation that is honestly trying to get along with labor—needs a union if he wants to be heard. The Church is only too glad to lend its strength and prestige to the cause of organized labor, because a man cannot be free as an individual but only as a member of a powerful organization."

This was a winning argument, not only with Catholic steelworkers but with all those who knew firsthand how hard it was to win a shop floor dispute standing alone against a foreman backed by the company. In October 2006, I spoke with Neil Crowder, who was one of the first SWOC organizers at Sparrows Point. He told me that he arrived on the Point in 1936, at the age of seventeen, and got a job in the labor gang with the help of a friend of his aunt who was a World War I veteran.

"It was hard to get a job down there then," he said. "So my aunt's friend wrote me a sob letter—'Please give this poor orphan a job.'" Within a short time, he saw how the workers were treated and resented it. Foremen had absolute power and workers had no voice at all. No matter how unfairly workers were treated, they had no choice other than to take whatever the foremen dished out.

He had his first personal experience with the arbitrary nature of this system two months after he started as a hooker, attaching cranes to loads. When his foreman accused him of working too slowly, he was sent to see the general foreman, a man named Edwards whose nickname was the Bulldog. When he tried to defend himself against the charges, the Bulldog refused to listen and sent him to the employment office, which demoted him back to the labor gang.

"That laid the groundwork for me to belong to the union," he said. "They weren't fair. When things went wrong, they would blame people that weren't responsible"—usually the least skilled workers. Most steelworkers, with families to support, were "terrified" to protest this kind of treatment, he said. "Either I was too young or didn't have enough damn sense to be afraid of anybody, but I wasn't."

One day in late 1939, he went to get his hair cut in Highlandtown.

"The barber said, 'Where do you work, kid?'" he recalled, "and I told him Sparrows Point. He says, 'Do you belong to the union?' I told him that I didn't know nothing about unions because before I went to Sparrows Point, I had worked as a telegraph operator in Philadelphia." The barber told him that SWOC was trying to get organizers inside the mills and explained what they wanted to do. "I said, 'That sounds like a great idea.'"

The barber sent him down the street to a men's clothing store where SWOC organizers had set up offices on the second floor. When he walked in and told the older men—organizers from the UMW— why he was there, "they almost hugged and kissed me," he said. They needed inside organizers, they told him, because when people on their team went to Sparrows Point and tried to hand out materials to steel-workers as they started and ended their shifts, "the guys would throw the stuff away. So they made me a shop steward right away, and gave me a bunch of buttons and other material." When he went to work the next day, Crowder started talking, and within a few weeks he had a number of men in his department signed up. "I was always a pretty good salesman," he said.

The foremen often played right into his hands. He knew that the union was "on the way in" one day when another "kangaroo court" resulted in the disciplining of seven workers. In the aftermath of that incident, he said, "I signed every damn one of them up." The basic issue, the one that motivated most of those who joined the union in the early days, was not higher wages or safety but simple fairness, he said. "You were promoted or disciplined at the whim of a boss." Most of the Sparrows Point workers wanted a union, he said, "but they were scared to death. The history of organizing steel was so bad. What they needed were people like me"—people who weren't afraid. "Even before the union, I would speak up. It doesn't make you popular [with foremen]," he said, but his co-workers trusted him.

His organizing efforts were made easier because he worked in a department that was staffed almost entirely by people who lived in the city. "Most of the guys who worked in the cold strip mill lived in Baltimore," he said. "I don't remember signing up anybody who lived in the town." In the beginning, union workers had to hide their SWOC buttons under their lapels, like members of a secret society. "But after I got them all organized, I said, 'Tomorrow's the day.'" That day, all the men who had joined the union wore their buttons openly. "The foreman saw them and his mouth dropped open," he recalled, chuckling.

Crowder's account of Sparrows Point organizing echoes those of historians who have studied SWOC's successful campaign to organize steel after decades of defeat for the Amalgamated. "No industry with steel's open shop history could have been organized in the absence of massive rank and file mobilization," noted the eminent steel labor historian David Brody. "A guerilla war for unionism ensued inside plants. . . . Only through the efforts of fellow workers could non-union workers be signed up."

It was slow going for a while. The flare-up of the Depression in 1937 after a brief reprieve had hampered organizing efforts. Steelworkers around the country were laid off or had their hours cut back. Neil Crowder was among those laid off at Sparrows Point in 1938. Nationwide, 28 percent of the steel workforce was laid off, and another 57 percent worked only a few days a week. But by 1939, when Crowder, back at the mill, began talking union to his co-workers, recovery was well under way at Sparrows Point, where every department was once again working at 100 percent capacity (compared with 55 percent capacity in 1934) and the shipyard had a $20 million backlog of orders.

The government also had a fine stick to wave around the heads of stubbornly anti-union companies like Bethlehem. With the drums of war beginning to beat loud enough to be felt on this side of the Atlantic, and with steel companies itching to win lucrative defense contracts, the National Defense Commission ruled that failure to comply with federal law, including labor law, would prevent companies from being awarded government contracts. "Bethlehem would never deal with the union until 1941, when they were threatened with the loss of war contracts," the Baltimore labor studies professor Bill Barry told me.

Caught between the rock of government pressure and the hard place of rank-and-file activism, steel companies were slowly being squeezed into surrender. By 1941, even the most stubborn companies were forced to admit defeat. Early that year, workers at Bethlehem mills around the country began taking part in targeted strikes organized by SWOC. Thirteen thousand workers at the company's plant in Lackawanna, Pennsylvania, struck to protest disciplinary action against union supporters in the mill. A few weeks later, over 90 percent of the workforce in Bethlehem, Pennsylvania, the company's hometown, walked off the job rather than vote in a scheduled election for the company union. The next domino fell at Johnstown, where the entire workforce walked out. A less dramatic but still effective one-shift strike at Sparrows Point in August illustrated the strength of union sentiment in Baltimore when workers refused to cross the picket line. Soon after, Bethlehem Steel agreed to NLRB-run elections in all its mills throughout the country. On September 25, 1941, Bethlehem's Sparrows Point workforce got its chance in the ballot booth, and SWOC triumphed by a wide margin, winning 68 percent of votes.

The support of black steelworkers was critical to the success of the organizing drive at Sparrows Point. As the biggest employer of African American workers in Baltimore, with fifty-five hundred blacks in a total workforce of 16,500, Bethlehem Steel had been a major CIO target. Arthur Murray, a veteran black steelworker from the Pittsburgh area, came to Baltimore to direct SWOC's outreach to the African American community, passing out union cards door to door in East Baltimore and encouraging blacks to trust white CIO leaders. Black ministers welcomed CIO organizers into their churches and spread news of drives, strikes, and rallies from the pulpit.

SWOC sponsored parades of black and white workers through all-white Dundalk—a daring move that illustrated the power of unity. The historian Roderick Ryon interviewed a Sparrows Point steelworker who recalled a turning point in the struggle when "a dozen or so blacks and ten or twelve whites who had worked on the same mill floor for eighteen years . . . sat down, debated the CIO's case, and as a group decided to join the union."

I asked Eddie Bartee Sr. if his father had been an SWOC organizer. "No, but my uncle was," he said. "And my father supported my uncle, who was vocal and out front and kind of mouthy." North Side residents tended to support the union, he said, because "we were the ones who had the most to gain."

The quiet support of black steelworkers like Bartee's father and the more open activism of men like his uncle helped turn the tide in the union's favor. The local SWOC director, Nicholas Fontecchio, admitted as much in an interview with *The Baltimore Afro-American:* "Had their vote been against us we would have lost the election. I want it known that we appreciate their support and we are going to work for the common good of all along the policy of the CIO which frowns on all race, color, or creed discrimination."

A similar drama was playing out around the country in industries that had long fought unionization. During 1941, over 2.3 million industrial workers went out on strike, in steel, auto, and coal, as well as other industries, to win the right to bargain collectively with their employers through the CIO and CIO-affiliated unions. In most of these strikes, the CIO unions were victorious. As at Sparrows Point, workers voting in the various CIO unions were not voting for communism, socialism, or any other radical ideology. What workers wanted, say labor historians, were "union contracts that carefully governed wage rates, disciplinary procedures, work rules, promotion rosters, and seniority." In place of the paternalism—sometimes benevolent but more often tyrannical—that had previously ordered their lives, workers demanded a system of rules and procedures that bound both employer and employee.

It's hard not to hear in that demand an echo of the principles upon which the United States was founded. In voting for union, workers rejected the principle of fealty—the automatic and unquestioning obedience one is expected to render to a lord or king—and chose the principle of contract or covenant, a mutual agreement that equalizes the relationship between worker and employer.

"The greatest achievement of the union," eighty-eight-year-old Neil Crowder told me, "is that it brought democracy to the workplace."

• LIBERTY •

Less than three months after Sparrows Point steelworkers voted for
union, the country was at war. Like many young men of the community, Wendell Doyle entered the service as soon as he graduated
from Sparrows Point High School. After training in Tennessee and
Florida, he was assigned to the aircraft carrier *Saratoga* as a turret gun-
ner in the Pacific theater. "I was in a night torpedo squadron," he told
me when we spoke in his apartment at a Dundalk assisted-living facility, surrounded by the delicate wooden animals he learned to carve in
retirement. "I made about fifty night landings."

"I guess you shot down a lot of planes," I said.

"Nah, I didn't want to shoot anybody," Doyle said.

"I thought that was part of the job."

"It was. It was." He paused. "I was in the naval raids on Tokyo and
Iwo Jima. They hit us with kamikazes, and we lost about three hundred men. We would lose five hundred men in a day, and you never
heard about it."

The southeastern neighborhoods of Sparrows Point, Dundalk,
Turner Station, Middle River, and Essex sent thousands of young men

overseas from 1941 to 1945. "Dundalk had the largest Selective Service board in the country," Harry Young, a volunteer at the Dundalk–Patapsco Neck Historical Society, told me. Despite the size of the draftee pool, many of those registered from the heavily industrialized communities never went overseas. "A lot of people were exempt because they worked in war-type industries," he said. "They froze them in what they were doing."

As a major defense installation, the company town was viewed as a possible target, and families there learned to endure regular blackouts for air-raid practice. "The wardens went around and told you ahead of time," Donald Lindemann recalled. "You had to turn out all the lights in the house for an hour and a half, two hours. And if the warden would see a light coming through your window, they would fine you $5. And that was a lot of money back then. You had to stay in your house and pull down all the shades."

Harry Young recalled both the pervasive sense of dread—"everybody thought we were going to be bombed, but we never were"—and the excitement of the time. "I owned all the paper corners in Dundalk from 1943 to the end of the war. I had all my paperboys selling papers on the streetcars. They'd come out of the Point and take the streetcar and they'd all be triple-headers, three cars linked to each other. They'd have eighty-five seated on each car and twenty or thirty standing. One right after another."

Just as in World War I, steel manufacturers reaped the benefits of vastly increased government defense spending, with Bethlehem in the lead. The War Production Board financed the rapid expansion of the facilities at Sparrows Point, adding a new coke oven battery, a seventh blast furnace, more open hearths, and new finishing mills. From 1942 to 1944, the blast furnaces at the Point produced a record two and a half million tons of hot metal each year. An even bigger source of community pride was the awe-inspiring record of wartime shipbuilding at Bethlehem's Baltimore yards.

"I remember when I was twelve or fourteen years old, coming across the streetcar bridge and watching the welding flashes on and off from all the ships they were building," Ed Gorman told me. "It was amazing. They worked all day and all night—daylight, four to twelve, and midnight. Just flashing and flashing."

The history of shipbuilding at Sparrows Point goes back to its earliest years, when a "marine department" was part of Frederick Wood's original blueprint for the plant. After Bethlehem Steel took over in 1916, the company began a huge expansion and modernization program, rebuilding old shipways and adding new ones and building new loading piers and floating dry docks. During World War I, the Sparrows Point yard delivered forty-nine vessels of various kinds to the U.S. Navy. But the yard's World War II production far eclipsed that earlier record. During the peak of war production, the Sparrows Point yard was delivering a ship every two weeks.

Bethlehem also operated a ship repair yard on Key Highway in Locust Point, and when defense contracts began pouring in during 1941, the company leased another shipyard in adjacent Fairfield. Jack Willis, general manager of the Sparrows Point shipyard, was assigned the task of expanding operations at Fairfield and assembling a workforce. Willis took forty experienced shipbuilders from Sparrows Point and used them as the nucleus of a Bethlehem-Fairfield workforce that would number more than forty-seven thousand at the height of the yard's operation. A *Sun* profile of Willis enthused that he "turned businessmen, insurance, automobile, and liquor salesmen, farmers, fishermen, artists and mountaineers into shipbuilders."

Bethlehem-Fairfield was originally contracted to produce fifty of the two hundred Liberty ships called for by the emergency shipbuilding program of the U.S. Maritime Commission. The design of the Liberty ships was adapted to mass production: the hulls were welded together, saving construction time and providing added strength. Liberty ships were not warships, though they were equipped with guns for self-defense. They were more like merchant ships, ferrying supplies, war materials, and men to the European and Pacific theaters of war, and also served as hospital ships for the wounded. Ships built at Bethlehem-Fairfield took part in every invasion in the European theater and in the Pacific, sustaining attack by aircraft, surface craft, and submarines. One shot down six enemy planes during an attack.

The keel of the first Baltimore-born Liberty ship, the *Patrick Henry*, was laid on April 30, 1941. Four months later, it was christened with great fanfare by the wife of the vice president of the United States. Within a year, the time it took Bethlehem-Fairfield workers to put a ship to sea, keel to launching, had shrunk to thirty days. In October 1943, *The Baltimore Sun* trumpeted the launch of a vessel twenty days and twenty-one hours after the laying of the keel.

In 1942, Bethlehem-Fairfield launched eighteen Liberty ships in August, nineteen in September, and twenty in October—an astonishing achievement considering that the vast majority of those working at Fairfield had never seen a shipyard before. From April 1941 to October 1944, these novices built and launched 384 Liberty ships, the largest fleet built by any single yard in the country during the war. Most of those ships not only survived the war intact but were afterward added to Bethlehem's fleet.

The Bethlehem-Fairfield workers were an ethnically and geographically diverse bunch, drawn to the state and to the yard by the promise of full-time jobs (with overtime) and the opportunity to learn more lucrative new trades. "Every state is represented among workers at the shipyard and 65 percent of them are from outside Maryland," *The Baltimore Sun* noted on April 5, 1944, in an article on the yard. "Ninety percent had never been employed in shipyard work before and 33,000 have been put through training"—becoming welders, burners, riggers, machinists, and electricians.

Some of those new craftsmen were low-tier Bethlehem employees who were finally given a chance to learn a trade when the need for skilled workers overrode old ethnic prejudices. Manuel Alvarez pointed out that it was during the war that his father and many fellow immigrants in their Highlandtown neighborhood moved out of the labor gangs at long last.

"When World War II came along, they gave anybody an opportunity who wanted to advance themselves to get a trade. So Mr. Garcia became a rigger. Mr. Lopez became a welder. Mr. Alvarez became a machinist. Our lifestyle changed dramatically," he added. "The table was full every day. We never again had to worry about food and basic clothing and rent." When I asked him why the company finally allowed immigrant men like his neighbors to become skilled crafts-men, he laughed. To meet production quotas, he said, "they would've dug you up out of the grave."

People come from everywhere down here during the war.
Virginia, West Virginia, Pennsylvania. It was during the war
that the big money started coming in.

—WILLY COHILL

The green leather cover of my maternal grandmother's battered date-book for the year 1941 is long lost, but its faded pages record a history shared with thousands of other families who came to Baltimore during the war years to work in its shipyards and mills. The entry, in my grandmother's neat handwriting, for January 4, 1941, reads: "Mr. and Mrs. Alphonse Milito and family came to Baltimore, Maryland July 1942 lived at 206 W. 27th Street Baltimore MD then moved to 2957 Liberty Parkway, Dundalk MD on Jan. 20, 1943." On January 30, she wrote, "Started to work for Calvert Distillery." Then, on June 10, 1943, "Went to work for Maryland Drydock." There is also an entry in my mother's childish scrawl: "My birthday is March the 9th. I moved to Dundalk and I am going to be eight years old."

The adjustment to life in Baltimore was hard for my mother, she said. She was a shy child, and she hadn't wanted to leave her friends, grandparents, aunts, uncles, and cousins behind in Pennsylvania to live among strangers. By then her father was an experienced steelworker, having worked his way up to shearman at the U.S. Steel plant in Van-dergrift. "He did piecework and was making good money when good money wasn't being made [during the Depression]," her older brother, Alphonse, told me. But on a wartime visit to Baltimore, my grandfa-ther found out that "he could make much more money here," my mother said. "Wages were much higher, and during the war years, the town was booming. So they decided to move."

She had just settled in and was making new friends in Dundalk when her father began bringing home an Italian POW interned at nearby Fort Holabird for Sunday dinner. "When my father found out from his relatives in Pennsylvania that one of their cousins was a prisoner of war and was being kept there, he started going to pick him up on Sundays," she said. Both Italian and German prisoners were held at Fort Holabird, an army camp in Dundalk. The German prisoners weren't allowed off the base, but if they had a sponsor, Italian prisoners could get a pass for a few hours on Sunday afternoons.

The POW cousin was "very nice and thrilled to be able to leave the camp and come to the house," my mother recalled. "My mother and father would speak Italian to him, and he was very handy and would make these little belts out of newspaper and plastic for us." But even though she liked him personally, my mother was ashamed and embarrassed by his presence. In Vandergrift she had been surrounded by a crowd of Italian relatives, people like her. But in Baltimore she became aware for the first time that "people were very prejudiced against Italians. Back then, some people would change their names from Italian-sounding names. And we had this man coming over on Sundays with a giant POW on his back, and with all the prejudice that existed in those days, it really bothered me."

Italians weren't the only ethnic group to discover that wartime solidarity did not erase prejudice. The huge influx of defense workers into Baltimore during World War II, including many whites from the Deep South and Appalachia, at a time when African American employment at local factories and mills swelled, greatly increased racial tensions. In July 1943, white riveters at the Sparrows Point shipyard walked off the job, successfully demanding that Bethlehem remove the fifteen African American laborers it had enrolled in a training class for riveters. Eight hundred black shipyard employees then staged a counterstrike, which led management to agree to reinstate the men. This in turn led to a march by white shipyard workers, thousands strong. The white marchers surrounded the black demonstrators, and a violent climax seemed inevitable. The situation was defused when Sparrows Point police escorted the black demonstrators from the yard.

The near riot at the Bethlehem shipyard was not an isolated occurrence. White women at the Western Electric plant in Baltimore walked off the job in August, a month after the Sparrows Point incident, when an African American woman was promoted to a supervisory position. Just as in the case of the black riveters at the Sparrows Point shipyard, white employees resisted the efforts of black employees to rise above low-level jobs into skilled or supervisory positions.

New CIO unions like the United Steelworkers of America and the Industrial Union of Marine and Shipbuilding Workers of America found themselves in a difficult position. Founded on a platform of racial equality, they were committed to protecting the rights of all employees, not just whites. But pushing for blacks to advance at the same time they were attempting to convince whites to join was not a recipe for successful organizing and growth.

In the early years of the Steelworkers union, shop stewards on Sparrows Point had to personally recruit each new member and collect dues every payday. "Back then when you first started working, the shop stewards would eyeball you because they weren't allowed to make union contact with new employees for thirty days," Ed Gorman recalled. "But when my thirty days were up, the washer shop steward, Neil Crowder, came over with a union card, and I signed it. I think back then they gave the shop steward a bounty, something like a dollar a person, for everyone he signed up." Neil Crowder confirmed this. But in his case, he used the bounty to pay the first month's dues for new recruits. "It seemed like a good idea and a good introduction to the union," he told me.

During those early years, shop stewards like Crowder had to work hard to sell the benefits of the union to sometimes reluctant employees. Austin McLelland was hired just after graduating from Baltimore's Thomas Edison High School, where his teachers in the machinist program were deeply anti-union. "When I went down there, there was no compulsory union," he said. "And I didn't particularly like the union, from what I learned in school. But then when I saw what working conditions were like [at Sparrows Point], I did join."

Bob Strasbaugh did not. "I was approached many a time when I was still hourly, and I would say, 'No, I don't want to join.' It wasn't a closed shop," he pointed out. Donna Young, Harry's wife, told me that her father, a shipyard draftsman, and his friends never joined the union either. "Like a lot of the people who came down here from Pennsylvania during the war to work in the shipyard and the steel mill, they were Republicans. They were people who had been through the Depression in their late teens and early twenties, and many of them, like my father, would have gone to college," she said. "They only worked in the steel mill because that was the first work that came up after the Depression."

Though they registered as Democrats in Maryland, where Republicans were few and relatively powerless, her father and his friends were conservatives, she said. They were philosophically opposed to trade unionism, particularly the kind championed by the "radical" CIO, which was known to have many communist members. But near the close of the war, when Soviet tanks began rolling into eastern Europe, Communist Party members were drummed out of the state CIO, even though many had played an important role in the struggle for unionization at local factories.

Passage of Maryland's Ober law, which made records on "subversives" available to employers, including Bethlehem Steel, not only helped purge communists in the state CIO but also suppressed leftist conversation among workers. Manuel Alvarez saw the change in his immigrant neighbors after the war, when a rising standard of living, together with anticommunist rhetoric by politicians, squelched previously heated discussion of workers' rights. "I think they were afraid that they would lose what they had, that they would be ostracized in the community," he said. That fear was not groundless. Austin McLelland told me that during a postwar strike, he saw a fellow worker seized by federal agents. "I was walking the picket line with him when all the sudden the federal government picked him up and said he was a communist."

African American workers lost their most powerful white supporters when communists and socialists were purged from leadership positions in the state CIO and its member unions. Even with signed union cards in their pockets, they found that they were still expected to accept second-class status in the mills and in the hall. Unlike the AFL craft unions that preceded them, CIO unions aggressively recruited black members, saying explicitly that "we want African-Americans to be part of this union," the historian Roderick Ryon pointed out. They also promised to fight for higher wages for the lowest-paid workers, "and that meant African-Americans," Ryon said. "But what the CIO did not do was promise to open up those privileged positions to blacks, and it did not bring blacks into positions of leadership in the union."

Black steelworkers, whose support for SWOC had helped guarantee its victory in the 1941 vote on the Point, soon found that the union was just as uninterested as the company in tearing down the wall between "black" jobs and "white" jobs. For example, when Lee Douglas arrived on the Point in 1946, fresh from the Marine Corps, he was hired as a laborer. Every black, he said, was hired as a laborer and usually assigned to one of the traditionally black units like the coke ovens or rigging.

Black laborers worked in the finishing mills, where they might be trained to fill in as replacements for white workers temporarily, but "you could never become part of that unit," Douglas pointed out. "They would hire a white straight from the street, and he would go right into the unit, while we're working there and can't become a member of the unit. It was very frustrating for everybody."

The USWA didn't challenge this situation, he said, because any attempt to change the long-standing system of racial discrimination in job assignments and wages on the Point would have been violently resisted by white steelworkers, and union officials understood that reality. "The union did not do much to help the black workers because 70 percent of employees were white and only 30 percent of employees were black," he said. "So the union had to cater to its strength, which was understandable at that time. The union could not be supporters of black rights because whoever come up with it would be voted out."

For Douglas and other black veterans returning home to work on Sparrows Point, the situation was familiar. Assigned to an ammunition company on Guadalcanal, Douglas participated in the invasion of Peleliu Island in September 1944. On the ship transporting the twenty-five hundred members of the First Marine Division and their associated black ammunition company, "whites were in their area, blacks in theirs," he said. His all-black unit was scheduled to go in on the first day of the invasion, September 15. Instead, they were assigned the gruesome task of fishing the bodies of white marines killed in the invasion out of the ocean because "the propellers were grinding them up. For two days we were dealing with them bodies."

When his unit finally joined the battle on the third day, something strange and unexpected happened. "For a short period of time, you became one," Douglas told me. In the heat of battle, the boundaries between black and white suddenly dissolved. "We went in together and we fought together." But once the battle was won, the wall of segregation snapped into place again. "After we had finished with the island, we went back to the same black situation."

Still, the experience changed him. He returned to Sparrows Point in 1946, he said, and "started working for equal rights for colored. I became the first black shop steward in my mill in 1947. Being overseas helped me. The Marine Corps taught me how to come together and do the unexpected. I started talking to all the black workers, explaining to them that we must go to the union hall and take a stand. I started getting up on the floor and talking about how bad things were in the mill. Which they didn't want to hear. But I would speak right on."

Some white veterans also came home from the war with a different outlook on the familiar scene at Sparrows Point. Austin McLelland, nicknamed Li'l Abner or just Abner (for the cartoon character) by his older colleagues, had worked in the coke ovens machine shop before going overseas. The thing that struck him most forcefully when he returned to the Point was the segregation. In the locker room, he said, "blacks and whites were separated by a partition ten feet high." In the lunchroom, blacks "had to go in one door and you'd have to go in another," with a long rail up the middle of the restaurant dividing black and white, who were served by different cashiers.

The situation frustrated him, he said, not only because "they were our friends and I didn't like leaving my friends" but also because it prevented them from talking about work practices. "When you work on the same job and something is kind of dangerous, you talk about what you are going to do next," he explained. "Well, it would have been safer if we could have talked while we were eating."

When he went to work in the pumping station, he noticed that one of his African American co-workers, a laborer, was particularly skilled at identifying problems with the engines. "He could tell which one we had to work on, and it saved a lot of time and money." McLelland said that he pointed the man's skill out to the foreman in an attempt to get him promoted out of the labor gang. The foreman was noncommittal, but McLelland kept pushing. "Finally he said, 'Look, Abner, there's no blacks in the skilled trades here, and there's not gonna be. So you just forget that.'"

Our ultimate aim is a more perfect Union, industrial tranquility to our members, provision for the common defense, promotion of the General Welfare and a full measure of Equity for our members.

—FROM THE CHARTER OF THE UNITED STEELWORKERS
OF AMERICA LOCAL 2609

In 1936, when efforts to organize steel were just getting off the ground, laborers at Sparrows Point earned only forty-six and a half cents an hour. By 1947, the standard hourly rate for steelworkers in Job Class 1, basic labor, had doubled, to just under a dollar an hour. By 1952, those employees were making $1.52 an hour. Those significant gains were not achieved without a fight.

In the immediate aftermath of Pearl Harbor, CIO officials had made a no-strike pledge to President Roosevelt, and they honored it despite the grumbling of members, even agreeing to a wartime wage freeze for defense workers. But when Philip Murray, president of the CIO, proposed a wage increase of $2 a day after the war to offset the loss of hours and to bring steelworkers' salaries in line with cost-of-living increases during the war, steel company management refused.

The United Steelworkers of America voted to strike, and on January 21, 1946, nearly eight hundred thousand men walked off the job, bringing the industry—flush with orders—to a grinding halt. The Truman administration quickly brokered a compromise, one that was to set an enduring pattern for decades to come. Steelworkers got their wage increase of eighteen and a half cents per hour—and steel companies raised steel prices 8 percent to offset their higher labor costs. "In the beginning, the company would give you pretty much whatever you wanted and then raise the price of steel," said Joe Kotelchuck.

The contract ratified by Bethlehem Steel in the wake of the 1946 strike recognized once and for all the United Steelworkers of America as "the exclusive representative of Employees for the purposes of collective bargaining." With that battle won, the union focused on eliminating wage inequities in the mills by establishing job classes, setting standard hourly wage rates for each job class, drafting rules for reclassifying jobs, and instituting new incentive wage rates for production workers.

The contract also established an eight-hour day and a forty-hour week as the standard, and overtime compensation of time and a half. Bethlehem steelworkers were now guaranteed six paid holidays a year, and employees scheduled to work on those holidays were to be paid overtime. After one year of service, employees were entitled to a week's paid vacation; those with twenty-five or more years of service were guaranteed three weeks of paid vacation. The contract also addressed seniority rules, grievance procedures, and safety and health, and—very important to returning servicemen—it guaranteed the right to reemployment on the basis of seniority. All future gains by Bethlehem steelworkers—and other industrial workers—were built on these hard-won fundamentals.

A series of postwar strikes not only steadily increased wages but also won benefits unimaginable to previous generations. After the big five-month steel strike in 1959 that won full health care coverage for hourly workers, Ed Gorman's father told him, "You can take this to the bank. That's the biggest raise you'll ever get in your lifetime." And the benefits won by union employees rippled outward. "It's a domino effect," Eddie Bartee Sr. explained. "A good example is Sears and

Montgomery Ward. Montgomery Ward was union; Sears was non-union. But everything Montgomery Ward employees got, Sears gave their employees. The only thing Sears didn't get was job protection."

Willy Cohill made the same point. He was hired in 1950 by Signode, a non-union steel strapping company based in Chicago that had just opened a new facility a mile or so from Sparrows Point. He had been a shop steward on the Point, so soon after he was hired on at Signode, he started trying to organize the place. The company got wind of his efforts and retaliated by laying him off. "But they sent the big shots down from Chicago, and we got it straightened out," he said, forming an in-house committee of elected representatives from each department. After that, Cohill said, Signode employees enjoyed all the benefits of their union brothers, save one: job security. "They would fire you for nothing," he said. "If you made one little mistake or they didn't like you, they would fire you."

Job security, subsidized health care, a comfortable retirement—within a generation all of these benefits won by organized labor were taken for granted by people who forgot (or never learned) how hard their parents, grandparents, and great-grandparents had fought to gain the workplace rights they saw as their due. "Without the unions, the lifestyle that the average so-called non-union person now enjoys would not have existed," Manuel Alvarez said. "They were the first ones who got a living wage, the forty-hour week, and on and on. These are things that, when you grow up with them, you accept without knowing where it came from. You don't give a damn where it came from. You just enjoy it."

• BOOM •

When I think of my late-baby-boom childhood in Dundalk, I remember penguins and POW bracelets, the Christmas train garden at the fire station, the summer parties at shore homes where you could win dolls and games by spinning a big numbered wooden wheel set up in the covered pavilion behind the house. I remember my father letting me pick his teams in the weekly football pools at the mills, and giving my brother and me coins to put in the jukeboxes in various taverns when we hung out with him on Sundays after he and my mother were divorced. Our favorite was called the Green Castle, though there was nothing castlelike about it. My brother and I shortened the name to Greenie's.

When my father picked us up on Sunday mornings, my mother told him to take us to mass, but we often skipped it to visit his cousin Donald, who lived near Our Lady of Hope Church. On our Sunday outings, Dad took us to circuses and ice shows at the Baltimore Civic Center, and he even took us to see the Beatles movie *Yellow Submarine*, though he himself had been a fifties teenager who styled his hair in a

DA and wore pegged pants and believed that rock 'n' roll started and ended with Elvis.

It was an enchanted childhood in some ways. Take the penguins. They were housed at Eastpoint, a shopping center on the northern border of Dundalk just below the city line, in a department store's refrigerated display window. No trip to Eastpoint was complete without a visit to the miniature penguins at Hochschild Kohn, frolicking in their little pool. Then we would walk to Hess Shoes, where live monkeys jabbered and climbed a tree inside a tall cage in the middle of the store, and salespeople took X-rays of your feet to prove to your parents that your toes had room to grow. Eastpoint was no mere shopping center for us Dundalk kids; it was a place of magic a lot closer to home than Disneyland.

For our parents, the beautifully landscaped shopping center symbolized something more vital than magic. It was the emblem of their newfound prosperity, anchored by Hutzler's and Hochschild Kohn, the Baltimore equivalents of Macy's, Nordstrom, or Gimbels. "When Eastpoint opened in 1956, people from all over the city shopped there," Harry Young of the Dundalk Patapsco Neck Historical Society recalled. "It was the number one shopping center in the area for a long time."

Eastpoint and the busy car dealerships that sprang up across the street on Eastern Avenue were like neon signs advertising an economic revolution. Released from the shackles of depression and war, Americans went on a buying binge the likes of which the country had never seen, and working-class Baltimore families like mine both produced and consumed the products that fed the postwar boom. An astounding 85 percent of all consumer goods at the time, from tin cans to household appliances, used steel in one form or another. "Steel was being used for everything under the moon," said Young. "And everything was being replenished. Mom needed another pot because the one she'd been using for five years was wearing out. You had to get a lot of cars out there because no one had bought a new one for five, six years. After the war, all the industry around here changed over from war pro-

duction to civilian. Then Korea breaks out, so you're back in war production again."

In Sparrows Point and Dundalk, many World War II veterans,
now young men with families to support, reenlisted when the Korean
War started. Bob Strasbaugh left a wife and three-month-old daughter
when he shipped out to Korea as a Marine Corps medic in 1950. Back
then, his wife, Nonnie, recalled, the community helped out the
women left behind. "We didn't get any money [from the Marines] for
three months. My milkman carried me till I got my first check. My
insurance man carried me. Marguerite, the landlady, carried me. I
don't think people would do it today."

Meanwhile, Bob was hunkered down behind the Thirty-eighth
Parallel. "I was with that bunch that was cut off at Chosin Reservoir,"
he told me. "Fourteen thousand against 150,000. It was tough. Forty
below. Summer gear." Less than half of the U.S. forces survived the
Chinese attack. I asked Bob how they managed it. He laughed. "We
fought our way out." When Bob returned home, he went back to work
at the Point, where he was promoted to foreman a few years later.

My father served in the Korean War too. Dropping out of Sparrows Point High School in 1951 after being caught smoking ciga-
rettes, he enlisted in the air force. He finished high school while
stationed at Nellis Air Force Base in Las Vegas and then went overseas, serving as an MP in Germany and later Morocco. One night he
was set upon by a group of local thugs and stabbed. He survived to
return home in 1954, joining his father, brothers, and cousins working
on the Point.

By then, industrial employment in Baltimore was topping wartime
highs. "The need for skilled workers is tremendous—tool and die
makers, machinists, electricians, welders, shipfitters, and mechanics
are in big demand," the manager of the Baltimore office of the State
Employment Service told a *Baltimore Sun* reporter in 1951. "Virtually
every high school and college graduate can have his pick of jobs this
year." Fourteen years later, with unemployment in the Baltimore area
below 4 percent, the personnel manager for a Baltimore industrial
concern told a *Baltimore News-American* reporter, "If you want a good

man in today's job market, you've got to swipe him from someone else."

Willy Cohill recalled that in those heady days of the postwar boom "there was so much work that when you were looking for a job, you could go anywhere. If you didn't like this place, you could go next door. There was always somebody looking to hire you." General Motors, Western Electric, American Standard, Westinghouse, Glenn L. Martin, Eastern Stainless Steel, Armco, American Can—the roster of companies where a kid just graduated from high school (or not) could find a good-paying job was seemingly endless.

In this competitive hiring environment, Bethlehem Steel had a built-in advantage: the high school sitting smack in the middle of the company town of Sparrows Point. Few of the young men who grew up in the town expected to do anything else but follow their fathers and uncles into the mills. They could hear the din of their future as they sat in their classrooms. "When I started high school, they were building the number 10 blast furnace," my uncle Ray said. "You're in school and all you hear is BA-BOOM, BA-BOOM 'cause they're driving piles, day and night. They drove piles twenty-four hours a day to put this blast furnace in. And the high school is right there."

I asked him if most of the kids from his class—the last to graduate from "old" Sparrows Point High School in the company town before "new" Sparrows Point High opened two miles away in 1952—had gone to work for Bethlehem Steel. "Probably not as many as you would think," he said, noting competitive jobs at Western Electric, Lever Brothers, GM, and American Standard. Often, the ones who chose jobs off the Point had seen their fathers' lives and health destroyed by steelmaking, he pointed out. "Some said, 'They're not gonna kill me like they did my father.'"

Still, the company did everything possible to bring those young men on board right after graduation. "They gave preferential treatment to those that had families down there," Roy Swaggert, whom I spoke with at a union retirees' meeting, told me. Swaggert's father arrived on the Point with his four brothers in 1934, he said, "and they all worked for Bethlem. One of 'em was killed in the shipyard." Two months before Roy graduated from Sparrows Point High in 1955, the company "came in and signed everyone up. I started working the day after I graduated. I had a twin brother that went down there the same time I did."

"The company actually had an employment table set up in the gym while we were practicing for our commencement," Harry Young told me. "I knew kids who graduated at seven at night, had a little party afterwards, and reported for work the next morning. They didn't even take a day off." Harry said that he was one of only 12 students in a class of 146 enrolled in the academic track. "Most of the boys took shop," he recalled—and at Sparrows Point, majoring in shop didn't mean making birdhouses. "When you took shop at Sparrows Point High, you were training to be a machinist, a sheet metalist, or some other trade," he said. Bethlehem Steel hired machinists to teach the classes and provided top-of-the-line equipment for the school, the same that was being used in the mills a whistle away from the classrooms—in effect, training its next generation of employees while they were still teenagers.

When he returned to Baltimore after World War II, Wendell Doyle was determined not to become a steelworker. "I wasn't going to work for Bethlem. I was tired of steel because my family was Irish and they all worked in the steel mills," he told me. So when it came time to get a job, Doyle worked first as a meatpacker and later as a salesman for the same company. But after he and his wife had a couple of kids, he concluded that "Bethlehem Steel is where the money is," and he surrendered to his fate.

"My cousin got me a job in the electrical department in the plate mill as a learner. Then you became a helper, and a C rate, B rate, then A, before motor inspector, which was the top hourly job. I went to night school and all that to learn," said Doyle, known as Wimpy by his co-workers for his love of White Castle hamburgers. He rose up through the ranks in the plate mill, becoming a turn foreman in 1956 and then an assistant general foreman. In order to take a promotion to general foreman in 1969, he had to shift to the pipe mill, where he stayed until his retirement in 1982. I asked if he had liked his job at the

Point. "It was noisy and dirty and I loved every minute of it," he said. "I liked the challenge of the thing."

Like Wimpy Doyle, John Bosse originally planned to look elsewhere for work. After graduating from Mount St. Joseph, a boys' Catholic high school in West Baltimore, in 1952, Bosse went to work for the city as a draftsman. But he too heard the siren song of Sparrows Point. "I just saw the opportunity to make more money," he said simply. "With the city, I was making like $110 every two weeks. Well, I went down to Bethlehem Steel and I was making eighty bucks a week. I was gonna be a millionaire!"

The Sparrows Point works exerted a kind of magnetic attraction, pulling young men away from less lucrative jobs in other areas. "I had an uncle who was a foreman at General Motors and another uncle in the police department. My dad was in law enforcement. So I could've went anywhere," Tom Capecci told me. But when he was offered a position as an inspector in the rod and wire mill in 1966, he joined another uncle and two cousins on Sparrows Point. Melvin Schmeiser was trained as an auto mechanic at Baltimore's Mergenthaler Vocational Technical High School, but two weeks after graduating in 1966, he too found himself working at Sparrows Point, in the Penwood power plant. The reason was simple, he said. "They were paying twice as much as the Pontiac dealer down Fleet Street, with more benefits and everything."

Naturally enough, Baltimore merchants and lenders treated Bethlehem employees like royalty. "People would say, 'Oh, you work for Bethlehem Steel!' We had the best benefits, the best health care," Donald Lindemann recalled. Pete Selhorst, a Bethlehem steelworker a generation younger than Lindemann, agreed. "Anytime you wanted to buy anything, people were like, 'Oh, you work at Sparrows Point, wow, come in, come in.' It was like red carpet from then on," he said.

This crimson carpet was rolled out not only for managers, foremen, and skilled craftsmen but for common laborers too—people who might not have much formal education but who (in a phrase I have heard from more than one retiree) "knew the mill" and got regular raises according to the terms of the USW contracts just like everyone

else. "It was bull work, hot bull work," said Bill Knoerlein, who
worked on the side of the mill that produced steel. "But it provided a
living for a lot of people."

> It was a dangerous job. But if it wasn't for Bethlehem Steel, I
> wouldn't have what I got today.
>
> —JESSIE SCHULTZ

During the boom, a surprising number of women also worked at Sparrows Point. Most of them were clerks in receiving or purchasing or in
one of the mill offices, but three to four hundred worked in the tin mill
as "tin floppers," inspecting sheets of tin plate used to can soup, soft
drinks, fruit, and vegetables. Women had worked as tin sorters on
Sparrows Point since the 1920s, but as American women abandoned
the thrifty habits of their foremothers and stopped canning their own
backyard fruits and vegetables, purchases of canned goods—and thus
tin production—boomed.

There was an art to "flopping" tin, Jessie Schultz, a former tin mill
worker, said, demonstrating the fluid motion for me in her living room
filled with porcelain angels. Jessie is eighty-five years old but looks
closer to seventy, and she is no one's idea of a steelworker. She is five
feet tall and must have weighed all of a hundred pounds soaking wet
when she was hired to work in the tin sorting room in 1948. "You had
to turn it and flip it real smooth, like this," she said, showing me how
to flip a sheet of tin without "kinking" it, as she was prone to do at first.
"When you're flipping tin, you have to take it and just gently let it
loose."

Forced to drop out of school at age thirteen to help support her
family when her father died of TB, Jessie had already worked in a
laundry, a bottling factory, and a distillery and as a seamstress sewing
buttonholes at a shirt factory before she arrived on the Point as a
young married woman with two children. Like Jessie Schultz, most of
the women who worked on the Point were not laboring for "pin
money" but because their wages supported families.

"Quite a few of the women who worked in the tin sorting room were single parents," Jessie's best friend, Phyllis Moskowitz, told me. "Plus, they were taking care of their mothers and fathers. Everybody, including me, would run to the phones on your fifteen-minute break to call home and see if things were okay, because we all had to depend on babysitters."

The job was physically grueling. Some of the thick-gauge sheets of tin were quite heavy, but even the thin ones, easier to lift, had sharp edges, so the women wore gloves at all times to avoid deep cuts. Fore-ladies prowled the room, checking "to see what you were doing with the defects, what you were putting into waste, which was not salvage-able," Moskowitz said. Sheets that could be mended were called sec-onds and were put into a separate pile. If you didn't sort at least a sixty-six-inch stack per shift, you were fired. To meet that quota left little time for socializing, and silence in the tin sorting room was strictly enforced.

"One of the biggest shocks I ever had in my life was when I walked in that factory," Moskowitz recalled. "Every night for about three weeks I went home and cried myself to sleep. I thought, My God, what have I done?" The severity of the supervisors, the toughness of her fel-low workers, the noise and filth of the mill itself, and the sheer physi-cal effort of the job stunned her.

Soon enough, she learned how to adjust to shift work by taking catnaps in the ladies' room when working the eleven-to-seven shift. "We had a concrete slab that had a pallet on it, like a mattress. If you had the time, which you usually didn't, you tried to sleep for a couple of minutes. They had a matron in there who scrubbed the toilets and kept an eye on things, and she would wake you up." About seven women could fit on the pallet, she added, and spaces were "first come, first served."

Inspecting metal at the tin pots was the women's worst job, she said. "That was how they coated the tin the old-fashioned way, before they had the plating lines. You had these poor men with the sweat just pouring off them, and you could tell they were in misery coating the sheet metal. And you had to stand there and observe and push your button for certain things before it went down in the bath to be plated if there were defects. The fumes would just about kill you," she said.

Because of the toxic fumes, the hot dip area was basically a roofed shed open on three sides, so workers were exposed to the weather at all times. "In winter I would wear a long coat and a hat and yet I was still so cold I was numb," Moskowitz said. "And in summer, well, the heat was indescribable. And you're standing on a cement floor the whole time. I got phlebitis in my leg from standing on that cement floor."

Despite the difficulty of the job, the tin sorters were a bit like a family, and their chief forelady, Elizabeth Alexander, a Hungarian émigré who ran the shop with military discipline for nearly forty years, "was like a mother to all of us—except a lot of the women didn't take it that way," Moskowitz said. Alexander, the highest-ranking woman on Sparrows Point for many years, was a tough customer, and most of the women who worked under her supervision quaked when they heard her step and smelled her heavy perfume.

"I'm only there thirty days and she comes up to me and says, 'Girlie, why did you put this sheet in the menders? What is wrong with this sheet of tin?' And I was so nervous I couldn't even find the defect," Jessie Schultz recalled. "I was looking and looking, and then I said, 'It's got that big roll mark right there and it's no good.' She said, 'I just wanted to see if you knew what you was doing.' I liked to choke her because she made me so nervous I couldn't even see the damn thing."

Members of Alexander's family who worked on the Point themselves spoke of her fierce protectiveness of "her girls" and the way she would "go nose to nose with some of the big bosses down there" to take care of them. "She took nothing from any of those guys, so they came to respect her," said her grandson Bill Knoerlein. "She made that tin mill, and the women in it, a place to be reckoned with."

There was a fair amount of flirting, dating, and just plain fooling around between the tin sorters and the men around them, most of the former tin sorters admit, though Alexander tried to discourage fraternizing—by any means necessary. Knoerlein recalled the time "some guy was pestering one of her girls and she literally knocked him on his ass." The lady was clearly formidable. "To be honest, I was afraid of her," said Julie Poholorec, a Czech émigré who was hired as a tin sorter in 1957. "She was hard lady, and she had an iron hand with the people. But the lady at heart is very honest and a very good person. I admire her for that."

Other female supervisors on the Point were equally stern as they attempted to win respect for themselves and their female employees in the intensely male environment of Sparrows Point. My mother's first job after graduating from Seton, a girls' Catholic high school in Baltimore, was in the purchasing department at Sparrows Point. "I hated that job," she told me. She and her co-workers were aggressively policed by their supervisor, a woman far more forbidding than the white-robed nuns at her high school. "There must've been forty women in that room, and someone was always walking around watching you," she said. "You had to punch in at a time clock, and you couldn't leave your desk without permission to go to the bathroom, and no smoke breaks. It was ultra, ultra strict."

Even though the job paid around $40 a week, she quit after eight months. She found "an entirely different atmosphere," she told me, at her secretarial job at Steelworkers Local 2610 headquarters on Dundalk Avenue. Not only was the atmosphere less like a prison camp for women, but unlike the all-white clerical pools (and tin sorting room) at the Point, the union hall offices were staffed by both black and white women. When she interviewed for the job in 1953, she said, the financial secretary "asked me if I minded working with black people, and I said no. Then I met Ann, who was about ten or fifteen years older than me, and we worked face-to-face. Maxine worked in the credit union a couple of halls away. Then there was Shirley, who was my age, and Floyd the photographer. They were very nice, sociable people, and we became friends."

When the bosses were out of the office, my mother said, she and her new pals would sometimes "party in Floyd's darkroom," drinking Scotch and taking photos. I still have a picture taken by Floyd of my mother wearing a straw hat and smiling a bit nervously. She and some of the other secretaries would attend evening union meetings to take notes. "I didn't have a car and would take a streetcar that ran down Dundalk Avenue, and Floyd would always walk out with me and wait for me while I got on the streetcar. Sometimes he would kiss me on the cheek, which would have been quite shocking back in the fifties," she said. "But we were really good friends."

Despite the good times, working at the union hall had its somber side. "I remember how the financial secretary used to say how the unions came into existence because they would work these poor guys long hours without any overtime and very unsafe conditions. And the unions were formed to safeguard these people from these abuses," my mother recalled. "He talked about how they would fall into these steel vats, and they couldn't even find the bodies. They would just have to take whatever was left and bury it."

You are a little harder when you come out of a steel mill than when you went in.

—AUSTIN McLELLAND

Even after unionization, Sparrows Point remained a very tough and very dangerous place to work. Bob Knoerlein, grandson of the sorting room forelady Elizabeth Alexander, worked three summers on a labor gang there while attending college. "I got exposed to some dirty, dangerous, backbreaking aspects of the Point," he told me. "And this is not to detract from the men who earned their living down there, but it was a very cold, dirty, hard place." When personnel noticed that he would be graduating soon and offered him a slot in the Loop Course, Bethlehem's prestigious training program for upper management, he declined. "I'm sure I could have made great money down there," he said. "But it didn't appeal to me."

Bob's older brother Bill didn't go to college. He started working at Sparrows Point in 1960 on the steelmaking side and stayed for thirty-eight years, retiring as a turn foreman in 1998. He said that he understands his brother's decision to look elsewhere for work. "For a great many years," he said, "Sparrows Point was a badass place." The number one rule was to keep the lines running, no matter what; health and safety ran a distinct second to tonnage. "A lot of the injuries and deaths at the Point could have been avoided if safety precautions had been put into place," LeRoy McLelland pointed out.

Working in the machine shop next to the coke ovens, Austin McLelland (no relation to LeRoy) often saw workers carrying injured men to the plant dispensary or the hospital. "They'd bring them through our shop," he said, "and you'd see their bones hanging out of their legs, or fingers chopped off, and they'd take them to the hospital to try and put them back together." He told me about seeing an electrician he called Uncle Herb electrocuted on the job. "Fifty thousand volts were running through the line, but they didn't like shutting down the electric when there was a problem because then they'd have to shut down all the coke ovens." When Uncle Herb and two other electricians went up into the scaffolding to repair the problem, "that fifty thousand got him," McLelland said. "They carried him out in a basket."

Union shop stewards spent much of their time in the postwar years fighting management about safety issues. Article 14, section 3, of the USW contract gave shop stewards the power to shut down a unit if conditions were unsafe. "Most of the time just the threat of invoking it would be enough to get the problem taken care of," Neil Crowder said, telling me about one time soon after he returned to the mill following the war when he threatened to shut down his shop. "I went through nineteen months in the navy and never came close to getting killed. Came back to Bethlem in '45 and within two weeks I almost got killed by a lid coming down on us." Crowder went to the foreman of the washer department, the notorious Bulldog, and said, "You listen to me. The number 1 line is down. The lid damn near killed me. You do something about it now or I'm gonna invoke 14-3." The problem was quickly solved, he said.

Another time, when he came in on a four-to-twelve shift, he learned that someone on the daylight shift had been "cut up real bad" because of improperly finished coils. But when Crowder complained to Bulldog, the foreman refused to look into the matter. On that occasion, Crowder said, he was forced to resort to his trademark "chair slam" move to get satisfaction. "When I would first go into the office, I would sit down in the chair close to [the foreman's] desk. If things didn't go my way, I would stand up and slam my chair against the desk." A show of force was sometimes necessary, he said, to prove that you meant business.

Shop stewards like Crowder served as the conduit between the rank-and-file worker and union officials, and the on-site mediator between the union and the company. They were not attorneys; most had only a high school education, if that. However, they needed to know the contract and to be able to write up workers' grievances in terms that would gain them a hearing. Shop stewards soon learned that their credibility depended on the ability to make the crucial distinction between a legitimate contract violation and plain old bitching about the job. "You had to watch out for the whiners," one former shop steward told me.

Zonemen were the next step up in the union hierarchy, representing whole departments of up to twelve hundred people. "None of the zone people were the type you could manipulate," LeRoy McLelland said. I asked Joe Kotelchuck what made a good shop steward or zoneman. "A guy that was conscientious, that took his work serious and tried to do the right thing," he replied promptly. "And someone who was willing to fight the company."

It was a very secure job, except for strikes and layoffs.

— ROSE MARIE WELLER

In 1959, Sparrows Point officially claimed the title of the largest steelworks in the world. At that time, just about everyone in Baltimore knew someone who worked for Bethlehem Steel. Whole families in Sparrows Point and nearby Edgemere and Dundalk often worked on Sparrows Point, their economic security entirely dependent on Bethlehem paychecks. My aunt Shirley Lewis, for example, went to work in the receiving office after graduating from Sparrows Point High School in 1956, joining her father, brother, and tin flopper mother on the Bethlehem payroll. "That's what you did around here," she said. "You got out of school and went down there to get a job."

She and my uncle Ray were high school sweethearts, and they married in 1960 after he served two years in the air force. He too found a job on the Point. "I got hired on at the peak," Ray told me, "when they had thirty to thirty-five thousand working down there. When I started in '56, they had thirty-five open hearth furnaces, ten blast furnaces, four soaking pits, four rolling mills, the plate mill, the skelp mill, the flange mill. You had the coke ovens, benzoil plant. But they peaked out at about '59, and you started getting foreign steel coming in. After that, it was just a gradual decline."

Ray's first few years on the Bethlehem payroll were similar to those of many young steelworkers, bumped from one job to another and laid off whenever production slowed in the department where he was assigned. He applied for a bricklayer apprenticeship in 1956, but because there were no openings, his first job was as a tin flopper. "But I only did that for a week. Then they went on strike and I was off for four weeks. I had earned $40, and it lasted me for four weeks, taking Shirley to the movies once a week. When I went back, they gave me another job, in the wire mill."

He did that job for about six weeks before his bricklayer apprenticeship came through. Then came the long strike of 1959, and after that was settled, he felt secure enough to get married. "When I first started in the brick department, they told me, 'We haven't had a layoff since 1937.' No cutbacks in the department since 1937. So I got married in April 1960, and about November, I was laid off. They hadn't had a layoff in twenty years!"

He was called back after a few months, and in 1968 he became a foreman, which helped insulate him from the regular layoffs that plagued hourly workers. The more seniority a worker had, the less he had to worry about layoffs, but for younger steelworkers and those who worked in mills where production varied according to the season, periodic bouts of unemployment were common.

"Tin plate was seasonal. When canning season came in during the summer, you worked. And then when winter came in, you were cut back," Donald Lindemann told me. "I was happy to have that job, but it's just that my job was seasonal and it was hard. I would go out and paint houses or anything on the side to make money. A lot of time, I'd get cut back to four days a week. I'd be making $62 a week, gross. Even after I had thirty years down there, I would get cut back to laborer. That's why I took a foreman's job."

When I was born in 1958, my father worked in the tandem mill, a finishing mill where workers could earn big bonuses tied to production. But as a junior employee subject to frequent layoffs, he spent a lot of time selling insurance or flipping burgers at Gino's. "The money was good and they had good benefits, but every year he either got laid off because he didn't have much seniority or they would go on strike," my mother recalled of my father's years on the Point.

Rose Marie Weller provided a similar account of the peaks and valleys of her early life as the wife of a Sparrows Point steelworker. She had two older children from a previous marriage when she married Cleone "Lee" Weller, and he adopted the kids. She had a good job herself, at Westinghouse, and she made even more money than her new husband, but after they had a couple of kids of their own, she said, "Lee made me quit. He said, 'Don't I make enough money for you?'"

Strikes and layoffs hit them hard then, particularly the 116-day strike of 1959. "We had four kids, a house payment, furniture to pay for, a car payment, gas and electric," she said. Her husband tried to get another job during the strike, but no one would hire him because they knew he would return to his job on the Point as soon as the strike was settled. Her elder daughter's boyfriend used to bring the family day-old buns and bread from his delivery job, and both grandmothers helped out, Rose Marie Weller recalled, in whatever way they could. The strike was settled after nearly five months, and in her opinion the steelworkers "lost more [in wages] than they ever won." Still, she said, when her husband was working again, "he was making good money."

I asked my mother what "good money" was. "Your father probably brought home $50 a week," she said. "But back then, that was a good wage"—good enough for my parents to buy a brick town house in one of the new developments springing up in southeastern Baltimore County for its growing population of industrial workers. With the GI Bill enabling veterans like my father to buy a house with no down payment and providing help with closing costs, they were able to secure a loan on a brand-new three-bedroom house with plaster walls, hardwood floors, and a finished basement with knotty pine paneling. With a mortgage payment of $80 a month, approximately 40 percent of my father's monthly earnings, and with my mother's salary added in, they were doing pretty well for a young couple—certainly far better than had their own parents, who started married life living either with family or in company housing. In this they were not alone.

In 1947, the average working-class family in Baltimore still rented, but by 1960, owner-occupancy rates in Baltimore's working-class neighborhoods were above 70 percent. In the county, acres of farmland between Sparrows Point and the city line disappeared as Baltimore builders began constructing and marketing row house developments for the area's burgeoning population of young industrial workers. "That all started around '52 or '53," said Harry Young, who was by then working for the Baltimore County Bureau of Land Acquisition. "The county had to extend sewer and water lines linking all the little communities together." The new developments became part of Greater Dundalk, which in the fifties expanded well beyond the original thousand acres purchased by Bethlehem Steel back in 1916. "When the row houses were finished, the population was about 115,000," he said. "If Dundalk would have been incorporated, it would have been the second-largest city in the state."

The rising standard of living for working-class families throughout Baltimore was driven by the booming postwar economy, which put workers and their unions in a strong bargaining position. In the immediate aftermath of World War II, fourteen and a half million Americans—35 percent of the civilian labor force—belonged to either an AFL or a CIO union. Workers in unionized industries boosted by the postwar economy enjoyed an unparalleled prosperity and security. As Alvarez pointed out, "when you went to work for a company, whether it was Bethlehem Steel or General Electric or General Motors, you knew that if you behaved yourself and worked hard, they would advance you. Your salary was compensatory to the work you did, and they made you feel like you were important. There were strikes, but you still knew that they needed you and you needed them."

During the boom years, Bethlehem Steel's operation in Baltimore was so huge that it required two USW locals to represent the nearly thirty-three thousand employees on the Point. Local 2610 represented workers on the steel side and craftsmen like bricklayers, iron-workers, and machinists. Local 2609 represented workers in the finishing mills. There was always a certain class tension between the two locals. "Our side was the old hard workers, the coke ovens, the blast furnaces. They [2609] had the clean mill jobs," said Tom Capecci, president of the 2610 retirees' group. "We were known as the Cinderella people," said LeRoy McLelland of 2609.

In the early years of the union, the two locals shared a storefront in Highlandtown, and they continued to share space in the hall the Steel-workers built at 550 Dundalk Avenue in 1944. Seven years later, 2610—which by then had over ten thousand members—built itself a bigger hall next door. Capecci told me that when he was hired in the mid-sixties, monthly union meetings were standing room only. Not only were all the chairs on the floor taken but steelworkers packed the balcony and spilled out into the lobby. "If you didn't get there twenty minutes before the meeting, you wouldn't get a seat," he said.

The meetings were not just crowded; they were often riotous. Hired in 1955, Eddie Bartee Sr. joined the union early on, mostly out of respect for his uncle, a zoneman who had helped organize black steelworkers at Sparrows Point. "My uncle says, 'Why don't you come to a union meeting?' and because he had been so nice to me, I went. It was round the time of the Democratic convention, and they were all hollering and screaming at each other, calling each other liars. I remember at one meeting, Lee Douglas was giving a report, and white folks was booing so bad they told the guard to make him sit down, and I was really scared there was going to be a fight, but Lee Douglas said, 'Don't you put your hands on me.'" Douglas, said Bartee, "would get on the floor and talk about discrimination in the mill when it was a very undesirable thing to do."

Back in the fifties, that's when all
the struggling started.

—LEE DOUGLAS JR.

African American men from Baltimore found jobs readily available at the Point during the postwar boom. "We were surprised because we had heard that they wouldn't hire anyone from Baltimore City, that they only wanted you if you were from the Deep South and wanted to get away from that mule," said Roosevelt Caldwell, who, with his childhood friend Eugene Levy, drove to Sparrows Point looking for work soon after they were discharged from the air force in 1955. Both had been trained as clerk typists in the service. The Bethlehem hiring office was unimpressed. "They said, 'Well, we don't have that kind of job for you, but you can come and shovel,'" Caldwell recalled. "They wrote on my application 'a big husky fellow,'" said Levy.

The two spent most of their days shoveling ore in the holds of ships docked at the pier, but depending on conditions, the labor gang they worked on would sometimes be borrowed by other departments on the steel side. "We were a feeder unit. Whenever a unit or department came short, we would be loaned out to them," Caldwell said. "The thing I disliked most of all was when they loaned us out to the blast furnace." As temporary employees, they were provided no special training or gear when they were assigned to the blast furnaces, the two men said.

"We would go over there, and the men who worked there had those big shoes with rubber soles because they were working with this hot metal," said Levy. "You could see that metal pouring like lava through a trough." They watched as men called cinder snappers straddled the flaming trough to remove bits of hardening iron. "You could always tell the cinder snappers because no matter what they had on, their legs or their feet would have sores on them," Levy said. "Because that stuff was splashing, it would burn them." Caldwell hated the blast furnaces. "I would leave there every day with a headache," he said, "from the smoke and the stench, sulfuric acid billowing. I don't go to church that often, but if hell is anything like that, I'll be on my knees from now on."

The two had more formal education than did most of their white co-workers on the docks and in the furnaces. Levy had completed a year at Alabama State University, and Caldwell began working on a bachelor's degree at Morgan State College one year after he started at Bethlehem. "There were a lot of well-educated [black] men down there, with degrees from Howard, Morgan, University of Maryland," Caldwell pointed out. In that era, he said, young black men were often told "to go to college, and when you come out, you can do anything you want. Oh no, no, no. You couldn't do anything you wanted"— which was one reason why so many African American men with college degrees worked as laborers on Sparrows Point in those days. The other was money: Eddie Bartee Sr.'s cousin was a professor at Morgan, he told me, "and I made more money than he did."

College degrees did not endear black laborers to their white foremen, some of whom—on the ore docks, at least—hadn't graduated from high school. The hostility was sometimes disguised as teasing. Caldwell recalled some white co-workers saying things like "Hey, schoolboy, how do you spell this?" and "Will you fill out this report for me?" Levy said that "one guy who worked over at the ships used to call me Professor. Everybody else called me Tank. I asked a friend of mine who worked with him, 'Why does he call me Professor?' And he said, 'Somebody told him you went to college.'"

Not all whites were "belligerent"—the word the two used to describe those who gave them a hard time. Caldwell said that his general foreman was a "fair guy" and helped him out when he was in college by arranging for him to have weekends off to study. Moreover, like and dislike on the Point didn't divide strictly along racial lines. "There were blacks who didn't get along with blacks," he pointed out, "and whites who didn't get along with whites. It was a complex world."

And the teasing could go both ways, as shown in a story Levy told about shoveling ore with a white co-worker on a hot summer night. "Around four in the morning we finished, and I said, 'That wasn't too bad.' He said, 'No, but the mosquitoes was tanning my hide.' He had on some kind of cologne or something. So I said, 'Damn, they didn't bother me. Don't you know mosquitoes don't bite black people?' He stood there for a good five seconds. Then he said, 'You shitting me?' I bust out laughing." Levy laughed again, recalling the incident forty years later.

Still, there were limits to the camaraderie. Once, when a white foreman was injured, Caldwell recalled, a few members of his crew went out to his house to see how he was feeling. "I don't know if they were in love with him or what, but they went down to his house, all-white enclave. Banged on the door. And this fellow looked out, saw them there, and said, 'If I ever see you so-and-sos down here again, I'm gonna fire every damn one of you.'"

Being a black steelworker on the Point at that time, he said, "was like being left-handed in a right-handed man's world. Left-handers are more evenhanded than right because it's a right-handed man's world. We acclimate ourselves to it."

Early in the postwar era, some African American steelworkers began organizing to fight discrimination on the Point, though they kept their activities low-key. "In 1952, we formed our organization, the Statesman," recalled Douglas. "We would meet every month in one another's houses." I asked him if he was able to find any allies among whites in those early days, and he said that "we had several allies"—Neil Crowder, for one. But it was hard for individual white workers to support their black friends and co-workers, he said, and impossible for them to single-handedly change the culture of white privilege on the Point. "They could not go but so far without jeopardizing themselves, and we recognized that."

African American steelworkers did begin moving into a few semi-skilled positions in the fifties. "When the first black guy, Hemphill, went into a crane, all the other crane operators walked out," recalled

Bartee Sr. "Hemphill had his problems because they didn't teach him how to operate a crane." But the man persevered, and after the precedent had been set, Bartee said, "that's where a lot of blacks got an opportunity to leave the labor gang and the lower-paying jobs because most of the crane operator and tractor operator positions were Job Class 7, 8, and 9."

But once whites got used to the idea of black crane operators, Bartee said, whenever a black man would ask to transfer to a position in one of the finishing mills, "they would say, 'Why don't you take the crane operator's job? That's a good job.'" In that way, crane operator became a "black" job. But black employees asking to apply for other kinds of skilled and semiskilled positions and apprenticeships were still told bluntly "That's a white man's job" well into the 1960s.

On Sparrows Point, generally friendly relations between blacks and whites on the job could not disguise the injustice of a system where black steelworkers were expected to accept limited possibilities for advancement without complaint—and to be grateful for the opportunities offered them. "They told us we had to get along with each other, so we did," one African American steelworker who declined to be interviewed for this book told me. Retired for nearly twenty years, he is still bitter about his experiences on the Point. "You want to know what it was like? It stunk," he said. "That's all I'm saying."

Eddie Bartee Sr. was elected to union office in 1963 when black steelworkers and their white allies in the union began working together to get a black elected to the governing council of Local 2609. Unlike most of those running for union office, Bartee had never been a shop steward. But he attended the classes for shop stewards and so knew a lot about the contract. "I was an agitator," he said. "I used to stir up a lot of stink by telling the guys their rights [under the union contract] and say, 'He's screwing you.' I was very good at that, and the guys thought I was smart. I wasn't smart. But I went from nothing to vice president and then stayed either vice president or president for thirty-two years. I never lost an election."

He had to display some nimble footwork during the sixties, when civil rights activists, including his old friend Lee Douglas, were using every means possible to pressure the company and the union. "I was right there with him," he said—but as a USW officer, he also had to mediate between the white union hierarchy and black workers demanding change. Once, a reporter interviewing him on camera after a civil rights rally at Sparrows Point observed that he, a black man, was vice president of a union that discriminated against blacks.

"I wasn't prepared for that question, even though I knew there was discrimination and I had been exposed to it. So I said to her, 'The officers are elected, and they didn't discriminate against me. But there is discrimination in the mills, and the union agreed to the discrimination before we came into office.'" When he went to work the next day, he discovered that his white union colleagues "were very pleased with my answer because it didn't incriminate them. There was a history, you see." It was an ugly history of collusion between union and company. "You just couldn't rise above that bigotry," said Roosevelt Caldwell. "They wanted to batten down the hatches on you."

The main mechanism used to protect "white" jobs on Sparrows Point (and in other steel mills) while seemingly adhering to the union contract was unit seniority. Under this system, a worker's seniority was based on the number of years he had spent in a particular unit, not in the plant as a whole. By assigning the majority of African American employees to just a few units, the company and the union created separate (and unequal) lines of seniority and promotion. Seniority was used to determine who was next in line not only for a promotion but also for a layoff. Benefits too (vacations, pensions, insurance) were tied to seniority. The unit seniority system effectively locked black employees into place because few were willing to trade away their seniority privileges for the bottom job in a "white" unit.

Steelworkers of color were often threatened with a loss of seniority privileges if they tried to buck the system. Melvin Schmeiser, a white steelworker hired in 1965, said that he "didn't even think about [discrimination] until I was there for several years, and then I couldn't see that something wasn't right. One of my best friends [a black man] had an all-daylight job because he was the second- or third-senior man in the department, with thirty some years' service. He was getting what they called the handyman rate, which was a Job Class 9. I was there a third his time but was three job classes higher—Job Class 12, untested." When his friend finally protested and asked to be promoted to a temporary millwright position, Schmeiser told me, "our foreman said, 'Well, I've got to give it to ya. But we might have to put you on turn work.' And the man had thirty-some years' service!"

Another method used to police the boundaries between "black" and "white" jobs was testing. "They set up a testing procedure because they knew that most black workers were not able to deal properly with fractions, algebra, and geometry, and they would make these tests to block them," said Lee Douglas. The ability to do fractions, algebra, and geometry was not necessary for most jobs on Sparrows Point, but even black workers who knew higher math found tests used against them.

Once, when there was a cutback in Eddie Bartee's department, a group of black steelworkers got laid off—including a teacher who had switched to working on the Point because, Bartee said, "he liked the freedom of the steel mill, and of course it was a few dollars more." When a position opened up for a steel man in the open hearth (a "white man's job"), the teacher requested a transfer, took the required test, and passed easily. At that point, the foreman administered another test. When the former schoolteacher passed that one too, they gave him another. "He passed all the tests they gave him till the last one," Bartee recalled. "The foreman looked at him and said, 'You ain't gonna pass this one.' And he didn't. He failed the last test they gave him. He should've got the job after passing the first test. But they didn't want no blacks on that job. They kept bumping it up till he failed."

"Our union did not represent blacks right," Neil Crowder confirmed. "They let that discrimination go on." Despite the "in unity is strength" rhetoric, many union members were no more enlightened than the rest of American society when it came to civil rights, Joe

Kotelchuck pointed out. "A lot of people had the impression that once you were in the union, you were for civil rights. But it wasn't so."

You couldn't find a more devoted group of men.

— RAY SWAGGERT

Retirees from the World War II and Korea generations still meet regularly at various locations around Baltimore—the McDonald's on Wise Avenue, the food court at Eastpoint Mall—to reminisce about the old days and to tell and retell stories of their years "down the Point." Truth to tell, any social gathering of Baltimore's senior citizens will turn up more Bethlehem retirees than the most enterprising journalist could interview in a year. The common thread running through all of their stories, whether happy or sad, is their loyalty and dedication to their jobs and to each other. "I was hypnotized from the minute I walked into the place," LeRoy McLelland said.

Despite their affection for the Point, it doesn't take much talking for most retirees to admit that the camaraderie among workers and good wages aside, their lives as steelworkers were far from easy. Shift work was brutally hard on the body, for one thing. In the tandem mill, where Ed Gorman worked, "one week we worked Sunday and Monday four to twelve, off Tuesday, come in Wednesday, worked Thursday midnight, off Friday, daylight Saturday," he recalled. "Your bowels don't get a chance to be functional. They don't know whether they're coming or going." In the tin mill, everyone worked rotating shifts. "One week you'd work two daylight [7:00 a.m. to 3:00 p.m.], two three-to-eleven, one eleven-to-seven. Or you could work three eleven-to-seven and two daylight and then go back to three-to-eleven," Phyllis Moskowitz recalled. "You never knew how you were going to work."

Few people who worked rotating shifts at the Point ever seem to have gotten enough sleep. "I never had a set schedule until I became a foreman," Donald Lindemann, who also worked in the tin mill, told me. "Our schedule changed every week. We'd work four to twelve Saturday night, and they'd put up a new schedule [that night], and you'd see you were scheduled for Saturday night midnight. I didn't sleep too much. I'd work a double, say four-to-twelve and midnight, come home, sit on the step and drink a couple of beers, lay down at ten, get back up at two, and then go back to work four to twelve. I did it a lot of times. That's the way we were. Kept going and going and going."

Not only was that kind of schedule hard on the body, but it made family life difficult too. "I worked turn work for fifteen years. Three-to-eleven was tough for the kids and tough for my wife. You don't see them," Wimpy Doyle recalled. "When I was young, I slept ten hours a day on eleven-to-seven. Then when I got older, I wouldn't sleep three hours." Rose Marie Weller recalled that her husband, Lee, "might not speak to you for two or three days because, as I found out later, he was exhausted all the time. They really worked them. I don't know how he did it. He would work on three to five hours' sleep every night."

"I would come home from working midnight and take the two kids to elementary school and come home and go to sleep," Ed Gorman told me. "Then I'd wake up when they come from school and we'd have supper at four-thirty. I'd get up early to eat supper with the kids. What other professions do you wake up to eat supper?"

Without question, the long hours took their toll on workers' relationships with their wives and children. Rose Marie Weller described for me a typical evening with her husband when he was working daylight, the shift most conducive to a normal family life. After showering at the plant and leaving his dirty work clothes there, he would shower again at home, she said. Then he would "eat his dinner and hardly talk, except to ask the kids what they were doing in school. And then he'd come in and watch television and read his newspaper and sit in the chair with the cat in his lap. I'd finish washing the dishes and come out, and him and the cat would be fast asleep. I wouldn't wake him up because I knew how little sleep he got. About ten o'clock, I'd say, 'Lee, wake up and go to bed,' and he'd say, 'I want to watch the news.' So I'd sit in the chair with my book. And he'd watch the news and then go to bed."

During winter storms, workers were expected to stay beyond their shifts and help keep the roads and railroad tracks within the complex clear. "When it snowed down there, Lee wouldn't come home for two or three days," Weller said. "'They've got a bench in the shower room,'" he told her. "I'd go in there and lie on the bench and sleep till they come out and woke me up and said, 'Come out and shovel.'" Roosevelt Caldwell recalled that when it snowed, "they would pay you double to stay. You really didn't have a choice. They would call out for food, bring in cots, and everything."

"Some of the guys worked so much overtime that they developed psychiatric problems," Tom Capecci said. "Or their marriages fell apart. They'd work so much that their wives would leave them or cheat on them." He told me a funny story about one man who turned a blind eye to his wife's infidelity until her paramour ate some leftover pizza he had planned to have for dinner when he got home from work. "You can have her," he said, "but stay away from the food!"

In *Wives of Steel*, Karen Olson, a professor of history and anthropology at Community College of Baltimore County, noted the toll that steelmaking took on family life and one of its less savory results. "Long hours and changing shifts left many steelworkers chronically exhausted and excluded from a central role in family life," she wrote. "These arduous conditions often fostered drinking after work as one of the few accessible ways to relax after a shift, and a pervasive bar culture encouraged drinking as part of a masculine ritual that was obligatory for steelworkers."

Most steelworkers phrase the fact more positively. "We'd sit there and drink our beers and shoot a little pool, and then here's the three-to-eleven shift coming in," said LeRoy McLelland. "Maybe we spent a little more time [in the bars] than we should," he said, but drinking together "created more harmony and solidarity than the union hall did, because not everybody went to the union hall." Not all steelworkers drank heavily, and some, like my uncle Ray, didn't drink at all. But for many others, stopping by the bar to have a few (or more) beers with friends after work was a habit they were not inclined to break. "I had guys that would work eleven to seven, go out on payday to drink, and then come back to work for the next shift," Wimpy Doyle told me. "They had a lot of alcoholics. Some were worth saving."

As children, my brother and I spent a fair amount of time in the North Point Road bars with our father, begging him for coins to put in the jukebox and playing shuffleboard while he socialized with his friends. He was not alone in his habits; most of the men we knew lived similar lives, as my mother recalled. "They were hardworking people, but steelworkers would get off work at seven in the morning and go into a bar. Then go home to sleep. When they worked three to eleven, same thing, into the bar. Eleven to seven, into the bar." My mother had reasons to object to this lifestyle, and my parents divorced when I was a young child. They remarried when I was twelve years old, though my father didn't stop drinking entirely till I was in college.

Unlike many of the retirees I've interviewed, my father didn't seem to love making steel. In his mid-forties, he enrolled at Dundalk Community College and then at the University of Baltimore, carrying a full course load while working full-time at Signode with his friend Willy Cohill. He graduated with a bachelor's in political science, and for the last fifteen years of his life, he worked as an insurance investigator for the Maryland State Department of Licensing and Regulation. His new job required him to travel around the country, examining the payout records of every insurance company that did business in Maryland, checking to be sure that they were not defrauding their customers—work that sounded dull to me but that my father enjoyed. He spent a great deal of time working in New York City, where he became an avid theater patron, attending Broadway and off-Broadway plays two or three nights a week. Near the end of his life, he took pride in the fact that he had visited all but one (Colorado) of the fifty states and numerous foreign countries.

"Your father was a diamond in the rough," my mother says whenever she is asked to describe him. I believe that there were quite a few men like my father at Sparrows Point in its heyday, men who became steelworkers not by choice but by convenience. Once he found work that permitted him to indulge his love of travel and conversation, he became a much happier man than he was in my childhood. I regret that he had so few years to enjoy his new life. He was diagnosed with lung cancer in 1995 and died two weeks after his sixty-fifth birthday, after a four-year fight with his disease.

When I think of the people who worked at Bethlehem Steel in the years of the postwar boom, I think of my father and my uncles. In some ways, they were a blessed generation. Born into depression and war, they reaped as adults the benefits of the longest economic boom in American history in what now seems a golden age for working people. But they worked harder than most people today can imagine working, and in the end many of them paid a heavy price for their good luck.

❖ SMOKE ❖

On a sunny May morning in 1968, every single window of every house on F Street in the company town of Sparrows Point shattered. Sleeping steelworkers were thrown from their beds, and children in the elementary school a quarter of a mile away screamed in terror as an ear-shattering boom rent the air. The world wasn't ending, though it probably seemed that way to people living in the town or working in the plant that day. A gas leak at one of the four steam-generating stations on-site caused an explosion that killed two steamfitters—both thrown twenty-five feet from the building—and injured twenty-two others.

The boom was heard in Baltimore, and it rocked the Sparrows Point peninsula. A *Sun* reporter visiting the town after the explosion noted that in houses fifty yards from the steam station, "plaster ceilings collapsed and walls cracked. Glass was imbedded in some walls. Furniture was toppled." Leonard Crowl, a steelworker who was thrown from his bed by the impact, told the reporter, "I'm moving away from here tonight and I'm going to live a good distance from the plant. I've been in two wars and worked in steel plants for most of my life but this is the most shook up I've been in a long time."

Crowl wasn't the only one who was shook up. By the late sixties, the consequences of living cheek by jowl with the biggest steel mill in the world were creating massive headaches for residents displaced by plant expansion and for government officials tasked with monitoring health and safety. The rapid growth of Sparrows Point in the postwar years was a devil's gift. The bigger the plant grew, the more families depended on Bethlehem wages and the more eager state and local officials were to appease the company. At the same time, it was no longer possible to ignore the toxic impact of nearly a century of steelmaking on the environment. As production and employment soared, so too did the amount of filthy water pouring into the bay and of particulate-laden smoke pouring from the stacks of the open hearth furnaces. What do you do when your state's biggest employer is also its worst polluter?

In May 1945, Bethlehem's president, Eugene G. Grace, had predicted that postwar employment at Sparrows Point would exceed thirty-five thousand. Almost every year throughout the early fifties, the company crept closer to fulfilling that prediction by announcing capital improvements geared to boosting production at the Point. For every new coke oven, blast furnace, or finishing mill added or rebuilt, new workers were hired. By 1952, the Sparrows Point works was supporting over twenty-five thousand families in Baltimore, about sixty-five hundred more than during the World War II employment peak. Boosting steel production from eleven to fifteen tons per minute—the goal of a 1956 expansion—increased the Sparrows Point weekly payroll to nearly $3 million. Steelworkers' salaries kept cash registers ringing and bank accounts building from Dundalk and Highlandtown to West Baltimore and beyond.

But progress always has a price. As production was ramped up at the Point, the air and water in the southeastern neighborhoods grew increasingly foul. In 1958, steelmaking on Sparrows Point consumed 861 million gallons of water each day, far exceeding the amount of water consumed in the entire metropolitan Baltimore area. Salt water from the Patapsco River supplied most of the Point's needs. The rest was treated effluent from the nearby sewage plant. At various stages in the steelmaking and finishing processes, the water became contaminated with sulfuric acid, lead, cyanide, benzene, chrome, and other toxic chemicals. "And they would pump it right on out," Donald Lindemann told me, into the Patapsco River, which feeds the Chesapeake Bay.

Donald, the boy once known as Duckie for his love of swimming and fishing, said that when he was growing up on Sparrows Point, "you could look down into the water and see straight down twenty feet." When he and his wife traveled to the Caribbean in later years, he was reminded of the water around Sparrows Point in his youth, he said. "You could pick the fish you wanted, the water was so crystal-clear." But by the sixties, all that had changed. When he took his son Richard crabbing near the Fort Howard lighthouse, close by where British troops had landed in 1814, he pondered the colossal steel pipe pumping effluent from the works. "It was pitiful," he said. "I couldn't believe the filth pouring into the bay."

As the waters of southeast Baltimore County, which is full of little creeks and gullies and rivers, became more and more polluted with chemical runoff from the mill, the number and variety of fish in the bay and its tributaries dwindled. "Before the war, they used to say that the Chesapeake Bay could feed all of Japan," said Willy Cohill. "There was so much fish, crab, and oysters. Hardheads, grock, perch, and sunfish." But only the hardiest species survived the chemical onslaught, he said. "Now the only thing left is rockfish." I asked both Donald and Willy if people in the area noticed the changes as they were occurring. They said yes. "People knew what was going on, but there wasn't any environment protection in those days," Willy said. "So Bethlem just did what the hell they wanted."

By the early seventies, the pollution had grown so bad that when my parents took my brother and me to summer parties at friends' waterfront homes in the area, my mother wouldn't let us in the water. "Your toes will fall off," she would say when we cried and begged to be allowed to at least wade out a bit. Other parents at those parties did let their children submerge themselves in the cloudy waters as my brother and I sat glumly on various piers next to the chicken parts used to catch crabs. We never saw anyone's toes fall off, but one mother washed her children's ears out with alcohol every time they stumbled back onto land.

Cautious mothers like mine could prevent their children from swimming in the polluted creeks, but they couldn't stop them from breathing. In my childhood, the entire town of Sparrows Point, and every steelworker's car parked in the lots during shifts, were coated in a layer of fine red dust. When the wind shifted, the Dundalk neighborhoods closest to the mills were also tinted red. The red dust was ferrous oxide, and it was a consequence of technological advances in the steelmaking process that greatly increased production—while worsening the quality of the air in the neighborhoods surrounding the works.

"Things didn't start getting really dirty until they opened the number 4 open hearth," my uncle Ray Rudacille told me. "That's because the old furnaces were 160- or 175-ton furnaces. The number 4 was a 400-ton furnace. And when they introduced oxygen—piped in through two lances—it burned a lot faster."

When he started working at the Point in 1956, my uncle said, foremen in the open hearth would pass out cigars when they achieved an eight-hour "heat," charging the furnace with iron ore, scrap, and alloys at six in the morning and "tapping the heat" (pouring molten steel) at two in the afternoon. "You would've thought the melter foreman had a baby," he said, describing the celebrations that followed the achievement of making 420 tons of steel in eight hours.

After oxygen lances were introduced in the number 4 open hearth, the time it took to tap a heat was cut in half. Crews were putting out four hundred tons of steel every four hours. But that rapid pace of production fed by oxygen was also what created the red dust. Even after electrostatic precipitators to filter emissions were installed in the 1970s, "what they used to do—if they could get away with it," my uncle said—was to open the stacks, disabling the precipitators. "They'd get caught now and then," he said, "but by then they'd already have the heats out."

The red dust was not just an annoyance. It made some people sick. Harry and Donna Young moved out of Dundalk soon after they discovered their young daughter was allergic to iron ore dust. "She would get so sick," Donna Young, a Baltimore County science teacher, told me. "She would throw up. Her joints would swell up. They thought she had rheumatic fever, leukemia." After conducting allergy tests, doctors told her parents that "we had to get to an elevation of five hundred feet." So the Youngs bought five acres of farmland forty-five minutes north of Sparrows Point and its spewing stacks.

Eddie Bartee Sr. became concerned about the effects of air pollution on his children after attending a union safety conference in Chicago. Flying home, he pondered a disturbing fact he had heard at the conference: people who live in industrial towns die younger than people in nonindustrial towns. As the plane passed over Baltimore on the way to Friendship Airport, south of the city, he said, "we flew over Sparrows Point and I noticed that the grass and trees were red. We could see that from up in the air, but down here you didn't notice it. So I came home all gung ho and said to my wife, 'We've got to get out of here.'"

By then, the Bartees were one of an ever-shrinking number of families still living on the Point. Prior to the Great Depression, nearly nine thousand people had lived in the company town. In the immediate aftermath of World War II, six thousand remained. But as the works expanded, the town contracted. "The razing of company-owned houses in the heart of the Sparrows Point community that got under way some weeks ago is to permit additions to the blast furnace battery and another battery of open hearth furnaces," *The Baltimore Sun* reported in January 1956, when close to two hundred families received eviction notices informing them that they had sixty days to vacate their homes.

Throughout the next decade and a half, each improvement to the works led to another round of evictions and demolitions. The company offered bonuses of eight months' rent to those who vacated their homes immediately after receiving their notices. Five dollars was deducted from the bonus for every day a family remained in the home.

This get-out-quick bonus was the only relocation assistance Bethlehem provided to families who had lived in the town for generations. Because the monthly rent on company houses was so cheap—with some elderly widows paying as little as $20 and no one paying more than $80 as late as 1972—many families resisted moving for economic reasons. Others were simply reluctant to leave behind the beloved streets and houses where they had raised families and in many cases had been raised themselves.

But Bethlehem Steel's need for space to expand the works outweighed such sentimental considerations. At the time of the May 4, 1968, steam plant explosion, only 288 houses were left. By 1973, the managers' big houses with their prizewinning gardens, the D Street shopping district, the churches, the schools, the movie theater and pool halls, the "colored" community of I and J streets, and the bungalows had all fallen to the wrecking ball. Just short of a century after its founding, the town of Sparrows Point simply vanished.

The razing of the town saddened families who had lived there for three generations. Many had re-created in Sparrows Point the close-knit kin communities they had left behind down south, in Pennsylvania and New Jersey and New York, and overseas. Moving away was especially hard on the elderly, many of whom lost not only low-rent housing but also the social network that had sustained them for all of their lives. "It was hard to watch the town being torn down," a woman named Gwendolyn Zimmerman told *The Dundalk Eagle*. "A lot of people lived there their whole lives, raised their children there. All at once, everything was gone. To be torn up by your roots is not easy."

On the day Willy Cohill and I drove around the Point together, he showed me the spots where various community landmarks once stood: "This used to be Penwood Park, where they played the Steel Bowl"; "This used to be the bungalows here"; "This was the high school"; "This used to be the car barn for the streetcar." Where I saw empty lots or deserted roads or abandoned mills, he clearly saw another scene superimposed on the bleak industrial landscape, an afterimage of what once was—streetcars clanging as they pulled into the station, disgorging men in hard hats holding big steel lunch boxes, women hanging out laundry and hoping that the wind would blow the dust from the smokestacks out to the bay, kids with fishing poles slung over their backs heading off to the creek, and himself as an altar boy ringing the bells for 6:00 a.m. mass at St. Luke's during the war, the pews crowded with steelworkers praying before punching the clock for day-light shift at seven. A town of ghosts.

"My mom was there for forty-two years before they made it go away," he told me. Like many elderly residents, Cohill's mother moved to an apartment in Dundalk. It wasn't far away and it was surely a lot safer, but it wasn't home.

"I'd still be living down there if they didn't tear it down," eighty-three-year-old Ainsley Dickinson told me at a bungalows reunion. He was ten years old when his father was transferred to the Point in 1931. "My father got me a rowboat, and in winter I would go around the coves and pick up wood," he said. "I ride down there every once in a while. You can hardly tell there was once houses. We had some good times. I miss that old place." When I told him that I was thinking of writing a book about the town called "Roots of Steel," he thought for a minute. "You should call it 'Roots of Sadness,'" he said, "because nobody's working anymore and they lost everything they had."

Asbestos is taking them right and left.

—TOM CAPECCI

Whenever I ask people about the downside of living and working on the Point, without exception they all mention its effect on their health. "There were a lot of conditions in the mill that we were exposed to that were hazardous to our health, but we didn't know about it," said Eddie Bartee Sr. "For example, all the people that worked in pickling, their teeth are black. In Ed Gorman's area, a lot of people developed heart conditions. With the bricklayers, it was asbestos. But we just found out about that, what, fifteen years ago? But look at all the people who died of lung cancer as a result of asbestos and didn't know why."

Asbestos is a fireproof natural mineral. But in this case, "natural" doesn't mean safe or healthy. When inhaled, asbestos fibers settle in the lungs, which produce an acid in an attempt to dissolve the fibers; the acid in turn creates scarring of the tissue that may become so severe the lungs no longer function. This chronic, debilitating, and sometimes fatal condition is called asbestosis—but it doesn't appear for ten or twenty years after exposure. Mesothelioma, an incurable cancer whose only known cause is exposure to asbestos, takes even longer to show up—twenty to fifty years.

Lee Weller was still working at Sparrows Point when he learned that he was sick. In fact, it was a workplace injury that sent him to the doctor's office in the first place. A couple of days after he had returned to work from a vacation, said his wife, Rose Marie, "he was carrying two buckets of stuff down black steel steps, and some electricians who had been working there when he was out had left a long black piece of wire on the steps. He didn't see it and tripped over the wire and fell down the steps. The first thing his boss said to him was 'Don't report it. We've got a perfect safety record.'"

But Lee was in so much pain that his wife insisted he see a doctor. "That was on a Friday. Saturday morning I got a telephone call. The doctor said, 'Bring your husband in. We need to talk to you. We sent the X-rays to an expert. Your husband has cancer.'" By the time his metastatic lung cancer was discovered, Rose Marie said, "there was nothing they could do. They admitted him to the hospital, and he never came home." He died six weeks after the cancer was diagnosed, one week short of his sixty-first birthday.

I asked Rose Marie if her husband had been exposed to asbestos on the job. She said that though he had worked all around the mill, for years he made asbestos covers for pipes. I asked her if she blames Bethlehem Steel for his death. "No, I blame our ignorance for not knowing that Bethlehem Steel was doing this to him," she said. "He used to say, 'I'm so tired, so tired.' I thought it was because he was working so hard. We just didn't know."

The first lawsuit charging that Bethlehem Steel had evidence that asbestos exposure was causing lung disease in its employees was filed in 1981 by six former bricklayers. The Baltimore attorneys Peter G. Angelos and Howard J. Schulman presented evidence showing that as far back as 1952, company physicians administering physicals in the Sparrows Point dispensary saw evidence of asbestosis on chest X-rays and concealed it from affected workers. The suit charged that the bricklayers, some of whom began working for the company in 1936, were continuously exposed to billowing clouds of asbestos fibers as they constructed and maintained various brick structures like open hearth furnaces and coke ovens. The attorneys pointed out that by withholding the findings of those medical examinations, Bethlehem physicians deprived Sparrows Point employees of occupational disease benefits owed them by Maryland's workers' compensation law and prevented the Workers' Compensation Commission, the state health department, and other state and federal agencies from taking action to protect other employees.

Two years later, in 1983, fifty-five active Sparrows Point employees and their wives sued Bethlehem Steel in federal court. Though most were bricklayers, some worked other jobs. Because asbestos products were used throughout the works as insulation in furnaces and as pipe coverings, pretty much everyone who worked at the Point was exposed to a greater or lesser degree.

Bob Strasbaugh was diagnosed with asbestosis after a routine medical examination in 1983, two years after he retired. When the doctors informed him he had asbestosis, he told me, "I really didn't know too much about it, to tell you the truth, but I sure did find out about it."

"How?" I asked.

"Couldn't breathe" was his reply. When I was walking up to his door to interview him, I had noticed the big silver oxygen tank on the enclosed front porch of his Dundalk home. "I only use it a few hours a day," he said matter-of-factly.

Bob inhaled a lot of asbestos when he worked as a shearman in the rolling mill, cutting steel as it came down the line. Shearmen worked in small shanties called pulpits, where they sweated in summer and froze in winter. "Many a time in the summer, if you came up in that mill, I was up in the pulpit in my little shorty underwear with just my shoes on," Bob recalled. "And back then you had a blower system, and in winter your heat in the pulpits was steam, and all the pipes were wrapped with asbestos. So what happened, that asbestos after a while would crumble, and of course this blower would be blowing asbestos particles with the hot air. Of course, all your piping back then—these huge steam pipes—were all wrapped in asbestos."

Machinists got a lungful of fibers every time they cut into a piece of piping or a bearing that had been layered with asbestos to retard flames. "When you were running the lathes, it was like snow with all the asbestos blowing around," said Austin McLelland. "I would step back—for some reason I didn't think it was good for my lungs—and I would take a deep breath and hold it till I shut it off. So far I haven't shown any asbestosis, which is a break."

Donald Lindemann was exposed to asbestos in the tin mill. "We had 275 burners, pipes like twelve inches around, because we used millions of cubic feet of gas in eight hours. The pilots were like torches, and they would blow out that asbestos where it would round the wall of the furnace. Man, that stuff would get in my mouth!" Donald has "just a touch of asbestosis," he said—but he has watched as his brother and numerous cousins who worked at the Point succumbed to lung cancer. "My brother died of lung cancer at sixty-three. He got one Social Security check."

My father and my uncle Ray—Donald's first cousins—and three other Sparrows Point cousins on Donald's mother's side all died of lung cancer. Some of them also smoked, and their tobacco use compounded the damage caused by asbestos exposure. "Everyone down there was exposed to asbestos," the ironworker Joe Lawrence told me, "and all of the ones that smoked too died." Roy Swaggert and his twin brother, for example, started working at the Point the same month. "He died at fifty-five of asbestos," Swaggert told me. "I have it in both my lungs myself, but I never smoked. He did."

It would be a mistake to conclude, however, that only smoking steelworkers die of occupationally related respiratory disease. My uncle Ray never smoked, and the form of cancer that got him—mesothelioma—has no association with smoking. Its only known cause is exposure to asbestos. Mesothelioma has a very long latency period—people don't get sick until decades after exposure—but it advances quickly. Most people die within twelve months of diagnosis. "It was such a swift-moving cancer," Rose Marie Weller said, describing her husband's rapid demise.

In 1991, over ten thousand asbestos-related injury cases filed at the federal courthouse in Baltimore were consolidated into a single trial by Judge Marshall A. Levin. Most of the steelworkers were represented by Peter G. Angelos. The son of a Highlandtown tavern owner, he had done some legal work for the USW and was one of the first attorneys in the country to represent steelworkers in asbestos cases. Asbestos made Peter Angelos a very wealthy man; the year after the big class action suit was settled, he bought the Baltimore Orioles baseball team. Later, he won an enormous settlement in a class action suit against tobacco companies, which has helped fund cancer research in the state.

Angelos is not too popular with many baseball fans in Baltimore, who accuse him of wrecking the team, but steelworkers are grateful for his efforts on their behalf and don't begrudge him his millions. "If it wasn't for Peter Angelos, we wouldn't have been compensated at all," said Tom Capecci. "So what if he got one-third? He fought for us when no one else would. Until Angelos came along, no other lawyer wanted to take on Bethlehem for asbestos."

In 1992, a jury found that seven asbestos companies were liable for damages to 8,555 plaintiffs—many of them people who had worked in the Fairfield and Sparrows Point shipyards during the war. Damages awarded in those early cases were impressive, particularly in a community suffering the effects of deindustrialization. In those days, winning an asbestos lawsuit was like winning the lottery, except you paid for the ticket with your life, or that of your husband or father. "I remember one guy bragging about all the money he got and the new car he got,"

Capecci said. "Well, he was dead at fifty-two. Who cares about the money?"

"Men would come into the bar and tell us that they had gotten $50,000," Nonnie Strasbaugh recalled of those early settlements when I talked to her and her husband in the fall of 2006. "They sat there and bragged, didn't they, hon?" Bob nodded. "The nineties was when the so-called big money came flying in," he observed.

But the big money dried up pretty quickly as, one after another, the asbestos manufacturers, and later Bethlehem Steel itself, declared bankruptcy. Most litigants today receive a few thousand dollars. Some widows, like Rose Marie Weller, have never filed lawsuits, though they have been virtually impoverished by their husbands' early deaths. Many of these "wives of steel" were full-time homemakers and found themselves in difficult circumstances after their husbands' demise.

A Bethlehem Steel widow receives half of her husband's pension reduced by half of the amount of her own Social Security stipend. Women like Rose Marie Weller, whose husband started at Sparrows Point after World War II and spent his entire working life there, typically receive between $100 and $200 per month in survivor benefits. The loss of their company-paid health insurance after Bethlehem Steel filed for bankruptcy in 2001 compounded a situation that longtime USWA vice president Ed Gorman calls "obscene."

"The old ladies, I'd see their husbands' deaths in the paper, and they'd come up to me and say, 'I haven't gotten a pension check in a few months.' And I'd tell them, 'It takes three months to straighten that out, but I'm afraid that you are only going to get a hundred dollars.' That's why you saw so many old women working at Hutzler's and Hochschild Kohn," Gorman said. "Because no one can live on that. And that was before the breakup."

> Just about everyone we know from down there
> got some kind of cancer.
>
> —JESSIE SCHULTZ

Retired steelworkers suffer from a broad range of health conditions directly related to their employment, even apart from life-threatening diseases like cancer. Years of brutally hard physical labor have taken their toll on most. Jessie Schultz, a former tin sorter and labor gang member, has had surgery on both shoulders, but she still cannot lift either of her arms above her head. "I can't even comb my hair," she said. "When I go to bed at night, I have to lay down to put my nightgown on. It's torture, the pain is so bad."

Eddie Bartee's claim that workers in different parts of the mill are vulnerable to different illnesses is supported by the scientific literature. A series of reports published in the *Journal of Occupational Health* looked at deaths and chronic diseases among a group of 58,828 steelworkers who had been employed in seven Allegheny County, Pennsylvania, steel plants in 1953. Researchers tracked the men in the study from 1953 through 1966; the series of scientific papers analyzing the data was published in the mid-1970s.

For several areas within the sheet and tin mills, the reports noted "significant excesses in mortality," including "higher than expected" rates of heart disease and cancers of the lymphatic and hematopoietic tissues. A similarly sharp spike in those types of cancers had previously been observed in blast furnace workers. And the sheet and tin mill workers were more likely to die of nonmalignant respiratory diseases. The studies also uncovered high rates of respiratory cancers and cancers of the digestive system among coke oven workers. "Most of the deaths from cancers of the lung occurred in men who had worked at least fifteen years on the ovens," the researchers stated.

Steelworkers themselves didn't need a bunch of academicians confirming that fact. "The larry car operators, they had an old saying: None of them ever retired—they all died," said Blaine DeWitt. "That smoke would be so thick, and they'd have to stand right in the middle of it till the operator got all the coke loaded in."

Shortly before the first asbestos lawsuits were filed, Bethlehem launched a study of cancer rates among its Baltimore employees. The study claimed that the rate of cancer deaths among its shipyard and steel plant workers in Baltimore was actually *lower* than the expected rate for Baltimore—22 percent less for whites and 24 percent less for blacks. Maryland's Republican senator Charles Mathias wasn't buying it and asked the National Institute for Occupational Safety and Health (NIOSH) to take a look at the suspicious findings.

NIOSH analysts found numerous methodological errors in the study. For example, the researchers did not break down the worker population by job class and work area, failed to determine the cause of death of workers who left the company before retirement, and had used only company records to calculate worker deaths. The combination of errors basically invalidated the results of the study.

NIOSH concluded that there was enough evidence of occupational disease at Sparrows Point "to warrant control by the company of the substances to which these workers have been exposed." The agency recommended that deaths from cancers of the bladder, pancreas, and lung be examined more thoroughly "to determine if common exposures can be identified" and that the company set up a "special medical surveillance program for those employees who seem to be at increased risk." Those recommendations were ignored.

Everyone was aware of the potential for injury and illness—it was hard not to be when people were regularly being carted off to the burn unit. But the material benefits of working at Sparrows Point outweighed potentially catastrophic health effects. "It was always in the back of your mind that working there might kill you," Pete Selhorst said. "But it was a good-paying job, and you just don't give that up easily. In certain mills, people seemed to survive better," he said. "In the pipe mill, when they still had that. Rod and wire mills. In the finishing mills, the guys survived better because the air wasn't as dirty. They had to keep the place cleaner because it was a finished product they were making rather than taking dirt to make iron to make steel."

In the coke ovens, "a kind of macho attitude prevailed," he said, with workers doing whatever they had to do to get the job done. The noxious fumes and particulate they inhaled with every breath, the black gunk floating in their coffee cups, the thick, heavy smoke—those things were the price of employment.

> Pollution is a dirty word. So is unemployment.
>
> —*BETHLEHEM REVIEW*, APRIL 1977

Like steelworkers themselves, the State of Maryland long gave the company a pass on issues of safety and health. From the time the works was founded in 1887, its owners—first Pennsylvania Steel and later Bethlehem—managed their own affairs. That freedom from government oversight continued well into the final quarter of the twentieth century.

"Bethlehem's Sparrows Point complex sits like a separate state subdivision at the foot of Baltimore's harbor," the *Baltimore News-American* reporter Mark Bowden wrote in 1979. "It is a fiefdom, a private 3000 acre peninsula that makes most of its own rules and laws. . . . Finding out what's going on inside that fief, whether you're a county cop, a reporter, a federal safety official or just a curious guest, depends to a large extent on how much the company wants you to know."

As concerns about air and water pollution began to build in the 1970s, the long-standing hands-off attitude of government became slightly more hands-on—but only slightly, given the economic stakes. As Bowden noted, "the ups and downs of the company's economy are the ups and downs of Baltimore's economy." In 1977, the Sparrows Point works accounted for nearly 10 percent of all manufacturing employment in the state and was estimated to generate two additional jobs outside the industry for each job on-site. With the economic livelihood of the entire state depending on the Point's continuing productivity, it is not surprising that Bethlehem Steel was able to wrap state environmental officials around its benzene-coated finger.

Soon after a 1973 report by the Council on Economic Priorities (CEP) judged the Sparrows Point plant "one of the four or five worst water and air polluters among steel mills in the country," the deputy director of Maryland's Water Resources Administration soothingly noted that "the company is spending a helluva lot of money on problems that have persisted for a long time. It can't be done overnight." This from a state water official at a time when the Point was dumping 324 pounds of arsenic and 5,469 pounds of cyanide into the waters of Baltimore's harbor each day! As the CEP report noted, "a few thousandths of an ounce [of cyanide] can be fatal to humans, and even smaller amounts can be deadly to fish." I remember seeing the beaches at shore homes covered with dead fish, but I wasn't aware until I read the report that *five* fish kills were reported in local waters in 1971 alone. No wonder my mother wouldn't let us swim in those deadly waters.

Two years later, in December 1973, *The Baltimore Sun* reported that Bethlehem had worked out a deal with the federal Environmental Protection Agency and state water quality reps that would allow the company to discharge "substantially higher amounts of polluting oil and metals than the limits announced by the agency at a public hearing held in October." Meeting secretly with company lawyers in Philadelphia, two hours north of Baltimore, state and federal environmental protection officials signed a permit that vastly increased the amount of chemicals the company would be allowed to dump into the Chesapeake Bay.

This permit approved an increase in average daily discharges by 347 percent for chromium, 86 percent for soluble zinc, and 55 percent for soluble iron, and it eliminated limits on tin. The regulators also okayed a 50 percent increase in oil discharges and a 94 percent increase in the release of suspended solids. And Bethlehem was granted a fifteen-month extension for treating the thousands of gallons of pickle liquor—an acid used to smooth out finished steel—dumped into Baltimore's harbor and an extension of fifteen to twenty-seven months for reducing the temperatures of wastewater discharges (which were largely responsible for the fish kills).

A *Sun* article published the same year showed that the county, no less than the state and feds, pretty much let Bethlehem do whatever it liked on the Point: "The county office of Permits and Licenses exercises none of the normal control over construction plans, sediment control, setbacks, inspections, and permit fees for Bethlehem Steel projects." The county's chief supervisor of inspections told the reporter, "We don't inspect them. They have their own engineers down there. It's a set-up that's been that way for years with the county. Why? I can't answer. It was just the procedure when I came in and it's been that way ever since."

Prodded by federal regulators, Bethlehem eventually reduced air pollution at the Sparrows Point plant, spending an estimated $65 million on abatement equipment and cutting its particulate air pollution in half between 1972 and 1976. The plant was still perfuming the air of Dundalk and Sparrows Point with over three thousand pounds of sulfur dioxide per hour, but that was better than the previous average of 6,217 pounds per hour. By contrast, the company's scorecard for reducing pollution of local waterways remained dismal throughout the seventies. In 1977, the Council on Economic Priorities termed Sparrows Point's efforts to reduce its pollution of local waters "abysmal."

A big part of the pollution problem at Sparrows Point was the age of much of the physical plant. How could the company possibly meet late-twentieth-century environmental regulations while operating three one-hundred-year-old blast furnaces? Those ancient workhorses, imported from the Ashland Iron Works, had been built in 1874, producing iron at Ashland until 1880. Pennsylvania Steel had dismantled and reassembled them on the Point, where they were first tapped in 1889, 1890, and 1891, respectively. Overhauled by Bethlehem in 1959, they weren't shut down until the new computerized L blast furnace was tapped in 1978. Of the ten blast furnaces operating on the Point before Big L became operational, four had been built in the 1890s and two in 1920.

Such decrepit equipment was not only environmentally problematic but also unsafe for workers. Two men died of carbon monoxide poisoning at C furnace in 1978; blast furnace workers told *The Baltimore Sun* that a critical section of piping on the furnace called a distance piece was constantly slipping out of place and that the problem had been repeatedly reported to management but nothing was done about it. Although one of the men who was killed had been overcome by fumes a week before his death and sent to the dispensary, the problem was still not fixed, perhaps because the equipment was so old and shabby that a permanent fix was impossible. The company was trying to keep production going until the new L furnace was operating at full capacity. Moreover, experienced blastmen had been transferred to the L for training, leaving novices to run the rickety old units.

Things were just as bad at the coke ovens, where some of the old batteries were so leaky that "we had the MOSH [Maryland Occupational Safety and Health] lady in every day," Melvin Schmeiser recalled. In 1978, MOSH fined the company $11,000 for twenty-six counts of endangering workers' health by exposing them to dangerous amounts of coke oven gas leaking from the aging ovens.

After that, Schmeiser said, "every day [the MOSH rep] went up on the batteries. It was showtime when she came. 'All right, here she comes. Crank up the exhausters—they suck the smoke off. Extra luter-men, get up there and put stuff around the holes to keep the smoke from coming out.' The foreman took off his white hat and put on a yellow hat to help. And the lady looks around, takes her measurements, and leaves, and it's back to normal. Now the smoke is rolling off again."

Before the coke ovens were finally shut down for good in 1989, "we got fined every day," Schmeiser said. "They knew they weren't gonna pay the fines. They didn't put any money into it. Instead of rebuilding, they hired outside contractors to stand there with fire hoses. The batteries were starting to go, tilting and everything. At that point you knew it wasn't gonna be much longer."

Maintaining high rates of production took precedence over maintenance, he said, and as a consequence expensive new machinery, including a new coke oven battery installed in the mid-eighties, wore out long before it should have. "You can get fifty years out of a battery. They weren't gonna get twenty out of that one," Schmeiser said. "All they wanted was to push coke, push coke, push coke."

Bethlehem's official response to the challenges posed by aging equipment and stringent new environmental regulations made it clear that company management greatly resented having to deal with the environmental issue at all. "The job ahead is a horribly costly one. It's going to be tough, almost impossible, to earn that kind of money," a *Bethlehem Review* article stated in 1978. Noting that the company had spent $370.3 million "just to buy the hardware to clean up the air and water at its various operations," and that "the money did not cover the costs to operate or maintain that equipment," the article concluded that "we will all have to rearrange some of our priorities and we'll have to strike a balance—a reasonable balance—between environmental and economic concerns."

Though replacing ancient equipment with newer, cleaner, more efficient machinery would have considerably enhanced the company's ability to compete with overseas steelmakers using the latest technology, Bethlehem long resisted a strategic analysis and overhaul of its vast operations and instead took a piecemeal approach to replacing worn-out equipment and installing pollution control devices. This foot-dragging is clearly evident in company publications from the seventies, which insist that "pollution is not all man-made" and argue that "we will all be far better off environmentally in the long run if we realize that we cannot undo, in a very short time, a lot of mistakes and bad practices which have grown up over many generations."

Employees got the message. Pete Selhorst said that though the company paid lip service to environmental regulations and installed technology to monitor emissions, "the meters and printouts could be doctored. I know one instance with water pollution in the coke oven area where the instrument guy made it so that the recorder couldn't go past a certain point. So it was always in the clean-enough zone."

Eventually, Pete became a technician himself and found out how the game was played. He and the other technicians would set up a monitor, and a manager would come in and complain, "That's not what it's supposed to say." The technicians would respond that they had just set up the equipment and knew the readings were correct. "Well, it's not supposed to be there," the manager would say. Pete and the other technicians would simply reply, "What do you want it to say?" and adjust the equipment accordingly.

"It was such a dirty place. The A battery stack in the coke ovens was so bad—it was the dirtiest stack on the East Coast, probably, just constant black soot near the end. All they wanted to do was run the place," Selhorst said, environmental regulations be damned.

Well after the company was making a show of environmental compliance, long-standing practices of dumping and running continued unabated on the Point. Tom Capecci told me about "the pit" where he and the other truck drivers dumped chemicals and debris. "Whenever they had to get rid of something, they'd either dump it or bury it," he said. "Asbestos, sulfuric acid, benzene, you name it." Sometimes the landfill would start to smoke and the Sparrows Point Fire Department had to open it up and put out fires burning underground, he said. When I mentioned to him that some people in the community think that one day the works will be torn down and condominiums and parks built on the waterfront, he laughed. "They can't do it," he said. "The ground is too contaminated. It's like a time bomb."

• JUSTICE •

In 1971, a group of African American steelworkers from Sparrows Point visited a civil rights attorney newly arrived in Baltimore. Kenneth L. Johnson had grown up on a farm in Mississippi and in 1960 was one of seven law students from Southern University who attempted to integrate a whites-only lunch counter in Baton Rouge, Louisiana. After being expelled with his peers for bringing "discredit to the university," Johnson transferred to the Howard University School of Law in Washington, D.C. There he was trained by professors expert in constitutional and civil rights law, including some who had argued the *Brown v. Board of Education* case before the Supreme Court in 1954. Upon arriving in Baltimore in 1969, the young civil rights attorney helped file discrimination suits against the Prince George's County school system, the Baltimore police and fire departments, and other employers.

The Bethlehem steelworkers "had heard of my work in Baltimore," Johnson told me in 2006 as we sat on the wide front porch of his gracious home in Roland Park. "They asked me for help. Of course, they also didn't have any money, and someone had told them that I'd take on the case for free, which I did."

Later that year, Johnson filed suit against Bethlehem Steel and United Steelworkers Local 2609. Local 2610 wasn't included in the suit, he said, "because 2609 was the bad guy." Representing workers in the finishing mills, with their traditionally higher-paying, clean jobs from which blacks were long excluded, Local 2609 was, he said, "part and parcel of the discrimination" on Sparrows Point, using the unit seniority system to keep blacks out of competition.

Ken Johnson took on the Sparrows Point discrimination case during a period of reaction, when many working-class white people responded with fear and resentment to the changes unleashed by civil rights activism. Some of the resistance was based in economics. Donna Young, who grew up in Dundalk in the late forties and early fifties, said, "I think where the prejudice came in was when people started to feel like their jobs were in danger, when civil rights came about and people felt like, 'These people are going to take over my job—they are going to move ahead of me in seniority.'"

The remedy that would come to be called affirmative action attempts to rectify past discrimination by easing advancement for blacks in employment and education—enraged them. Why were African Americans being given help that they themselves were denied? Those who were the children and grandchildren of immigrants—the Irish, Italians, Poles, and Slavs who had arrived in America with nothing—pointed out that their ancestors too had faced prejudice and economic discrimination. They did not recognize, as many whites of that generation still don't, that one or two generations of struggle is in no way equivalent to four hundred years of systemic oppression.

That may be because many working-class whites still felt the sting of prejudice and limited opportunity based on class rather than race. People in Dundalk smarted under the "white trash" label applied to the community long before local disc jockeys started a campaign of mockery in the 1980s, targeting the way they looked, talked, and lived. Donna Young told me that in 1952, the mother of one of her freshman roommates at the University of Maryland moved heaven and earth to try to get her daughter a new room when she learned that she would be sharing it with two girls from Dundalk. "I didn't find out till after we had gotten to be good friends, but her mother had gone to the state legislator when the campus wouldn't do anything. We grew up with that idea that you were rough, tough, and nasty because you had grown up there." Now a teacher at a school in an upper-middle-class section of the county, Young recalled the shock of her students when she told them that she was from Dundalk. "Their jaws dropped," she said. "Here I am, a teacher. Do I speak incorrectly? Do I carry knives?"

When my mother went to work as a secretary for the State of Maryland in the sixties, she experienced the same kind of condescension from supervisors and co-workers. "My boss used to tell me that I should move to a nicer neighborhood like Roland Park or Towson," she said. The ubiquitous bumper sticker LIVE, WORK, SHOP . . . DUNDALK shouted the community's defiance, but beneath the bravado was a kind of fear of venturing out into that wider world, where better-educated, more-affluent people would look down on you. Why risk it? Best to stick with your own kind.

Right-wing politicians were quick to capitalize on this murky mix of anger, defensiveness, and denial by creating a socially acceptable target for white working-class anger. Who was to blame, they asked, for the social upheaval that threatened to upset their way of life? Who was pushing African Americans to challenge the old ways and encouraging rioting in the streets? The same people who looked down on working-class whites and dismissed them as white trash, of course: left-leaning middle- and upper-class whites—liberals!

It was as though we threw a rock through all the employers'
windows in the area.

—LARRY AGELOFF

In March 2007, I spoke with two men who played important roles in the Congress of Racial Equality's (CORE) campaign on behalf of African American steelworkers at Sparrows Point, five years before Johnson's lawsuit. John Burleigh, who is black, was CORE's director of employer relations; Larry Ageloff was one of two CORE volunteers (both white) who served as liaisons to the Bethlehem steelworkers.

In many ways, Bethlehem's practices on Sparrows Point were no different from those of most other employers at the time, Burleigh and Ageloff said. Refusal to promote blacks was the general practice in the area at that time by all employers, government as well as private. And in many ways, the Bethlehem steelworkers were in a much better position than the great majority of blacks in Baltimore. "The guys at the steel mill were relatively well off financially compared to what was available jobwise for most blacks at the time," Ageloff pointed out. Still, to the CORE organizers, the Bethlehem case represented an opportunity to deliver "a wake-up call to other employers. Every time you have some success, it affects others."

CORE officially became involved after two Bethlehem steelworkers, Francis Bernard Jones and Francis Brown, walked into the CORE offices on Gay and Eden streets in Baltimore in July 1966 to register a complaint about segregation and discrimination at Sparrows Point. At that time, locker rooms, cafeterias, and restrooms were still segregated, as was housing in the company town. Burleigh assigned the job of investigating violations of civil rights on the Point to Ageloff and his colleague Irwin Auerbach (now deceased).

"We went in and started interviewing people," Ageloff said. "Set up meetings and talked to people till we had a real handle on the problem. We outlined each division, got some idea of what percentage [of employees] were black and what their jobs entailed. We learned that a black couldn't become a truck driver, that the dirtiest, most dangerous jobs were black jobs. That their supervisors were white. Housing was a problem."

Word of the investigation spread among the black employees in the various mills and the shipyard. "As Larry and Irwin dug into what was going on, they brought more and more people in, and the picture really loomed into being much larger than we initially thought," Burleigh said. "It was like a ripple effect."

The involvement of an activist group like CORE, Ageloff pointed out, "is a two-edged sword. Not only does it cut against the discriminator, but it brings in more people who have been discriminated against." People who previously accepted injustice because it was familiar begin to see thing differently, he said, and realize "I'm a victim and I've been a victim all my life."

Cliff Lockman, a tin mill worker, told me that he and some of his friends became active in the civil rights campaign around that time. "You got involved to show you was interested in trying to do something, wanting to get out of the situation you was in, being held back and all." Tank Levy agreed that the efforts to overcome discrimination on the Point were given a big boost by the outside assistance. "Once CORE came in, the whole thing started snowballing," he said.

After a few months of talking, investigating, and building a group called the Steelworkers and Shipyard Workers for Equality, the organizers realized that it was time, Ageloff said, "to strike a blow at the company. Once you get people together, you have to deliver. You can't just be having meetings and doing surveys. You reach a certain point where you have to do something, or your patrons, who in this case were the workers, are going to leave thinking that it's more of the same old crap."

CORE and the Sparrows Point workers knew that they had to confront the problem at its root, "the head of the monster," in Bethlehem, Pennsylvania. One memorable day, four busloads of steelworkers pulled up at Bethlehem headquarters, ninety miles north of Baltimore, to protest discrimination on Sparrows Point. "It was warm here but it was cold up there, and there was wind coming down from the mills while we were picketing," recalled Lee Douglas. The company refused to let the protesters enter the building to meet with management—or even to use the restroom.

"I remember getting off the bus and seeing this big guy whose nose was like on the other side of his face. I thought he was going to beat the hell out of us," said Ageloff. "But they wouldn't even let us in the building. They locked their people in and they locked us out."

In response, the picketers themselves took control of the doors and refused to let anyone enter or leave the building until they were allowed upstairs to present their demands. "We held that turret door that turns around so that it wouldn't let anybody in or out because we had decided that we would go to jail," Douglas recalled. "That's the only way we knew how to deal with them. When you orderly, nobody care about you. When you disorderly, they want to see what the hell they can do to straighten it out."

The strategy worked, and a small group of protesters was escorted upstairs to meet with representatives of the company. The proudest moment of his career as an organizer and an activist, Lee Douglas told me, was "sitting at the table in Bethlehem, Pennsylvania, after we had laid out on the table the things we wanted and they said to us, 'Before you get back to Sparrows Point, these things that you have requested will be in the making.'"

It wasn't quite that simple, of course. As in its past dealings with union organizers, the company wasn't about to give in that easily. Even so, it was a victory, and "it sent a current through all the workers—that we had gone up against the company and won," said Ageloff. "That was a lovely day."

Two weeks after the trip to Bethlehem, CORE organized another caravan—this time to the Department of Labor in Washington, D.C. They didn't find the door barred against them as they had in Bethlehem, but they were told that the secretary of labor, W. Willard Wirtz, whom they had asked to see, was out of town. "So we sat down and waited [for him to return]," Ageloff said. "And sure enough, in a couple of hours he met with us."

Lee Douglas recalled that trip a little differently. "The secretary didn't meet with us, but he sent someone else down," he said. In either case, CORE and the steelworkers had finally gotten the government involved, and just like SWOC organizers in the forties, they had discovered a potent weapon to use against the company in their quest for justice: the threat of losing profitable defense contracts.

With the war in Vietnam escalating, Bethlehem was once again poised to reap enormous profits through defense spending, as it had in World Wars I and II. In 1966, the Sparrows Point plant alone had more than $50 million worth of federal contracts with the Department of Defense, while Bethlehem Steel as a whole enjoyed $92.1 million of government business. Those contracts could be abruptly terminated if the company was not in full compliance with all relevant federal legislation—in this case, the Civil Rights Act of 1964, which mandated fair housing and employment, and Executive Order 11246, signed by Lyndon Baines Johnson to protect minority employees of federal contractors.

"That was our entrée," recalled Burleigh. "We said that they should provide opportunities for everybody if they were receiving federal contracts." Labor Department officials were forced to agree, and CORE and the Bethlehem steelworkers "came away from that meeting with a lot of promises," Ageloff said. Although for months afterward the Departments of Labor and Defense bickered over which agency was responsible for enforcing the law—"Labor would throw the ball to Defense, and Defense would throw it back to Labor," said Ageloff—the secretary of labor ultimately ordered a compliance review of the company, which resulted in a direct order for Bethlehem Steel to eliminate racial discrimination in its employment practices.

The ruling that followed the investigation, handed down in February 1967, led to "recommendations for improvement in virtually every area of the vast Sparrows Point plant," a *Sun* article noted, adding that "a commitment for improvement had been obtained from the company." Failure to meet the recommendations could result in "suspension or cancellation of present contracts or debarment from all future contracts." Once again the company had been arm-wrestled into compliance with the law out of fear of losing government money.

Throughout this intense phase of demonstrating and negotiating with the Departments of Labor and Defense, "we had CORE at the table with us," Douglas said. Burleigh and Ageloff's goal in the Sparrows Point case "was to get these government agencies involved, doing what they were supposed to be doing," said Ageloff. "The government may not have moved as quickly as we wanted them to, but they did move." Douglas agreed. "We forced the government to take a stand. If it had not been for the government, we would have remained in the position we were in."

However, as CORE's integrationist mission began to morph into black nationalism, and the Bethlehem case was taken over by New York organizers who rejected the grassroots approach of Baltimore officers like Burleigh and Ageloff, Douglas and other steelworkers grew uneasy with the group's increasing militancy. The New York CORE representatives started holding press conferences without the steelworkers, Douglas told me, and used inflammatory language that would not help their cause.

"They were talking about 'them white crackers down there, denying these blacks the right to get jobs' and all that," Douglas said. "I wasn't gonna let them come up with no stuff that's gonna cause us a problem when we go back to work. So I called my lawyer and discussed getting rid of CORE, and he told me how to do it without any problems. We were trying to do the right thing."

"Lee decided to pull up his tents shortly after the New York kids came to town," said Burleigh, "because they undercut negotiations that were already in progress." And, as Ageloff noted, "by that point the steelworkers and shipyard workers were self-sufficient. They really didn't need us anymore."

Over the next few years Douglas and his group continued to negotiate with the company to dismantle the mechanisms of racial privilege on the Point. The major concerns of steelworkers of color remained transfer rights, testing, and apprentice training. The company and the union took steps to eliminate the most blatant forms of discrimination, increasing the number of African American foremen from 63 to 101, for example, and adding twenty black men to a crafts apprenticeship program. "They stopped the worst of the discrimination," Cliff Lockman said. "You could get into other departments, even if you could only move up a certain extent."

But in a workforce of more than twenty-five thousand that was nearly one-third black, opportunities for promotion and leadership remained limited. There was only one black electrician in a unit of over three hundred, for example. Appointing a few blacks to supervisory positions and apprenticeships, cutting back on testing, and allowing transfers between departments were viewed as radical concessions by Bethlehem and the USWA. The activists, on the other hand, saw the concessions as Band-Aids offered as a substitute for open-heart surgery. It was time, they decided, to take their fight to the courts. As they had with CORE, they soon found an advocate with a shared agenda.

> The tone of civil rights or anything else in the country is set
> out of the White House. If it is a positive tone, things are
> positive. If it's a negative tone, things are negative.

> —KENNETH L. JOHNSON

Ken Johnson had been a Justice Department lawyer in Birmingham, Alabama, during the Johnson administration and witnessed firsthand the effect of the 1968 election on civil rights enforcement. "Nixon ran on a platform of a Southern strategy, and he vowed to appoint strict constructionist judges, meaning judges that would be hostile to civil rights, and he did," Johnson said. "When he and John Mitchell came in and started doing horrible things, I quit."

That decision brought him to Baltimore, where fear of social upheaval played a large part in delivering white working-class votes to Nixon and his running mate, the former Baltimore County executive and Maryland governor Spiro Agnew, in that critical election. During the campaign Agnew memorably proclaimed that "anarchy, rioting, and even civil disobedience have no constructive purpose in a constitutional republic." Many whites in Dundalk and other working-class neighborhoods in Baltimore admired Agnew for his public dressing-down of the city's black leaders after the 1968 riots, which he contended they had done nothing to stop.

On Sparrows Point and in surrounding neighborhoods, many black steelworkers were quick to dissociate themselves from lawlessness. Tank Levy recalled being approached by a white co-worker during the April 1968 riots in Baltimore, when an after-dark curfew was imposed on the city and surrounding counties. "He said, 'I don't know why I got a curfew. Y'all are the ones rioting.' I said, 'I'm not rioting. You don't see me out there.'"

In Turner Station, older men from the community drove around and warned young people that they were not to leave the neighborhood to join in the mayhem in the city. The young people stayed put. Just as Lee Douglas had jettisoned CORE when he began to perceive its methods as counterproductive, so too did Bethlehem steelworkers reject anarchy in the streets as unlikely to help their cause.

But either privately or publicly, most supported the vigorous organizing efforts of Lee Douglas, Francis Brown, Oscar Hoggs, and other leaders of the civil rights campaign on the Point. At its peak, the Steelworkers and Shipyard Workers for Equality claimed about twenty-four hundred dues-paying members, though only a couple of hundred regularly attended marches and rallies, and even fewer signed on to Ken Johnson's lawsuit against the company and the union. But the ones who did, Johnson said, "had integrity, fortitude, and they could not be bought off. They were very, very determined to make things right."

That became clear in 1974 when the United States Department of Justice unilaterally settled all pending discrimination cases against Bethlehem Steel and eight other American steel companies via two consent decrees in which the companies agreed to substitute plantwide seniority for unit seniority throughout the industry. The decrees, negotiated with the steel companies and the USW by the Justice Department and the federal Equal Employment Opportunity Commission, established a onetime payment of $30.9 million to fifty-five thousand black, female, and Hispanic steelworkers in compensation for past discrimination in work assignments and promotion.

Covering 245 plants and 73 percent of the nation's basic steel industry, the consent decrees were both revolutionary and reactionary. Revolutionary because they admitted past discrimination and offered reparations for it; reactionary because they prevented individual steelworkers from seeking their own justice.

"The thing was worked out somewhere in the Justice Department and the White House to get rid of litigation," Johnson said, "because there was litigation going on all over the country, and the steel industry wanted to put an end to it. So they went to the Justice Department and the White House and put together a settlement that included all the cases, even though people in the individual cases like my clients were not even part of it. They put us in a position that the only thing we could do was object to [the settlement], but we were overruled."

When steelworkers began receiving the checks meant to compensate for wages lost as a consequence of discrimination, they became even angrier. The average check was for approximately $600, less than a week's pay for most Sparrows Point steelworkers at the time. According to some estimates, the steelworkers were paid approximately one cent for every thirty-nine owed them. Moreover, by signing the checks, a steelworker waived his right to all future litigation against the company and the union.

Johnson told me that he advised his clients to decide for themselves whether to accept the money, but his own feelings on the matter were clear. "It was such an insult," he said, "but I knew that there was nothing else we could do. Five or a hundred or two hundred dollars was nothing, but better than zero in that you could at least pay the gas and electric for a couple of months. On the other hand, if you said, 'It violates my conscience to accept this,' then send them back."

The great majority of black steelworkers on Sparrows Point sent the checks back, Johnson said, a point I have been unable to verify. However, Tank Levy is the only person I've interviewed who cashed his check. His best friend, Roosevelt Caldwell, sent his back. Eddie Bartee Sr. sent his back. So did Cliff Lockman. "I sent it back because Johnson was supposed to be helping us out," Lockman told me, though he also said that he later regretted his principled stand. "Things didn't work out, and we lost out completely. We lost all that money, and the people that cashed theirs made out."

I asked him about the response of most of his friends and co-workers to the checks, steelworkers who hadn't necessarily taken part in the activism. "Nobody liked it," he said. "But they figured [the company] was giving you something, so they kept it. But I wasn't satisfied, and a bunch of others that I know that was in my group wasn't satisfied. So we sent them back." His own check "wasn't as much as I made in a week," he added. After all was said and done, he told me, some of the men who had cashed their checks laughed at those who had sent them back as a protest gesture. "You turned yours in and you lost out," they teased.

Ken Johnson said that he was enormously proud of the steelworkers who returned the checks because "they did what I would have done if they owed me $100 million and had offered me $1 million. I would have sent the million back. You can't buy integrity. I was just elated to run across people like that because a lot of people don't understand that there are concepts in life greater than me, and the concept of justice is one of them. And the steelworkers had that belief. I was very proud to be working with them."

Johnson himself didn't make "one red cent" from the case, he said. Under Title VII of the Civil Rights Act, individual judges could award attorneys' fees to plaintiffs in civil rights cases, but the Baltimore judge who heard the case, a Republican appointed by Richard Nixon, refused to do so. "His reason was that Bethlehem Steel and the union had done everything that we'd asked them to do." Johnson snorted. "We said, 'Wait a minute, Judge. They did everything that you and I and the court *made* them do.'"

Even so, he doesn't regret taking the case. "I was on a crusade," he said. "If my wife hadn't worked and paid the mortgage and the kids' schooling, I would have been in terrible shape, but she worked and didn't mind, so I was a lucky man. We changed the situation, and so not being paid doesn't bother me and never has because that's not what I was in it for."

When you look at what we've been through, it's amazing the difference where we came from and where we ended up. We made it, more or less, to the top.

— ROOSEVELT CALDWELL

In the winter of 1974, a partly handwritten, partly typewritten statement of defiance was taped to walls around the Sparrows Point plant days after the eleven-to-seven shift on the coke ovens had walked out, demanding job reclassification and an end to "filthy hazardous working conditions":

WE WILL NOT GO BACK TO SLAVERY! The man says that we are breaking the law and must go back to work! We will not go back to slavery! Slavery days are gone! The court never did a thing about the discrimination classification. The court did nothing for the men that died last year, and the years before, in the coke ovens! We are out on strike to end these conditions. When working men go out on strike, then working people unite and stand together they are no longer slaves! We have shown that by uniting and striking that we are not slaves. WE ARE HUMAN BEINGS!!! WE WILL NOT RETURN TO SLAVERY!!!

The January 1974 wildcat strike in the coke ovens, led by the zoneman Johnny Fair, was a largely black protest, though it was supported by some rank-and-file white steelworkers who were equally disgusted with conservative union leadership. "That was one of the most effective grassroots actions I saw on the Point," said Len Shindel, one of a group of young radicals hired in the early seventies who were determined to "move the union to the left," returning it to its roots as a revolutionary defender of workers' rights.

"There were always a certain number of socialists and communists down there," Ed Gorman, a former USW Local 2609 vice president, told me. "We had four or five groups—socialists, Maoists, flat-out communists—that would sit in union meetings and throw out these unanswerable questions. One time I said to [district director] Dave Wilson, 'If they ever got together, they'd kill us all,' but they couldn't because the ideologies were different and they were always arguing among themselves."

One thing that the different leftist groups did agree on was the need to assist black steelworkers in their struggle for justice. During the 1974 wildcat strike, they posted their own flyers exhorting union members in other departments to support the coke oven workers and applauding "the militant leadership of the RANK AND FILE. Black and white workers are standing together to fight the company no matter what the officials say, and are determined to win the fight for better pay and conditions, and against the discrimination the company uses to divide us and keep us down."

The coke ovens wildcat strike—like the consent decree checks returned to Bethlehem—showed black steelworkers refusing to be bought off and demanding justice, with whites in the unfamiliar role of followers. Blaine DeWitt was working in the coalfields—one of only twenty-some whites in the majority black labor force—at the time. "I was used to being in the majority, and there I was in the minority," he said. "For the first six months it was hard. I'm not saying I didn't have any prejudice, because that's the way I was raised. But I got used to it."

The strike started on a Saturday, he recalled. "I walked into the number 1 clock house, where the coke oven people punched in, and a bunch of union people were in there. They said, 'We're going on strike.' A lot of us guys were still real young, and we're all like, 'Okay!' They told us to come up to the union hall that night. So we just turned right around and walked out. They had supervisors out there threatening us. My foreman, Al, put his arm around my shoulders and was trying to talk me into going in. I said 'Al, I'm going with the boys.'"

Nearly every hourly employee in the ovens went out, he said, save for some old-timers who weren't union members and were afraid of losing their jobs. By Tuesday evening, when the strikers had been out of work three days, "we were all fired up," DeWitt said. "People were saying that if we stayed out a couple of more days, the [basic oxygen furnace] was going to go out, this and that is going to go out. Because the working conditions were shit everywhere."

Len Shindel worked in another part of the plant but with the other leftists was actively involved in drumming up support for the strikers.

He and the members of his group hoped that the insurrection would spread, he said, forcing the union to take a more radical stand for workers. The flyers they posted in support of the strikers urged other workers to follow their lead: "We can all learn from what the coke oven workers are doing. . . . If the rank and file of the whole plant is organized and UNITED against the company, there is no way they can defeat us."

Though the strike wasn't officially sanctioned by the union, which faced stiff fines the longer the workers stayed out, "Local 2610 knew what the deal was," DeWitt said, and the leaders of the strike were under a great deal of pressure from both the union and the company to return to work. When the company went to court to impose an injunction on the union and threatened to jail the shop stewards, the zoneman Johnny Fair called a meeting, said DeWitt, "all of us crammed into this little room at the hall, guys sitting around and sucking on bottles. It was a screaming match. Finally, old Johnny stood up and said, 'Who wants to go back to work tomorrow?' Some are hollering yes, and others are hollering no. Finally, he puts his hands up in the air and says, 'Fuck it. Go back to work tomorrow.'"

Though short-lived, the strike was a success. "The coke ovens wildcat set the standards for coke oven workers nationwide on safety and clean air rooms," Selhorst said. "Before that, if you had a cup of coffee, you'd have all this debris—benzene-soluble particulate matter—in your coffee. But the wildcat won clean air rooms, places to cook your food, to eat your food, and take breaks when you weren't working." Organized and led by black steelworkers, the wildcat measurably improved working conditions for everyone—and showed that the days of blacks "acclimating" themselves to discrimination and toxic working conditions had ended on Sparrows Point.

After the consent decrees, with plant service the key factor in determining promotions, senior black employees made rapid progress in advancing into skilled positions. By transferring out of their old units, they were able to leapfrog ahead of men who had worked for years in their new units as successive openings up the line of promotion became available.

"Let's say you had a guy working on a tractor servicing my number 1 tandem mill," Ed Gorman told me. "He'd bid on a job and come in as a laborer. Then, next job opening, he becomes a scaleman. Next job opening, he's on the mill, whereas it took me seven years to get there. Then, in only nine years, he gets to roller [the top job on the line]."

Seniority rosters were "reracked" so that when a position opened up, the more senior transferred workers would be promoted ahead of the incumbents from the unit. The reracking, meant to remedy the effects of past discrimination, worked very well to advance men who were old enough to have accumulated a solid amount of plant time but young enough that they didn't mind starting over again at the bottom of a new department and whites ultimately benefited just as much as blacks.

"I transferred from the labor department to a production unit, first to the skin pass unit and then to continuous annealing. Just kept going up the ladder from lowest to top job," said Cliff Lockman. "I can't speak for anybody else, but I went as far as I could go, to the top job in the department, operator."

Men who chose not to transfer out of their original units also benefited from the new system, with some, like the ore dock workers Roosevelt Caldwell and Tank Levy, gaining white hats as the company tried to move more blacks into supervisory positions. "Guys were being promoted because they wanted blacks for foremen. You know, 'Tank over there is a good guy. He's got a little education, so put him in the job,'" Levy said. "It was a dramatic change. You had no problem advancing."

Even black men too close to retirement to personally benefit from new promotional opportunities appreciated the improved climate. "The Man knocked down the wall," Robert "Moe" Buchanan, who started working at the Point in 1945, told me when we chatted at a union meeting in 2007. He was talking about the wall in the locker room, but his comment could apply equally well to the whole system of race-based employment at Sparrows Point. Buchanan remained in the labor department until he retired, but he told me that "it looked like a new day" on the Point after the consent decree. "I was surprised at how smooth it went," he said mildly.

The smoothness was a matter of perception, however. The dismantling of the unit seniority system created a great deal of anger and resentment among people who felt that their opportunities for advancement were being blocked by people who were given unfair advantages. Resistance was particularly strong in the high-wage finishing mills. "When that first influx came in, the white guys didn't want to teach the black guys," Ed Gorman told me. "The first thing they'd ask is, 'How much seniority you got?' Then they were like, 'I'm not gonna teach him anything. Why should I teach him something when he's gonna take my job?'"

Eddie Bartee Sr. told me that some whites—men he had considered friends—gave him the cold shoulder after the impact of the consent decree began to be felt in the mills. "I had a preacher friend. We used to talk about religion. It hurt me when he wouldn't speak to me." The pervasive anger and resentment negatively affected people's ability to do their jobs too, he said. "I had good white buddies that we worked together as feeder, feeder helper, and floor hands, and when the consent decree came, they stopped speaking to me. They'd be working daylight and I'd be working three to eleven, and most of the time when you came in, you'd say, 'Okay, we're running such and such a thing' or 'Look out for this.' If there was something going on that would make it easier for you, they'd tell you. No more."

"The skill level honestly and truly went down," Gorman confirmed. "By the white guys not teaching the black guys what to do, the black guys only had a fundamental idea, and they then had to teach other black guys." He became so concerned, he said, that he set up a training program. "I didn't want people to get killed. Forget about yourself, you could kill someone else."

White workers who *were* willing to train black men sometimes confronted hostile peers. Ken Johnson told me about the first black man to be made an electrical helper, only to find that his white colleagues would not train him. "Electrical work is very, very dangerous if you don't know anything about it," Johnson said. "It can zap you out. One mistake and no forgiving. So a white steelworker felt sorry for him and knew that it was wrong. He says, 'Look, I'll train you, but it has to be done on the sly, because if they find out that I'm doing that, I'll have a hard time too.'" The black apprentice understood, and the training was carried out in secret. But the white electrician's co-workers got wind of it, and the next day he found human feces in his lunch box.

It took a very long time for things to settle down. The consent decree provided for implementation committees to be established in each local union to oversee day-to-day seniority issues. Francis Brown, a black steelworker who had been extremely important in the civil rights struggle, was appointed chairman of the implementation committee for Local 2610. Brown passed away before I could speak with him, but his friend Len Shindel told me that "Francis always said that he was set up to fail by the bureaucracy in the government, union, and the company. He was a high school graduate given a big job with no secretary or support. He was under pressure from his black constituency to interpret the decree as broadly as possible to allow black workers to overcome years of racism."

Meanwhile, his (white) counterpart in 2609 "was under pressure to narrow the decree's impact in the mostly white units of the finishing mills," Shindel said. Rollers and assistant rollers in the tandem mill unit of the cold mill were among the highest-paid workers in the plant, and even into the late 1980s, almost all the highest-paid jobs were held by white workers. Some shop stewards encouraged their peers not to train workers who had transferred from the steel side, Shindel said, and when later cutbacks should have led to a reracking of seniority, with transfers (both black and white) from the steel side moving up, foremen and shop stewards instead violated the reracking provision of the consent decree so that junior rollers and assistant rollers could maintain their status.

As a zoneman, Shindel supported reracking and consequently found himself under fire by some whites. "I remember one white skin mill roller telling me that I had ruined his life," he recalled. "And there was a section of white workers claiming that everything was reverse discrimination." But some black employees could also be difficult. "There were a few black workers, narrowly nationalist black workers, who spent a lot of time filing charges against union reps when they didn't get what they perceived they were entitled to. And a lot of the time they weren't really legitimate complaints."

Union reps got caught in the cross fire, he said, telling me about a day when, soon after arriving at work, he came across a white worker verbally attacking black workers' performance on the job. Shindel confronted him, and a foreman came over to ask what was going on. The white worker replied, "Shindel's taking up for the niggers." He walked away from the dispute, he said, "and I'm walking down the mill, and no more than three hundred feet away, one of the black workers jumped on me and said, 'All you're doing is looking out for the white guys here.'" He shook his head ruefully. "One minute I'm taking up for the black liberation struggle, and the next minute I'm a racist. I said, 'Fuck it, I'm going home. This is too much for one day.'"

From Shindel's perspective, "there was infancy on both sides." Still, the frustration various individuals and groups felt was to a certain extent understandable, he said. "The whole thing was a real bitch, leaving folks on all sides tense and unfulfilled." Gorman concurred. "It was bad times," he told me. "We lost the camaraderie."

The adjustment period was made even more difficult as it coincided with the early signs of an economic crisis in the American steel industry and the first round of mass layoffs since the Great Depression. "Eddie [Bartee] and I were full-time union guys, and we had to be," said Gorman. "Because it was turmoil."

They only hired women because they had to, and they only did for women what they had to on a corporate level. A lot of men felt that women didn't hold their own down there.

—MARY ELLEN BEECHNER

The 1974 consent decree mandated equal opportunity not just for steelworkers of color but for women too. Some of the women whose lives were changed by the ruling were new hires, but some were former tin floppers or had worked in other parts of the mill prior to the ruling. Mary Lorenzo, hired in 1971, worked on the halogen line in the tin mill with former tin floppers transferred there when the old tin sorting room was closed. The older women jealously guarded their turf in the ladies' locker room, she said, and were clearly of another generation. "It was so funny, one lady wore white gloves all the time. While she was working."

Some former tin sorters, including Jessie Schultz and Julie Poholorec, transferred to labor gangs when they were in their fifties. "Some of those women would go down and have to clean up the troughs and wear boots up to the hip," Lorenzo recalled. "It was dirty everywhere down there, but this was really dirty, like tar. Oil and stuff from where the rollers dripped down. But they did it."

Lorenzo was laid off the year after she was hired, went back to work, and was laid off again. By then she was divorced and a single parent, so when they started hiring women in the coke ovens after the consent decree, she bid in. "That must've been about '76 or '77," she said. "There were a lot of girls out in the coalfields then, but it was still new, because some of the men acted like they never seen women before, hanging out of the cranes whistling and hollering and carrying on."

She was thirty-six at the time. "I was put up on the batteries, and I was working in a mud mill. It was the hardest job I ever had in my whole life. That's where they would take clay and the coke, and when you push the coke, it would fall on the run, and you would go out and get that in a wheelbarrow and bring it in, and you mixed it with clay in a big round trough to make mud. Then you would shovel it up and put it in the wheelbarrow, and they would take the mud and seal up each oven with it. The first time I stuck my shovel in the mud, the suction was so strong that I couldn't get my shovel out."

After watching her struggle for a while, the men proposed a solution. "It used to be where around two o'clock was the last time you had to fill up the trough for the guys," she said, "because it gave them enough mud for the next shift. So the guys, when they seen that I was trying, said, 'Look, Mary, we'll shovel the mud. You go out and clean the run.' So they would have their batch of mud done at one-thirty or something, and I would go out and clean up all the runs." She wasn't as strong as many of the men, she said, "but I always pulled my share."

All in all, she found the men in the coke ovens fine to work with. "When I first went there, the black men were the ones who helped me the most because they knew what it was like," she said. This point was mentioned by other women too. "The black men had the dirtiest, nastiest jobs in the place, but they were the most gentlemanly to me," said Mary Ellen Beechner, who was hired in 1975. "I don't know if it was because I was a white woman or what, but it used to almost make me sad in some ways." Julie Poholorec said, "Black men I didn't have no problem with. They was decent. Other women didn't have complaint with them either, I don't think." Some white men who felt threatened when women started competing for traditionally male jobs were a different story, she said.

Julie began working on the labor gang after the tin sorting room was closed, she said, because "I didn't have nobody to support me. I had to work so I can live. So I took any kind of job." She found that some of her new co-workers weren't too happy to see women in previously male domains. "Some women was in Washington marching for women's rights when I was working for the first time with men, and one of the men looked at me and said, 'Why ain't you in Washington marching for women? You want to get men's jobs.' I said, 'Look, mister, I don't want your job. I want a job so I can survive and pay bills like you pay.' But they wasn't nice at all. They was angry."

A few were kind and tried to ease her transition. "My foreman was very nice and decent," she said, and he pointed out certain men who were opposed to having women in the mill and warned her to avoid them. "He said, 'Those sons of bitches would sell their own mother.'"

The attitude of the foreman seemed to be a critical factor for a woman moving into a previously all-male environment. If the foreman was friendly, the woman would be okay, even if some of her male co-workers were hostile. But if the foreman didn't want women in his unit, she was in for a rough ride, which is what happened to Mary Lorenzo when she left the coke ovens to train as a refrigeration mechanic.

"This one foreman I had, he didn't want me there," she said, "and I just couldn't do anything right. I'd come home with my rider at night, and I'd be crying, saying, 'I shouldn't have to put up with that.' And he'd say, 'I know.'" But her male co-workers too were afraid of the man. "They didn't think that what he was doing was right, but if they came out for me, then they would be next." And some of the men, she said, "thought it was funny because they didn't want you there either."

No matter how bad things got, though, she was determined not to give up. "No matter what he did, I just wasn't going to quit," she said, "because there was no place I could make money like I was making there." This determination to tough it out seems to be a shared trait of the women who integrated departments. When Julie Poholorec and the two other women in her department were being harassed by their supervisor and one of the younger women threw down her broom and stalked off, Poholorec told the man, "Mister, I have to work, so I don't care what you do, I'm not quitting."

Mary Lorenzo stuck it out too, although she eventually was forced to file an EEOC suit. At first, she said, "all I would do was cry. Now I know that once they get you crying, they've got you. That was my problem back then. At the time I didn't really know what sexual harassment was. I thought sexual harassment was that they were trying to get you to go out with them or something."

One aspect of life for female steelworkers that was clearly sexual harassment although few complained about it was the hard-core pornography displayed throughout the plant. "There was pornography everywhere, absolutely everywhere," Mary Ellen Beechner said. "I remember walking into one shop where I was going to do some lead sampling to make sure people weren't being overexposed, and they had pictures from *Hustler* magazine, I mean really hard-core stuff, wallpapering the walls. I put my hand on the table and it was all over the tables, under plastic and all. I felt so uncomfortable."

As her job took her around the plant, she found pornography "most everywhere you went in offices and on the floor, openly displayed." She didn't ask that it be taken down, she said, just as she kept her mouth shut about a foreman who regularly referred to the women under his supervision—as well as his own wife and her friends—using demeaning terms for female genitalia. "He used to make my skin crawl," she said. "My husband would say, 'I'll go in and talk to him,' but I'd say, 'No, that will just make things worse.'" If she'd had more courage, Beechner said, "I would have brought him up on charges, but I wouldn't be there today if I had done that. It would not have gone over."

Mary Lorenzo told me that she "never complained about those pictures. They were in the shops that I was in, but I never said anything. I remember when they were taken down in refrigeration. A foreman came over and just happened to see them and had them taken down. But I never said anything because I knew it would be just another sore spot raised up on me."

Some battles, she and the other women said, were just not worth fighting. The battle that did matter, the one that was worth fighting and winning, was proving that you could do the job. Beechner, a college graduate who worked as a boiler foreman, a chemist, a chemist foreman in the metallurgical lab, and a safety and health technician, told me that she "would never let anyone see my weaknesses. I would do whatever I needed to do to get the job done."

She worked through two pregnancies on Sparrows Point. "It's interesting being pregnant in a steel mill," she said. "It's an oddity. People would come up and put their hands on your belly, and you'd be like, 'I don't even know you.'" But at six months pregnant, she climbed down a thirty-foot ladder into a settling basin to test the water. "Don't tell me I can't do something, because, doggone it, I'm gonna do it," she said. "I'm six months pregnant and climbing over all this pipe and then down a ladder, and all these millwrights are clapping and going, 'Yeah!'"

Her attitude was very similar to that of Darlene Redemann, hired in 1976. Shortly after she arrived, Redemann became one of the first women trained as a crane operator. Later, she transferred to the cold mill, where she became the first female roller, the top job on the line. "I was the first woman to run a mill," she told me with pride. Getting there was a bit of a struggle, but her account of her years on the Point is punctuated with a great deal of humor, as when she told the story of how she learned to operate a crane. A few women had been trained as crane operators during World War II, she said, though not in the center [control] cab. But shortly after she was hired, she said, "they started wanting to make it discrimination that women weren't allowed to run the center cab cranes. So I got in."

On her first day, she was alone in the crane, operating the three hoists while her trainer on the floor shouted instructions. "And he was telling me to lower the block. So I was lowering the block, and he was screaming and freaking out because the other boom was going down. And I looked, and it was actually my boob that was lowering the boom!" Redemann, a grandmother who retains a voluptuous figure, mimed her panicked response as we chatted in her kitchen. "So I took my arm and threw it up, and then I got it pinched, so I couldn't stop the other boom." She laughed as she recalled the ludicrous solutions her male co-workers proposed to avoid such problems in the future: having her stand on blocks in the crane so her breasts would be above the controls; making a wire vest for her to wear; inserting a clause in her personnel file that she must wear a bra at all times.

To a certain extent, she understood the resistance, she told me. "My supervisor was like, 'I didn't want you women in this mill.' Then when that happened, he was really alarmed, like, 'What am I in for? These women are gonna start getting their breasts caught.'" Rather than feeling ashamed and giving up, she good-naturedly accepted the teasing, learned the job, and worked as a crane operator for twenty years. "Darlene is pretty tough," her friend Len Shindel commented. "She had her own way of dealing with stuff."

Throughout the years, particularly in the early days, she and the other women had to deal with plenty of harassment, mostly centered on the prejudice that women just couldn't do the job. "You had a lot of guys that were like smaller height and not that manly built," she said, "and they would make allowances for that. But they looked at it like you were a female and so you couldn't do it. Like we would have metal plates that they wouldn't ask the smaller guys to get but would make us get. Later on, when I was a union rep, I won a case for women who were being discriminated against and taken off the job because they couldn't lift this forty-pound brass plate, and at the same time neither could the smaller men. That was a big step back in '78."

She had been on the job for only four weeks when she joined the union. "The guy that was training me was a real fanatic about unions," she said. "So the whole time he was training me, he was quoting me inserts from the contracts. He was a real gung ho fighter, so he practically embedded it into my brain." Eight months later, she was elected shop steward for her unit, and from there, she said, "I just went all the way to the top," becoming an assistant zoneman and then, in 1987, a zoneman (the first woman on the Point to hold the job).

"When I ran for the position, there was only about 10 percent women in the mill, and I ran against four men," she said. "It was overwhelming the number of votes I got." A few years later she transferred to the floor and started working her way up to roller. "People said that she wouldn't be able to do it," Shindel told me. "But she did. And her crew is mostly men, and she has their respect."

Redemann's experience seems to prove the truth of something that Beechner told me about being a woman on Sparrows Point. "By and large, they accepted me perfectly fine," she said. "Even though the idea of women working down there wasn't popular and still isn't. It's sort of like . . . hate the race, but not the person. You know how they used to say that [white] Northerners hate individuals but love the [black] race, where Southerners hate the race but love individuals. Well, I think it was similar to that."

Despite the challenges she endured as a woman in the "very macho environment," Beechner loves working at Sparrows Point. "I love the people," she said. "As much as they can be very macho and crude at times, I like them. There is a certain honesty, and we all look out for each other. We've been together for thirty-two years. We know each other's families. We know each other's sorrows. We know each other's joys. That is the warmth of the place."

• RECKONING •

On the third Tuesday morning of every month, Tom Capecci flicks on the lights at Steelworkers Local 2610, and a steady stream of retirees trickles in to claim places at the long tables. Arranging themselves in cliques as fixed as any in a junior high cafeteria, ironworkers sit with ironworkers, machinists with machinists, bricklayers with bricklayers, coke oven workers with coke oven workers. When Capecci calls the meeting of the seniors' group to order at eleven, the men (and a few women) rise to say the Pledge of Allegiance with their hands over their hearts. Next comes a minute of silence for recently departed members of the local and then a quick summary of the latest news about pensions and health care. By eleven-thirty, the real business of the meeting commences—a hearty lunch and conversation. "That's why most of them come," said Capecci, a tall, silver-haired man, "to talk about old times."

The only jarring note in the proceedings is the enormous illuminated bingo board on the stage at the front of the hall—the union has been forced to rent the hall to a bingo entrepreneur to help pay the ballooning gas and electric bills. The Steelworkers are none too pleased with the arrangement. The bingo players "tear the place up," Capecci said, adding that both this hall and 2609's next door would probably be sold soon anyway. Technically, the two locals have merged to form Local 9477. Still, retirees continue to meet separately in their own halls, just as they did in their days of active employment, when the two Bethlehem locals on Dundalk Avenue were rivals and brothers, with 2610 the roughneck and 2609 the technician.

"We were like a family in those days," Capecci said, reminiscing about the bygone years when his local had over ten thousand members and meetings were standing room only. "And the company knew that as a family we gave 110 percent." But somewhere along the line, he told me, that solidarity evaporated. "The young ones down there now are different. They will cut your throat for overtime." The me-first attitude of the younger steelworkers and their disdain for the union were among the reasons he opted for early retirement in 2002. "I had to represent a lot of those guys in my last years down there, and they don't care about the union or about each other. At the active union meetings now, they get maybe twenty-five guys." Still, he said, "I would've stayed if I'd known that we would lose as much as we did."

Capecci's bitterness is shared by many others who signed on to work at the Point in the late sixties and seventies. Unlike the previous generation's, their years on the Point were far from secure. Hired near the end of the postwar boom, they experienced a short period of stability followed by thirty years of layoffs, terminations, and concessions, culminating in a bankruptcy that cut deeply into their pensions and eliminated their health insurance. Their time on the Point was shadowed by frustration and anxiety; having survived all that, they found themselves stranded less than ten years from retirement—too young to stop working, too old to start over again somewhere else.

But if they were more cynical than the World War II and Korea vets who had preceded them, they differed too from the generation that followed them into the mills—"kids" more interested in making money than in fighting the company and without much sense of solidarity. "It all started to change in the mid-nineties, when they started hiring a lot of guys, new employees, from non-union shops," Capecci said. "People who accepted the attitude of 'If you want to move up, do what I say.' They say, 'The company is treating us good. I'm making $100,000.' I just tell them, 'Someday you're gonna need the union.' But that's the way the companies got them now."

At one of the retirees' luncheons, after Capecci handed me the mike and invited me to introduce myself to the gathering, I met Albert Wolfkill, a former pipe fitter with forty-four years of service, who told me that he lived just around the corner from my aunt and uncle. He also said he had some magazines that I might want to see, so I stopped by his house after the meeting. It turns out that Wolfkill has nearly every issue of *Bethlehem Review*, the company's employee newsletter, from 1969 to 1989, a collection he plans to donate to the local historical society. Like a stack of old *Playboys*, Wolfkill's stash of *Bethlehem Reviews* reflects the innocence (and hairstyles!) of another era. But the articles also reveal how a series of economic and technological shocks led to massive job losses and a reshaping of the workforce.

Reading through the newsletters, I felt at second hand the paranoia and confusion that dogged workers during the years when U.S. companies began losing their edge, and the outlook for Bethlehem employees, and for American industrial workers as a whole, began to darken. It all seems inevitable, in hindsight—but was it? Beginning with the shocking announcement of a plunge in profits in 1971, the articles increasingly depict a company under siege, encircled by relentless adversaries. I envisioned a hapless victim being slowly advanced upon by zombie hordes: the government and its death by a thousand cuts of regulation, the Steelworkers union with its insatiable hunger for "fringe benefits," rising energy costs coupled with inflation, and the biggest, scariest monster of all, Foreign Steel, which each year swallowed a bigger and bigger share of Bethlehem's market.

The language used by Bethlehem scribes to characterize the threat posed by foreign imports is significant. A flood is an unforeseen natural catastrophe, but American steel executives' surprise at the "rising tide" of imports now seems impossibly naïve. Could they really have believed that the postwar dominance of U.S. industry would continue forever? American investment dollars poured into Europe and Japan after World War II. New steel mills equipped with the latest technology were built through not only the Marshall Plan but also the Export-Import Bank, an organization whose mission was to provide loans to foreign companies to finance the purchase of American goods. From 1945 to 1978, the Export-Import Bank provided $38.7 billion in overseas loans—$2.3 billion of which was used to boost foreign steel-making capacity. About 85 percent went to eleven countries whose steel exports to the United States increased nineteenfold in a twenty-year period.

Japanese and European steelmakers were the first to siphon off business from American firms, but by the late seventies they too were facing stiff competition from steelmakers in developing nations like Brazil. Steel imports into the United States increased steadily beginning with the 116-day strike of 1959, when domestic customers first started buying from overseas mills. "When the company went back to work, they had lost customers," Ray Rudacille told me in 2005.

Bethlehem might have won some of those customers back, he said, if they weren't also operating at a technological disadvantage. "Don't forget that Europe and Japan were starting with practically brand-new mills in 1950, where Bethlehem was running old mills and incorporating new technology into the old mills. They should have modernized when Bethlehem was making money back in the fifties. But they didn't want to rock the boat because they were doing good. They started modernizing too late."

The basic oxygen furnace (BOF), invented in Austria in 1952, didn't go in at Sparrows Point until 1965. Instead of installing a BOF in the late fifties, Bethlehem built the biggest open hearth furnace in the world. "When Bethlehem built the number 4 open hearth, open hearths were practically obsolete," my uncle said. Instead of replacing open hearths with the newer, cleaner, faster BOFs capable of churning out two hundred tons of steel every forty-five minutes, company engineers jerry-rigged oxygen lances into the number 4 open hearth. The oxygen sped up the steelmaking process, cutting the time it took to produce a 425-ton heat from eight hours to four, but it was still nowhere near as efficient as the BOF.

"One of the things we all used to talk about is that whenever new stuff came in, Bethlehem always brought up the rear," said Bill Knoerlein, who worked on the BOF when it was finally installed in the sixties. "They were never the first to jump on the bandwagon with new technology." He and others attributed the company's slowness to adopt new technology and new ways of doing things to its fuddyduddy management, both in Bethlehem and on Sparrows Point. "All the people they had running the place were old farts," he said. "It was a typical old-time company."

Another new technology, the continuous caster, which greatly sped up and simplified the process of converting molten steel to slabs, was developed in the early sixties, but once again Bethlehem management waited far too long to invest in the new equipment. In a continuous caster, steel is poured directly from a BOF ladle into a tundish (a large reservoir that prevents a break in the flow of steel while the ladles are changed) and from there to the strands of the caster, which produces glowing steel slabs. Three hundred tons of molten steel could be converted to ten-inch-thick slabs in forty-five minutes—compared with the twelve hours it took to produce the same volume of steel in the traditional manner.

A few small American companies had imported the technology, developed in Germany, in 1962. Bethlehem installed its first continuous caster at its Burns Harbor, Indiana, plant in 1975, but at Sparrows Point, slabs were produced the old-fashioned way until 1985, when, with much fanfare, Bethlehem installed the nearly twenty-five-year-old technology. "Bethlehem's management would never accept a new concept until someone else proved it," Wimpy Doyle said dryly.

Sparrows Point steelworkers who kept an eye on foreign producers wondered just how they were expected to compete using half-a-century-old equipment. Ed Gorman, who worked as a roller in the tandem mill, told a story that illustrates their frustration. "We entertained a group of German steelworkers in the middle seventies, maybe '78. And we met with them in Bethlehem's main office the first day after they toured the plant. Bethlehem Steel labor relations people were at the head of the stage, and they told us if we wanted to ask questions, we had to direct them to this one guy because none of the others spoke English. So I said, 'You saw the forty-two-inch tandem mill. In Germany do you have any plants as old as that one?' Because our tandem mill was built in '36. And this guy rattled off an answer in German, and the head guy translated. He said, 'Yes, we have old mills. We have new mills too, but we also have old mills.'"

Later that day, union officers hosted a luncheon for the Germans at the hall. Gorman had trucked in cases of German beer, hot dogs, and sauerkraut. With the translator busy elsewhere, "the guy that had answered my question in German came over to me," Gorman said. "It turned out he spoke wonderful English. And he said, 'He didn't tell you what I told him. After the war, the Russians took all our steel mills. The Marshall Plan built us brand-new ones.'" Gorman shook his head, relating the story to me. "It was like we were running the grand prix of steel driving a Volkswagen."

Other steelworkers on the Point drew the same conclusion, particularly those given the opportunity to see the competition up close. "One year they sent people from the electrical department over to Japan," recalled Wimpy Doyle. "There was nothing there less than ten years old. The mills themselves, all new equipment. We bombed them and rebuilt them. We did the same thing for Europe." I told Doyle that my father used to say the Japanese won the war. He nodded. "The Japanese made a quality product. We thought that we were the best. But then you weren't the best anymore."

In *Crisis in Bethlehem: Big Steel's Struggle to Survive*, published in 1986, the Bethlehem newspaperman John Strohmeyer discussed the reasoning behind the company's failure to adopt new technology—a "failure of vision" it shared with other big American steel producers—during the prosperous fifties and sixties. "Why bother with this untested stuff? We're doing very well without it" was the generic response to new technology developed overseas, he pointed out.

There were no technical people in top management, one of his sources told him, which led to an inability to recognize the critical need to keep pace with technological advances. Even discoveries made in Bethlehem's own research and development lab languished for years before being implemented in its mills. "We were making evolutionary changes when a technological revolution was going on," the former manager of primary processes research at Bethlehem told Strohmeyer.

The boardroom was similarly hesitant when it came to exploring new markets. Strohmeyer interviewed two former Bethlehem executives who saw clearly the challenges and opportunities of globalization before most people had even heard the word. In the early fifties, Robert H. Gray and Talbot Shelton were able to persuade Bethlehem executives to consolidate the company's international operations— twenty-one subsidiaries involved in the buying and selling of raw materials—in a Nassau office, which would then buy steel from Bethlehem and sell it for the best prices on the world market. Plans were in the works to build a finishing mill in Belgium, which would roll semi-finished slabs manufactured in Sparrows Point to sell overseas. But the company closed the Nassau office in 1959, and plans for the Belgian mill were "torpedoed" soon after, Strohmeyer wrote.

Plans to engage in foreign steelmaking partnerships, like the need to invest in new technology, fell victim to the tunnel vision of top management. "Bethlehem Steel just wasn't interested," Gray told Strohmeyer. " 'Why rock the boat?' That was their favorite expression. 'We're doing well at what we're doing' was another. You'd talk about continuous casting and that sort of thing, and they'd think you were crazy. There was leadership but not entrepreneurship."

Management's lack of interest in developing new markets and investing in new technology was coupled with a cavalier approach to customer satisfaction. As equipment on Sparrows Point aged, the quality of steel and finished products manufactured there began to suffer. But that didn't seem to bother management, Tom Capecci and other steelworkers have told me. "Bethlehem cared about quantity, not quality," he said. "We lost a lot of good customers because of it."

When he was working as an inspector in the tin and rod mills in the sixties and early seventies, Capecci said, he "would red-tag bad batches and then go down to the docks and find out they were shipping them anyway." He protested and was overruled on more than one occasion. "They wanted to fire me one time because I wanted to reject a quarter-million dollars' worth of steel. The orders from the top were to pass it. The attitude of management was 'If the customer doesn't like it, we'll ship 'em another hundred tons,'" he said. "The rule was to get that tonnage out. Get the quantity out and don't worry about the quality."

Bethlehem's first instinct when confronted with the threat of competition was not to modernize operations, nor to focus on quality or customer service. Instead, it was to urge employees to work harder. Newsletter articles throughout the seventies hectored employees about the need for increased productivity to justify their wage and benefit gains and to meet the challenge posed by imports. No doubt there was room for improvement in that area at Sparrows Point.

By the late sixties, "you had a lot of featherbedding down there," Tank Levy told me. On the ore docks, where he worked, "there were some guys who did absolutely nothing," he said. "They were called checkers. They might go in to check two or three cars and they were through for the day. And you'd say, 'Hey, we need some help over here.' And they'd say, 'It ain't my job.'"

Blaine DeWitt told me that when he began working in the coalfields, he was a real go-getter, wanting to make a good impression. He quickly learned that his industriousness wasn't winning him any friends among his co-workers. "When I first started, the guys wanted to know how come I'm doing so much work. One guy took me aside and told me, 'On Monday we don't work because you're hungover from the weekend. On Tuesday we don't work because it's payday and you're going out afterwards. On Wednesday we don't work because you're hungover again. On Thursday we work. On Friday we don't work because the weekend is coming.'" For employees like these, working as little as possible was viewed as a victory against the company.

Wayne Morris, who went through the Loop Course after earning a degree in industrial management from the University of Maryland, said that one of his greatest frustrations as a foreman was watching new employees being indoctrinated into this devil-may-care work culture. "All the bad habits, bad attitudes, and bad ideas would get passed on to the new guy. I always said that the only way they would ever be able to change the system down there was to take everybody working there, line them up, and do a St. Valentine's Day." He mimicked a machine gun. "Wipe them all out, and probably most of the foremen along with them, and start fresh."

Wimpy Doyle, who worked his way up through the ranks to foreman, was a bit less harsh in his assessment of the average employee. "Eighty percent of the men were good workers, and 20 percent were bad," he told me when I asked about laziness and bad attitudes among his crews. "There are certain people that don't want to work, okay? Always the case. You'll find it in an office too."

Moreover, in many mechanical and maintenance departments, cycles of intense work could be followed by periods when people had time to sit around and watch Colts games or nap, he pointed out. "On a seven-day turn, you'd have two days when you couldn't breathe, with cranes breaking down and all that. Then you'd have two days where you didn't have anything to do. If you changed a lightbulb, you were lucky. A lot of maintenance is hurry up and wait. You've got to hurry to get the mill running and then wait around."

A good foreman would know when to push and when to allow his crew to relax, he said. But he admitted that the troublesome 20 percent of hourly workers, backed by a union that would file grievances on their behalf when foremen tried to discipline them, contributed to the slippage in productivity. "I remember one time a bunch of millwrights were playing cards and the whistle blew and one of them said, 'Them sons of bitches, they never let you alone.' And he had played cards for seven days and let his helper do all the work!"

Some were able to get away with that kind of goofing off because of the sheer number of employees on-site during any given shift. By the early seventies, the number of Sparrows Point employees had fallen from its postwar highs, but many folks have told me that there were still far more workers on the Point than was necessary to maintain operations. "When I started, there were twenty-four thousand people down there, and they could have run the place with fifteen to eighteen thousand," DeWitt said.

New equipment was beginning to reduce the number of workers needed to perform certain tasks—repairing the brickwork in an open hearth, for example. "When I went down there, to tear out a furnace took huge manpower," Ray Rudacille recalled. "You'd have maybe a hundred and fifty laborers, fifty at a time with tongs tossing the bricks out, and when they'd had all the heat they could take, the next wave would go in. By the time I left, pulling out an open hearth got down to a bulldozer with one operator, a Gradall [forklift] with two operators and four laborers, maybe a dozen men total to tear a furnace out, compared to the hundreds it took before."

Increased automation on the ore docks, in the coke ovens, on the BOF, and in some of the finishing mills similarly began cutting into the numbers of laborers needed in various areas. What to do with the excess workers, many of them older men nearing retirement age? Management's solution was to hand them brooms in place of shovels. "In the seventies they tried to equalize their employees so there was no discrimination," Darlene Redemann pointed out. "But at the same time, they had people there that they didn't need. It would amaze me because they'd have eight people sweeping a hallway." Make-work assigned to employees awaiting retirement was an old tradition in American steel mills. Everyone knew how hard those men had worked in their younger years, and no one begrudged them their sinecure. Younger workers' indolence is harder to justify, however, as is their hazing of people who actually wanted to work. "I got called a company man a lot," Blaine DeWitt said. "I wasn't trying to make waves, but I didn't mind working. You had a lot of stupid rules down there of what you could and couldn't do."

One of the rules strictly enforced by the union and by fellow workers was not doing any task that exceeded the boundaries of your assigned job category—and there were thirty-two job categories on Sparrows Point, each with its own contractually defined responsibilities and limits. "An electrician would never do mechanical work," Wimpy Doyle said. "A troubleshooter would never do maintenance." The reason for this was job protection, Eddie Bartee Sr. told me. The union was committed to protecting every man's job, he said, and the way to do that was by making sure that "you don't do my work and I don't do your work."

Bartee admits that in practice this could be extremely wasteful of time and resources. "Let's say a mill breaks down, and the operating people say, 'We think it's electrical,'" he said. "So the electrical people come out and say, 'No, it's mechanical.' So the electrical people go back to their shanty, and the mechanical people come in and say, 'Yeah, it's our problem.' Okay, now you got to go back and get the electrical people back to shut off the power in the mill. Then let's say that there is a helper motor involved. You've got to call the millwrights to take the helper motor off the roll. Then the mechanics come back and take the old roller off and put the new roller in. Then the millwrights got to come back to put the motor back on the roll."

Sparrows Point steelworkers and union officers may have read *Bethlehem Review* articles about the economic threat posed by imported steel, and slapped BUY AMERICAN stickers on the family Chevy, but they don't seem to have noticed a connection between such inefficient job practices and the company's shrinking profit margin. Like Bethlehem's executive board, steelworkers long assumed that the problem posed by imports would be solved by government intervention, not by any action they themselves might take on the shop floor.

Meanwhile, management's most visible effort to respond to increased competition was an expensive failure that eroded employee morale. "They made a lot of white hats in the seventies," Tom Capecci said. By mid-decade the workforce was beginning to look like an inverted pyramid, he and others have told me, with an expanding number of salaried foremen at the top and a decreasing number of hourly workers at the bottom.

The reason for the sudden explosion of white hats seems to have puzzled even those who became foremen themselves during that period. My uncle guessed it was related to job safety. "Someone read an article that said you needed so many supervisors for so many work- ers," he said. Roosevelt Caldwell thought it was because they wanted to make more black men foremen. Others believed that it was an attempt to weaken the union, since the company often chose new white hats from the pool of shop stewards. "When I first got there in '73, the union guys would be skimmed off," Pete Selhorst told me. "If you wanted to be a boss, be a shop steward first. They skimmed off the leadership as much as they could. So they did have good people. Leaders are leaders. A good percentage of [the former shop stewards] were actually harder on the rank and file than the other ones."

The company tried to recruit him, Tom Capecci said, but "I never wanted to wear a white hat." As time went on, "it got to be a boss for every four workers down there," he said. "We tried to tell them they were top-heavy with management, but they didn't want to hear it." It seems clear from old copies of the *Bethlehem Review* that the sudden increase in the number of foremen on the Point was related to upper management's anxiety about their anemic profit margin. "A return of 4.7 percent on revenues in a capital-investment industry such as steel does not represent an adequate return on investment," Bethlehem's chairman, Stewart S. Cort, wrote in a 1972 letter to employees. "We must improve that rate of return to remain a strong company."

The company's strategy to return to the fat profit margins of old was to decrease the number of man-hours required to produce a ton of steel and finished products in order to bring Bethlehem's productivity more in line with that of overseas competitors. The way they proposed to do that was not by asking the people actually doing the work how operations might be made more efficient—information that many would have been happy to offer, as there were still a lot of people on the Point who took pride in their work and in the company—but to vastly increase the number of foremen and to push them to push workers harder to boost production.

"You know that drawing of two horses pulling a wagon?" Melvin Schmeiser asked me. "The Bethlehem way was to put one on top of the other with a whip. Take one out of harness and put him up on the seat with a whip."

The increase in the number of white hats had precisely the opposite effect of the one intended. Ray Rudacille told me that when he started in 1956, a turn foreman and maybe one other foreman worked each shift. "You might have fifty, sixty, seventy men out there on the turn. The men didn't rely on the foremen. The bricklayer would go on and lay the job out and tell the helper what he wanted. You didn't have the foremen out there watching you and telling you what to do."

In those days, bricklayers "used to run to the job," he said. "Well, when they did all this micromanagement and the foremen started telling you where to go, you'd get your assignment and piddle around, finally get there, and wait for them to tell you what to do. It was less efficient, and the men didn't take responsibility because it was taken away from them."

Rank-and-file resentment grew especially acute when a man from outside a department was made foreman over men who had worked for years in the department. In bricklaying, Ray told me, men were promoted mostly from within, which was how he first became a foreman. "There was no real hostility because if he was a good man, people would say, 'He deserves it.'" But one day Ray was transferred from the brick department to the mechanical department "with no training whatsoever," he said. "One Sunday they said, 'You're gonna be a mechanical turn foreman,' and so that Sunday morning I'm sitting in the office, and there's nobody there but me, and the phone rings. 'Eighty-six furnace, slew cable.' I said, 'What the heck is a slew cable?' Now I've got to go downstairs and tell the men, 'Eighty-six furnace, slew cable,' and I don't know what it is."

For the first few years he would go on just about every job with his crew, he said, to learn the ropes, but in the beginning he had "no idea what those guys did for the most part." Naturally, men who had been in the department for years resented him. "You had men who had been looking to be foremen, and I walk in out of nowhere and I'm the foreman and he's still hourly. So there was a lot of animosity."

> It was common knowledge that Bethlehem was the worst-managed company that made a profit in the United States.
>
> —MELVIN SCHMEISER

Bethlehem Steel enjoyed its first-ever $3 billion year in 1972, racking up $3,138,177,000 in revenue as steel imports actually declined by

3 percent from the 1971 level. Nonetheless, 1972 "was not a good year," according to *Bethlehem Review*. "It fell far short of our expectations on many accounts. Net income—what's left over after all bills were paid—fell to 4.3 cents on the dollar of revenue." Where did the money go? Not to investments in new and improved facilities. As the *Review* notes, these expenditures during 1972 were "well below previous years." (The company did find the money to open a fancy new corporate headquarters, Martin Tower, in 1972, however.) By contrast, 1973 was a good year for all American steelmakers as worldwide demand for steel—and therefore orders and production—shot up. At the close of the year, Bethlehem was reporting "record production, near-record shipments, and the best earnings (adjusted for inflation) in our history."

But by the second half of 1975, right around the time the full effects of the consent decrees were beginning to be felt in the mills, the miniboom went bust, leading to "dismally low production, both of raw steel and finished products, short workweeks, layoffs and shutdowns, disturbingly low return on reduced sales dollars, and a forced slowdown in our long-range capital improvement program," moaned the *Bethlehem Review*. Total revenues for 1975 were over $5 billion, but the company couldn't seem to find the profit in that number. The 1975 return on revenue was 4.8 cents on the dollar, compared with 6.3 cents the year before. The end-of-the-year report for 1975 was bleak: "Steel shipments down 27%, pre-tax income down 54%, net income down 29%, return on revenues down 24%, and employment down 7%."

Bethlehem's response was to raise prices, a move that baffled the U.S. government, the media, and the company's own employees. Its chairman, Lewis Foy, defended the 6 percent price hike for its sheet steel products in the December 1976 *Bethlehem Review:* "Are buyers willing to pay our prices? There's only one way to find out, and that's by letting the market decide. If our country intends to preserve some semblance of a free market system—and I hope and pray we do—that's the course we have to take whether we're talking about steel, cement, automobiles, or chewing gum."

Despite the Adam Smith rhetoric, Bethlehem executives weren't quite so jazzed about the value of free markets when it came to competition from imports and later from American minimills. Foreign steelmakers were the major target of American steelmakers' ire in the seventies. Overseas producers weren't "playing fair," they argued; they were "dumping" steel in America, practically giving it away. "Why can foreign steel be shipped to this country and sold at or below our prices?" Foy asked Bethlehem employees in the June 1977 *Review*. "Simply because our foreign competitors are as a rule either government-owned or government-subsidized in one way or another. We believe that foreign producers, in periods of slack demand, dump steel here—that is sell steel at prices below their full production costs. They do this to maintain high levels of operation and employment."

Imports of steel hit a record-breaking 21.1 million tons in 1978. Despite the implementation of a trigger price mechanism designed to alert the government when foreign steel was being sold below production costs, the flood of imports became a rout later that year when in December, mighty U.S. Steel fell to second place behind foreign producers—a defeat that led to much breast-beating in Pittsburgh, Bethlehem, and Washington. It was the first knockdown punch in American industry's long boxing match with overseas producers and an ominous foreshadowing of worse to come.

> W. W. Woods, president of Local 1742, said he did not think
> the coming union election had anything to do with the
> shooting. He suggested that whoever shot Mr. Corum might
> have mistaken him for a Communist.
>
> —*THE NEW YORK TIMES*, JULY 28, 1976

In the midst of the uproar over imports, automation, and productivity in the mid-seventies, a third-generation Chicago steelworker named Edward Sadlowski launched his campaign for president of the USW. The thirty-seven-year-old Sadlowski was more than two decades younger than his adversary, Lloyd McBride, and had been elected president of his ten-thousand-member South Side local at the astonishingly young age of twenty-five. In 1972, he became director of the biggest USW district in the country, with 130,000 members. Throughout its history, the Steelworkers had generally avoided the bare-knuckle tactics of other unions, but during the hard-fought campaign of 1976, Sadlowski supporters were threatened, beaten, and, in one horrifying incident in Texas, shot by opponents.

A great deal was at stake in the election, which came at a time when the Steelworkers were facing the first real challenge to what had become a fairly comfortable lifestyle. The union itself had grown (in the words of one observer) "soft, pompous, dull, a bit lazy and distant from its membership . . . more than a little like the old Employee Representation Plans which the Steel Corporations set up in the early thirties to head off Phil Murray's organizing drive." The Pittsburgh author of this editorial—the labor priest Charles Owen Rice—wrote that "Sadlowski would be a tonic for the USW's tired blood. Tough realists are good for this country, its people and its industries."

Ed Sadlowski was a populist, but he looked forward, not backward. He did not mourn a lost golden age of steelmaking. In fact, he embraced new technology, recognizing that though jobs would be lost in the long run, working conditions for steelworkers would vastly improve. In January 1977, he told a *Penthouse* interviewer that as a consequence of new technology, "no man will have to be subjected to the blast furnaces. We have already benefited from what our brains have produced technologically. We've reduced labor forces from 520,000 fifteen years ago to 400,000 today. Let's reduce them to 100,000."

The McBride team immediately seized on this quote to accuse Sadlowski of promoting job elimination, but Sadlowski and his supporters fought back by pointing out that Abel, McBride, and the rest of the USW leadership were failing to acknowledge or plan for the effects of job loss due to automation and imports. They argued for a proactive, not reactive, stance by the union, and they proposed some fresh ideas—encouraging workers to retire at thirty years, shortening workdays to six hours, requiring companies to retrain employees displaced by new technology, and eliminating overtime—to meet the challenges faced by the rank and file.

"I'm opposed to overtime when people are laid off," Sadlowski told a cheering audience in Buffalo, where layoffs were beginning to winnow the ranks of junior workers with young families at Bethlehem's Lackawanna plant.

Sadlowski was also a fervent believer in union democracy. He promised that if he was elected, the rank and file would vote on every contract. There would be no more "secret" deals between union leaders and the companies, like the Experimental Negotiating Agreement (ENA) of 1973 negotiated by I. W. Abel. Termed the No-Strike by workers, the ENA prohibited a nationwide steel strike for three rounds of contract negotiations, with both the union and the steel companies agreeing to accept binding arbitration for any issues left unresolved prior to signing contracts in 1974, 1977, and 1980. In return for their no-strike pledge, the USW won a 3 percent minimum annual pay raise, plus cost-of-living adjustments (COLA) tied to inflation.

In his study of the American Steel Industry's decline, *And the Wolf Finally Came*, the labor journalist John P. Hoerr calls the ENA "the most incredible money-making machine ever invented in collective bargaining." Average wage rates jumped from $4.27 per hour in 1972 to $11.91 in 1982, he points out. "COLA alone contributed $5.11 of the increase. In that ten-year period, the steel wage rate climbed 179 percent, while inflation rose 132 percent. Compounding was the key to this phenomenal rise. Each year, the COLA hikes were added to the base rates, thereby raising the value of the next 3 percent raise and boosting vacation, overtime, and holiday pay."

Like the Department of Justice consent decrees, the ENA was initially opposed by the rank and file. Many steelworkers were furious that the union had traded away their right to strike without a vote. Leftists on Sparrows Point and elsewhere were beyond angry. They were apoplectic. "This vicious deal states there will be no strikes until

1980. With skyrocketing prices, injunctions, unsafe conditions, we need *more* strikes, not less," a leaflet distributed by the Committee to Smash the No-Strike Deal fumed. "The right to strike cannot be let go, this is our main defense against exploitation and oppression by the monopoly capitalists."

The radicals were correct that steel manufacturers were "trying to ease their crisis in profits by using the union leaders to help them impose labor peace" by signing the no-strike pledge. Steel companies signed the ENA hoping it would eliminate "hedge buying" by customers during the years when union contracts were being negotiated. Fearful of being cut off during a prolonged strike, customers would order large quantities of matériel during the months leading up to contract deadlines, forcing production into overdrive. This frantic activity would then be followed by a painful bottoming-out when the feared strike failed to materialize. Steel companies hoped to pacify jittery customers by signing the ENA to avoid the boom-bust cycle that played havoc with their balance sheets. With characteristic shortsightedness, management "coveted no-strike for its presumed benefits but couldn't digest its costs," said John Hoerr.

In retrospect the radicals were right to oppose the no-strike, though they did so for the wrong reasons. Not only did the agreement send employment costs zooming upward but it also prevented a realistic reappraisal of market conditions and hardheaded bargaining between steel companies and the union over the critical issues confronting the industry during the seventies. "Management gave up too much to solve a problem that was only a manifestation of the industry's central problem," said Hoerr. "It had lost its competitive-cost advantage."

Because Sadlowski's Time for a Change slate lost the February 1977 USW election, it can't be known what difference a Sadlowski presidency might have made during the dreadful decade that followed. Unlike McBride, Sadlowski was not viewed as a company stooge by workers, so they may have been more likely to trust him when five years of red ink in the early eighties forced steelworkers to accept (with great bitterness) the "giveback" contracts of 1983 and 1986. It is possible that Sadlowski's reputation for independence may have given him the credibility to persuade workers that change was needed and to have fought for the kinds of changes that would have cushioned some blows for workers. Of course, they might just as easily have turned against him when he, like the unfortunate McBride (who had a heart attack during the 1983 contract negotiations and died shortly afterward), told them they needed to accept concessions.

Some of Sadlowski's ideas were taken up by a group of younger steelworkers on Sparrows Point. Len Shindel, who in 1980, with his friend Paul Revell, founded the Job Protection Committee to fight job elimination, was one of them. Shindel came to Sparrows Point in 1973 as a communist. He left it in 2001 as a trade unionist. Working on the Point during the agonizing eighties and nineties taught him the limitations of ideology, Shindel told me. "You can't be like, 'Everybody else is over there, but I'm gonna drag them all over here where I am.' You have to meet people where they are, and you have to go through what they are going through, right or wrong."

Shindel and his radical friends found that Sparrows Point steelworkers weren't interested in overthrowing—or even debating—the system. They were interested in concrete issues affecting their economic security and working conditions. Shindel discovered that "if you paid attention to real issues and tried to be a real friend, people responded." Initially conceived in opposition to the USW, the Job Protection Committee caught the attention of District Director Dave Wilson and soon "became a joint effort between the leftists and the union officials over issues of technology," Shindel said.

Throughout the next two decades, he and many of his former comrades in revolution worked with the union officials they had formerly denounced to address rapidly changing conditions at Sparrows Point during a period when the options there and at other steel mills around the country were steadily narrowing. By then, however, the complacency shared equally—though manifested differently—by management, workers, and the union had brought them all to a painful reckoning.

You'd have a nervous breakdown every Friday, not knowing if
the place was gonna shut down or if you'd be laid off.

— DARLENE REDEMANN

By the dawn of the eighties, the company had entered the first stages
of an illness from which it would never recover, though the company's
new CEO, the accountant Donald Trautlein, plunged the patient into
the kind of aggressive treatment program that is just as likely to kill as
cure. In 1980, with raw steel production and shipments of finished
products at their lowest point since the early 1960s, Bethlehem laid off
over eight thousand workers. Two years later, Trautlein called a halt to
steelmaking at Bethlehem's Lackawanna plant and merged its operations with Johnstown. In the same year, he closed plants in Seattle and
Los Angeles. Between 1982 and 1983, Bethlehem shuttered the pipe,
rod and wire, and nail mills at Sparrows Point, transferred its strand-
ing operation to Williamsport, and sold off all the company's ship
repair yards, including the one on Baltimore's Key Highway.

These successive amputations slashed the total Bethlehem workforce by 37.5 percent, from eighty-five thousand to fifty-three
thousand employees. "When business picks up—and it will—some
additional hourly employees now on lay-off will be recalled, but it is
unlikely that the majority will return to work for Bethlehem," Trautlein commented in a *Bethlehem Review* editorial titled "Trimmed
Down as a Way of Life." Despite the deep cuts, Bethlehem finished
four consecutive years (1981 to 1985) in the red. The 1985 losses
alone topped $185 million as total Bethlehem employment continued
to nose-dive, from forty-four thousand in 1982 to twenty-seven thousand in 1985.

Trautlein turned over the chairmanship of the bleeding company
to its president, Walter Williams, on March 1, 1986, after six years as
CEO (during which the company sustained a walloping $2.03 billion
in losses). In a period when workers were being laid off by the thousands and whole operations were being shut down (including the
research and development lab), the former CEO had awarded himself

an 11 percent pay raise and approved severance packages of $1 million each for thirteen retiring vice presidents.

On Sparrows Point, the security enjoyed by the postwar generation of steelworkers was replaced by a cloud of suspicion and anxiety. "Every year it was like, 'Are we gonna get laid off? Are they gonna close this part of the plant?'" said Pete Selhorst. "It was really depressing." Morale plummeted. Rumors flew around the plant like bats. Even people who liked their jobs found it hard to keep their spirits up in an atmosphere so drenched in mistrust. There were some bright spots. The continuous caster went online in 1985. "That was supposed to be our salvation," said Darlene Redemann. The hot strip and plate mills were both modernized in the eighties, and a new coke oven battery was built. The nearly twenty-year-old BOF vessels, which had each produced over twenty-five million tons of steel, were replaced to prepare for the continuous caster, and the giant L blast furnace was partially relined.

These investments signaled Bethlehem's continued commitment to Sparrows Point. But with the entire company on such shaky ground, even new equipment didn't help tamp down workers' fears that the end was near. Indeed, some of the long-delayed improvements actually added to the insecurity. "It was very threatening when whole operations were being shut down because of the new technology coming in," Len Shindel said. "The company would say, 'We're not eliminating any jobs' or 'This isn't going to reduce the workforce,' and next day you'd read an article in the newspaper saying the workforce is going to be down to ten thousand in five years."

At first, he and the members of the Job Protection Committee "were fairly nihilist," he admitted, "saying, 'We don't need any new technology.' But later we corrected our position and said, 'We need to have a greater say in how the technology is introduced.'" Part of the problem, he said, was the autocratic manner in which everything was managed and the way that staffing new facilities got mixed up with the still-problematic issue of race. For example, when the company built an experimental pellet plant in the coke ovens, management "hand-picked the crews to work in the new facility, and they were mostly white." In the nearly all-black coke ovens, this was—naturally enough—viewed as a racist provocation, and coke oven workers picketed the USW district director's office.

Similarly, when Bethlehem built a beautiful new cold rolling mill in the late nineties—its last major investment on Sparrows Point—the company brought in a consultant to administer tests to decide which workers from the old cold mill would be invited to apply for jobs in the new mill. The consultant used focus groups to prepare a test with a built-in 25 percent fail rate to weed out less-educated candidates.

"That was the roughest thing I ever had to do in union office," Shindel said. "To see a guy or a woman who had busted his or her ass in the old mill not even get a chance to go to the new mill that's cleaner and safer. In most cases they could probably have absorbed the training. It's not brain surgery. But there was a cutoff because it was computerization, a new technology. When they [the company] are spending all that money, you're not going to tell them they can't have a test."

Jobs that had once been filled by men and women with a high school diploma (if that) increasingly required more education and training. Bill Lloyd, an electronics foreman, told me that when he first started working at the Point in the sixties, a high school diploma was all that was needed to be hired as an electrical helper. By the nineties, however, to be considered for a helper's slot, a candidate had to have graduated from a technical school and mastered the basics. The company would then take them to the next level by training them on the new equipment at the Point.

Even in the coke ovens, technology changed the work. "A lot of computers went in," said Melvin Schmeiser. "Up on the batteries, you used to have somebody pull off the door and scrape it. Now you had a machine pull the door off, and these arms came up and scraped everything off. Instead of having five people on this machine, you'd have two."

"There was a sense of inevitability about many of the changes," Len Shindel said. But that doesn't mean they weren't painful for all concerned. For example, relations between the two locals, 2609 and

2610, deteriorated as large numbers of workers on the steel side were displaced by technology and transferred to the finishing side. Their seniority entitled them to bid on openings in the mills, but they weren't exactly welcomed with open arms.

Transferring to the tin mill from the coke ovens "was like going to a whole new company," Blaine DeWitt told me. "The tin mill people were prejudiced against the coke oven people. They thought that all we did was work in the slop and the dirt, and that's just the kind of jobs they give us. I used to put in a lot of eighty-hour weeks over at the mill. That's the only way you could make any money."

Like Blaine DeWitt, Melvin Schmeiser transferred to the finishing side when the coke ovens were shut down. Because he was a mechanic with a decade more seniority, he was in a slightly better position than DeWitt, at first bidding into a plantwide labor pool—"I got into what they called the ball gang, a roving gang of mechanics"—and then being hired as a temporary employee in the cold sheet mill. Eighty percent of the employees in the mill at that time were "on loan," he said, meaning that they had transferred to the mill after their own units were shut down but were working as temporary, rather than permanent, employees in that mill.

"Some people who transferred over when the pipe mill closed had been in the sheet mill for ten years!" Schmeiser said. "But they were still classified as retention, which means that you are at the bottom of the pole for seniority. So people with twenty-eight years of plant service were getting laid off before people with ten and fifteen years." Some of the so-called temporary workers were also forced to work shifts again, while permanent cold mill employees with far less seniority had all-daylight schedules. As they had after the changes set in motion by the consent decree, the finishing mills were undergoing a forced integration—in this case of workers on the steel side with those on the finishing side, the latter trying to guard their turf and the former fighting for the jobs to which their seniority entitled them.

Just as the black men who bid on previously "white" jobs had, the displaced employees found their competency questioned. They, in response, jeered at the "spoiled brats" of the finishing mills who had never worked under the brutal conditions steelside. Technology displacement and layoffs made the shift from unit to plant seniority an even greater source of racial and class tensions than it likely would have been in fatter times. "The industry declined at the same time as black and women workers began moving into the skilled trades," said Len Shindel. "So a lot of the affirmative action issues were never really resolved. The crafts were never integrated. They still aren't."

> Do your own job, but don't do anyone else's; Don't work overtime during layoffs, scheduled or not; Don't let the foreman fill in when you are short-handed; Speeding up does not make up for low incentives; Don't work unsafe!
>
> —JOB PROTECTION COMMITTEE FLYER

Throughout the eighties, the Job Protection Committee fought a doomed rearguard action to defend workers from practices that reduced the number of jobs and threatened the health and safety of workers. Two of the most contentious issues were overtime and contracting out. During Job Protection Week in January 1981, the committee distributed a flyer that noted: "It is our local's official policy that members will not voluntarily work overtime during a lay off. This is very hard to enforce and is left up to the individual."

But as crew sizes were cut back, more overtime was offered or, in many cases, required. When I spoke with Melvin Schmeiser, his wife, Alice, angrily denounced the company for the years in which her husband worked sixty to eighty hours a week. Retirements, cutbacks, and layoffs fueled a situation where many departments were undermanned and remaining workers were compelled to work one double shift after another.

"It was mandatory overtime, to a certain extent," Melvin Schmeiser said. "They weren't supposed to schedule you more than two doubles a week, but they had ways of getting around that. Say they schedule you for doubles Friday and Saturday. Well, the next week your scheduled doubles are Sunday and Monday. That's four doubles in a row!" Men working four consecutive sixteen-hour days became "like zombies," he said, and their exhaustion led to serious accidents, as did the pressure on mechanics to keep the mills running while making repairs. "Near the end that's why so many people were getting hurt."

Hourly workers at least had the union to fall back on if they were asked to perform unsafe tasks. The contract workers who helped fill the void left by the layoffs and cutbacks had no such protection. In one of its dubious management decisions in the seventies, Bethlehem imported contract workers into many of its mills, including Sparrows Point. The number of contract workers on-site mushroomed during the eighties and nineties, as full-time permanent hourly employees were laid off or retired (membership at Local 2610 plummeted from 11,393 in 1971 to 2,286 in 1995). Union men saw the trend coming but were powerless to stop it. "The company started giving work away," Tom Capecci told me. "Langenfelder [a heavy equipment operator] made millions down there."

Bethlehem preferred to hire contractors, rather than bring its own employees back from layoff or hire new people, because, Capecci said, "they didn't have to worry about benefits for those guys. They didn't have to worry about vacations, sick leave, medical, disability if someone got hurt on the job." The problem was "those guys would get hurt all the time because they didn't know what they were doing. I would try to tell them, 'You can't do that,' and they would say, 'I have to do it.' The companies would go up to all these dying steel towns up north and hire these guys for $5 or $6 an hour. They wouldn't give 'em no safety masks or nothing. But what were the guys gonna do? They had no choice. Living in a town with no jobs and they had to feed their families. 'You crawl and eat dirt or you don't have a job,' that's what one of them told me."

Not all of the contract employees were outsiders. My brother, Jeff, worked on the Point for a company called Mobile Dredging and Pumping for two years in the mid-eighties. "With our family history," he said, "I always thought it was my fate to work down there." But by the time he graduated from high school in 1979, Bethlehem was cutting back, not hiring. So he worked as a commercial painter for a few years until he was hired by Mobile Dredging, an industrial cleaning service, in 1985. "It was the filthiest, nastiest job imaginable," he told me. He vacuumed debris (both wet and dry), sludge, waste oil, chemicals, and acids into big trucks to be dumped at various locations on the Point. "I worked in every conceivable place you could go in that plant," he said, "on the steel side and the finishing side."

There were about thirty Mobile Dredging employees permanently assigned to the site, and my brother agreed with Capecci that they and other contract employees were not protected from the hazards of the job. His boss—"he looked like Bluto from *Popeye*, and he thought he was always right about everything"—would often order employees to do things that were manifestly unsafe. Once, my brother and his crew were sent to vacuum out a tank, he said, and "when I got like twenty feet away, I could smell the gas coming out of the tank. So I called up my boss and told him it was a fresh-air job"—meaning that the crew needed to "go in under the bottle" (wear oxygen masks) to do the work. "He was like, 'You're full of shit. The fire department was already there and did a gas reading and it's fine. Get your crew in there and start doing the job.'" My brother refused to take his crew into the tank. "I told him that I wasn't gonna be responsible for getting those guys killed. He said, 'If you don't want to do the job, you're fired.'" My brother took his men back to the trailer and went home. "Come to find out," he said, "they took another reading, and it *was* a fresh-air job. So he called me up and basically smoothed it over. But that's the way it was." Another time, Jeff said, he noticed a contractor's crew stripping asbestos off of pipes without respirators. "I went up to one of the guys that was doing it and said, 'You know you can get cancer from this stuff.' And the guy said, 'I'm fifty-two years old. What do I care? I'm making X amount of dollars pulling this stuff off.'"

That kind of attitude drove Tom Capecci and the other union men crazy. "I felt sorry for those guys," he told me. "They had every dirty job down there, and they wouldn't have no safety equipment or nothing. No respirators. Sometimes with the ammonia or limestone, it would suck the oxygen right out of the air and you couldn't breathe.

I'd see them crawling around the stacks vacuuming. We couldn't do much for them because they weren't union, but we'd call our own safety man over to try and help them. Their supervisors would say, 'You have no power over our men. They have to do what we tell them.'"

Like my brother, many of the contract employees were men who, in a different era, would likely have been union members themselves. Now they were doing the same jobs for less money and certainly under less safe conditions. Even so, my brother said, they were well paid, and the fact that they were working among union men probably had something to do with that. "I made pretty good money, around $14.70 an hour. And we were a twenty-four-hour emergency response, so I put in a lot of eighty-plus-hour weeks," he said.

Occasionally, things could get tense between the contract workers and the unionized Bethlehem employees. Most of the Bethlehem employees, my brother said, "didn't care about us. We would go in and do these filthy jobs, and you would have four or five guys just standing around looking at you or barking out orders. But I remember one guy, a big union guy, coming up to me in a bar one time and saying what pieces of shit we were for stealing their jobs."

My brother maintains that one reason companies like Mobile Dredging were brought onto the Point is because some Bethlehem employees, protected by their union, got lazy. Others have also raised this issue. At non-union Signode, a stone's throw from the Point, "we worked," said Willy Cohill. "We didn't have anybody laying around sleeping like at Bethlem." Roosevelt Caldwell and Tank Levy said that once they were made foremen on the ore docks, they became frustrated by the nonexistent work ethic of some employees.

"Sometimes you would have to wake them to get them to go to work," Levy said. "Sometimes you'd literally have to beg them to go to work." Former co-workers gave him a hard time, he said, when he tried to get them to step to it. "They'd say, 'You was a sorry son of a gun when you was in the gang, and now you want to work the hell out of people.' I would just say, 'Well, the shoe is on the other foot now.'"

"Growing up in Dundalk," my brother pointed out, "you were always sold on the idea that unions were all good." But working on the Point in the eighties, he saw "the reverse side of it, the bad part of it," which he believes contributed to the undoing of the company. The worst of it was a kind of laziness and lackadaisical attitude bred by the knowledge that the union would stand behind you, no matter how badly you screwed up, because that was their job. That was why you paid your dues. Not everyone on the Point had that attitude, he admitted, but enough did that it became a problem.

"You had a lot of guys down there who were still hard-core Bethlehem guys, who had their whole heart and soul in that place, like our uncle. That plant meant everything to them," he said. "But you had a lot of others where it was just a paycheck to them. I remember that coiled steel coming off the line looking real pretty, and then I'd see it get all banged up by a forklift driver. At that point they would have to scrap it. And they didn't care. It was just like, 'Screw it.' Or you'd see guys hanging around the canteen for an entire eight-hour shift. They would sit around and do nothing and know they would get paid for it and the union had their back. I think the way the system was, some people took advantage of it after a while."

Cliff Bawton, an Edgemere tavern owner who worked at the Point from 1964 to 1969 before getting a business degree from Johns Hopkins, had a front-row seat on the decline. After buying Friendly's Tavern, a popular steelworker hangout less than a mile from the plant, he watched "the attitude go downhill. A lot of that had to do with bad relations between the union and the company." He heard stories of sabotage by workers angry when they couldn't get a day off, "a lot of unsafe conditions," mills shut down while waiting for parts that were already there. "The right hand didn't know what the left was doing," he concluded.

I never understood how people could stay high in the mill,
but they did.

—LEN SHINDEL

Shop stewards and zonemen knew better than anyone how the stresses of job elimination, affirmative action, new technology, and all of the other changes that haunted the Point in Bethlehem's final decades affected the physical and mental health of employees. "You were like a social worker, a marriage counselor. I was bailing people out of jail, getting people back with their families," said Darlene Redemann. "It was like a jack-of-all-trades just to have this union position."

Drug abuse and alcoholism became major problems. There had always been a fair amount of drinking on the job at the Point and before and after shifts at Mickey's and other nearby taverns. "Mickey's was crazy after daylight shift and three to eleven," Blaine DeWitt said. "They'd be shooting craps behind the car wash. The old-timers would be there drinking knotty head gin and Wild Irish Rose. They'd be sitting there on a crate and then would keel over. Later on, there was plenty of weed."

The drug problem on the Point "wasn't unknown to management," Redemann said. Shindel shared a story that illustrates that point, recalling the day a group of Sparrows Point employees got arrested smoking pot in a van outside Mickey's. "It happened to be two consecutive crews that ran the mill," Shindel said. "So the company went down and bailed them out so they could get the mill running."

The incidence rate at Sparrows Point for mental health referrals for treatment of drug abuse and alcoholism was 40 percent greater than the national average, Shindel told me—and the problem went beyond booze and pot. "There was a lot of heroin," he said. "Some jobs people might work an hour a day. So you work the hour and then you nod out and your buddies protect you. It was very, very prevalent."

One foreman in the coke ovens was a known heroin addict, Shindel said. "People thought he was basically a good guy with some problems." Management was aware of his drug problem but let it continue because he was "ratting out" other users. "Supervision knew where all the drugs were, and it was a number they could pull anytime they wanted."

A 1988 article in the *Sparrows Point Spirit*, a local version of the *Bethlehem Review*, described the "plant subculture" of drug use on the

Point in an account of one steelworker's journey from addiction to sobriety. "It was a hushed, sheltered underground society of booze and drugs," the article intones, describing how Pete Ross, an African American steelworker from Baltimore, was introduced to alcohol and marijuana at work shortly after being hired at the age of eighteen in 1969.

"I began doing drugs both on and off the job," Ross told the *Spirit*. "I was using hallucinogens such as LSD in combination with alcohol, marijuana and everything else. If I got a little too drunk or high, I could sleep it off somewhere. Somebody would always cover for me. I would come to work under the influence and would think nothing of it."

As his addiction worsened, Ross considered suicide, but on the recommendation of a co-worker who was also an addict, he contacted the Bethlehem employee assistance program. By 1986, Pete Ross had achieved sobriety and become one of the program's success stories— volunteering to be profiled in the *Spirit* to inspire others—but many alcoholic or addicted workers either did not seek help or were unable to remain sober. Bethlehem paid for one-month inpatient treatment at various rehab facilities, and I've heard that a good number of folks on the Point racked up two or three stays at such places.

Shop stewards and zonemen spent plenty of time on addicted and alcoholic employees. "I really had my hands full because it was a constant problem," Darlene Redemann said. Shindel agreed. "If you were in union office, you wound up being a drug counselor half the time," he said.

In addition to dealing with the way that employees' personal problems affected their job performance, shop stewards and zonemen in the eighties also helped set the tone for the manner in which their units responded to contentious issues like the integration of black and steel side workers into the finishing mills, technology, and job elimination. Coming down on the wrong side of a contested matter could lead to losing the next election and going back to full time in the mill.

"I really took a lot of heat and ridicule for those eliminations," said Redemann. "That was when they were saying, 'Okay, we're gonna eliminate three guys off the mill now that we got this automatic shearer.'" Partly as a result of the controversy, she lost her second election for zoneman.

Some shop stewards were tempted to pander to the worst instincts of the rank and file. "In the late eighties, a couple of shop stewards in one of the finishing mills were open racists who encouraged their peers not to train transferred workers to promote," Shindel said. "Management tried to keep them in their positions, despite numerous run-ins over discipline, including the firing of one of them for smoking dope on the job." The employee won his case in arbitration, Shindel said, and remains on the job today, one of the lucky few who survived the upheaval of the eighties and nineties.

"It was an endless battle," said Tom Capecci, describing Bethlehem's final fifteen years. "Our manpower dropped more and more. So many stupid decisions were made. Like our plate mill was making a million and a half dollars a month profit and they closed it. Why? Because they wanted to eliminate jobs. Everything was just falling apart."

• LEGACIES •

The Golden Gate Bridge.

The Chesapeake Bay Bridge, George Washington Bridge, Verrazano-Narrows Bridge.

Madison Square Garden.

The Waldorf-Astoria Hotel, Time-Life Building, Metropolitan Opera House.

The U.S. Supreme Court Building.

Each of these iconic structures was built with Bethlehem steel. The Manhattan skyline owes much of its distinctive character to the Bethlehem Gray beam (the sideways H adopted as the Bethlehem logo), which helped engineers build skyscrapers taller than ever before. Yet the two tallest buildings ever built in Manhattan, symbols of American economic power, share a darker history with the company.

In 1971, Bethlehem's steel fabricating division bid $117 million to provide the materials to build the twin towers of the World Trade Center, beating out U.S. Steel's $122 million bid. Both companies lost out to a consortium of fifteen steel fabricators, many of them using Japanese steel, that bid in at $83 million. As a consequence of their suspiciously close bids, the Port Authority of New York and New Jersey filed a price-fixing suit against Bethlehem and U.S. Steel.

Bethlehem's painful bond with the twin towers was amplified in the devastating autumn of 2001. Little more than a month after the towers fell, Bethlehem Steel too collapsed. The economic upheaval that followed the 9/11 attacks was the coup de grâce that finished off the long-ailing company, one year short of its one hundredth birthday.

The company had enjoyed a few years' reprieve after the massive cutbacks and layoffs of the early eighties. In September 1985, Ronald Reagan approved a five-year plan to limit steel imports to 18.5 percent of U.S. consumption to give the industry "breathing space" to regroup. All the players connected with the industry realized that this was their last chance to reform operations. Bethlehem modernized equipment, flattened its traditionally top-down management style through the creation of on-site labor-management participation teams, and focused on quality and customer service.

The USW agreed to a contract that further reduced the company's employment costs. Base rate wages had already been cut $1.25 an hour in the 1983 contract with elimination of cost-of-living adjustments. Sunday premiums, vacation, and holidays had also been cut. In the 1986 contract, base rate wages were slashed another $2.35 per hour.

"We didn't like concessions. We fought them," admitted Len Shindel. But the rank and file realized that it was a question of survival, and they accepted the financial sacrifices to help save the company. "Most of the guys understood that it was either give back or you're out," said Tom Capecci.

At Sparrows Point, employees also worked harder—and smarter—for their reduced wages, signing on to initiatives with names like Priority One and Statistical Process Control focused on quality assurance and customer satisfaction. Their efforts restored the Point to profitability in 1988 after eight successive years of losses. Reject rates for the hot strip and tin mills dropped from 17.19 percent in 1986 to 7.47 percent in 1987. The plate mill, which in 1986 was shipping only

20 percent of its products on time with a 6 percent reject rate, by 1988 was shipping 96 percent of its output on time with less than 2 percent rejects.

Overall, Sparrows Point workers achieved a 23 percent reduction in man-hours per ton, from 6.2 in December 1981 to 4.8 in December 1987—and by the fourth quarter of 1987, Bethlehem as a whole had posted its first profit in five years. Driven by a spurt in demand for steel, 1988 was even more profitable, with the company reporting a net income of $403 million and tonnage of finished steel shipped per employee up one-third in two years, from 360 tons in 1986 to 495 tons in 1988.

Despite these positive developments, new devils began to stalk the company. The first was the relative strength of the U.S. dollar compared with foreign currencies, a macroeconomic trend that propelled the cost of U.S. steel far above that of foreign steel in the nineties. Bethlehem execs bore no responsibility for this development, and they had little power to fight it. The second calamity was one they brought on themselves and that, some economists argue, finally consumed them. Thousands of forced retirements in the eighties and nineties, combined with sloppy bookkeeping, created a demographic nightmare where an ever-shrinking number of active employees were responsible for generating profits sufficient to support an ever-expanding number of retirees.

"Every time it closed a plant, [Bethlehem] accelerated the retirement of longtime workers, rang up a bill for shutdown benefits, and put new burdens on a benefit plan that by the 1970s the company acknowledged was underfunded," *Fortune* pointed out in an "autopsy" of the company published in 2004. "From 1980 onward Bethlehem had five CEO's who, on the one hand, agonized about the legacy costs they inherited and, on the other hand, created new ones by plant closings and layoffs and even by labor settlements that added to the benefit burden. It was a never-ending, ever-expanding mess."

Determined to cut employment costs, Bethlehem lured both salaried and hourly workers into retirement with a series of generous buyouts. In the beginning, "they kicked them old guys out with like a $150,000 lump-sum payment," Blaine DeWitt said. This lump-sum pension was offered to senior salaried workers at the start of the company's plunge into insolvency.

"Top management could always do it, but they never let the first-line supervisors take the lump-sum retirement until '81 or '82," John Bosse told me. "There were strings. You had to be fifty-five, prove that you could manage the money and that you were in good health. I have a friend that went on salary a few years before I did and walked out of there with almost a quarter of a million dollars."

Bob Strasbaugh, who retired in 1981, and Wimpy Doyle, who retired in 1982, both took the buyout. "They only offered [the lump-sum deal] for about a year," Doyle told me, "but I'm still living off it." During his years in the mill, he had also saved 4 percent of his salary in the Bethlehem Savings Plan, a kind of pre-401(k) company match program.

"You had to take 2 percent in Bethlehem stock and 2 percent in cash. They matched 4 percent. When I got my lump sum, I sold my Bethlehem stock right away." He invested everything, and despite a $19,000 loss when the market plunged in 2001, he has fared far better than those who retired on regular pensions. "Some of those guys who got the lump sum have more now than they walked out with," Bosse said.

My uncle Ray Rudacille retired in 1985. Unlike Doyle and Strasbaugh, who started working on the Point in the 1940s, he was nowhere near retirement age, being only forty-seven—albeit with twenty-nine years of service, fifteen of those as a foreman. Like other senior employees who were persuaded to retire during the eighties and nineties, he was offered a $400 monthly pension supplement to sweeten the deal. Five mechanical foremen left at the same time he did, my uncle said. I've since been told by others that the company purposely alienated older, better-paid workers so that they would "choose" to retire.

"What happened was I asked for a day off," my uncle said. "No, 'too valuable a man,' they couldn't give it to me. Two weeks later, they want to send me back to the brick department. I thought, If they don't want me to work, I'm not staying here. I guess I copped an attitude."

The purging of senior employees who had not yet reached retirement age picked up in the nineties. "Everybody lived in terror and dread when we were with Bethlehem because they kept cutting people and cutting people. Every year they'd cut 10 percent of the salaried workforce," Mary Ellen Beechner said. "It got really ugly because people would say, 'Well, my job is important, but that job should be the one to go—that person is a lazy bum' and so on. And with the gossip and rumormongering, it was awful, really awful."

Bill Knoerlein, a BOF foreman, and his brother-in-law Bill Lloyd, an electronics foreman, told me that salaried (non-union) employees were particularly hard-hit by pay cuts and job loss in the nineties. "When things got tight and they had to start watching the money, it was the salaried people who didn't have any protection who got hit. They cut our salaries several times," he said.

When paychecks were cut across the board by 3.5 percent or 5 percent, Lloyd added, "there was nothing you could do about it. You either grin and bear it or you quit." Lots of people quit. "When I left in '98, they were in the process of eliminating foremen," Knoerlein said. "As they retired, they didn't replace them. Instead, they paid hourly guys to supervise."

As manpower continued to drop, hourly workers' opportunities for overtime increased. Because Bethlehem calculated pensions based on a worker's highest sixty months of earnings, people started working as much as possible to build up their earnings. "That didn't catch on till the nineties," Eddie Bartee Sr. told me. "The goal was to get sixty months of high pay. One guy I worked with would stay in the mill after his shift was over to make sure that everybody from the next shift come in. Once, they caught him actually trying to work a fourth turn. He had worked twenty-four straight hours and was walking around like a zombie. He was making $100,000 a year when it was unheard of. But he got a real good pension."

"A lot of people couldn't work enough," Melvin Schmeiser agreed. "They would want to work all the overtime they possibly could. They'd be walking dead." Two years before Bethlehem declared bankruptcy—"and they knew they were going to declare bankruptcy," John Bosse and many others said—the company offered anybody fifty-five or older who had thirty years' service a buyout: $400 a month added to their pension until they reached sixty-two. This generous pension supplement, added to their substantial earned pensions, persuaded many younger steelworkers to retire rather than retrain when new technology eliminated their jobs or their units were shut down.

For example, Darlene Redemann's husband, Larry, a crane mill-wright in the old cold mill, was offered the extra $400 a month to retire early when that mill was being closed to make way for the new cold mill. "Believe me, my husband spent months and months calculating if he could retire," she told me. "He checked every avenue to see if he could lose his pension. They told him, 'There's no way—we got a fortune in the fund.' This was May of 2001. He went to a meeting and asked, 'Is there enough money in here that I'm gonna keep getting my pension?' 'Yes. No problem.'"

She and her husband "didn't have a clue," she told me, that the pension fund was in trouble. And how would they when the company agreed to generous pension upgrades in the 1999 contract with the Steelworkers? "For the last contract we negotiated, we had a substantial increase in pensions," Eddie Bartee pointed out. "For the love of money, I can't see why they would agree to that. The company was in trouble. They had not funded the pension plan like they were supposed to, but they are gonna give a substantial increase?"

My uncle had a theory about that. In that last contract, he told me, "they were giving money away. I guess they knew they were going bust, so they just gave away money to keep people working." That final boost in pensions followed a series of contracts in which the company had traded wage increases (or accepted wage reductions) in exchange for enhanced pensions and insurance benefits. "It was an 'oh promise me' kind of thing," said Ed Gorman, who retired in 1988. "My pension amounts to $1,000 a month—and for thirty-seven years' service, that ain't much," he said ruefully.

At the time he retired, he told me, cost-of-living adjustments that had been added to hourly employees' base pay since 1962 were not used in calculating pensions. "So when I retired, a huge chunk came out of my projected earnings, about $18 an hour. That's a pretty big clip to take off your pay. But after I retired, in the following contract, they allowed half of the COLA increases [which had been added back into the 1989 contract] in your pension calculations. Then they allowed the whole thing."

Throughout the nineties, Bethlehem's pension obligations continued to swell as more and more employees retired. When the company filed for bankruptcy in October 2001, Bethlehem Steel had 13,100 active employees versus 85,000 retirees. The value of its pension fund was $3.7 billion, but its unfunded obligation—the difference between the money in the account and what the company owed to its retirees—was $2.9 billion. When the Pension Benefit Guaranty Corporation (PBGC) took over the Bethlehem pension a year later, its accountants found that Bethlehem had substantially lowballed its unfunded obligation to retirees. The fund was short a walloping $4.3 billion.

Bethlehem executives had tried to make up the pension shortfall with private equity offerings that raised nearly $1 billion in the decade prior to bankruptcy. In 1988, Bethlehem's CEO, Walt Williams, announced that the company had deposited into its pension fund $170 million financed by a public offering of ten million shares of common stock. The *Review* failed to report, however, that some of Bethlehem's earnings during those years was set aside to annuitize a large portion of supplemental retirement benefits for top company executives. These executives, who wrote encouraging letters to employees about the company's improved bottom line, took the precaution of insuring their own health and life insurance benefits, "thus moving themselves largely out of the line of fire," said *Fortune*.

Meanwhile, workers at Sparrows Point were told that their improved productivity and attention to quality, their concessions in union contracts, and powerful new equipment would dig the company out of the hole. For them, Bethlehem's final years were like the proverbial roller coaster ride, with short spurts of exciting speed on a level course punctuated by a series of sickening drops.

"When we found out we were getting a new cold mill, we were up here," Darlene Redemann told me, raising her hand above her head. "Then they closed our plate mill when it was making a million and a half a month in profit, and we're back down here." She dropped her hand to knee level. "Then we move into the new mill and we think everything is great. It made the best steel you've ever seen in your life. Then *boom*, you're bankrupt. *Boom*, you lost your pension. *Boom*, somebody else bought you. Then they sell you too. That's how it was, and it's still going on like that."

Throughout Bethlehem's last years and subsequent changes of ownership, workers were constantly being told, she said, "If you don't give this up, you'll lose your job" or "If we don't get this order, the plant will close." The actual bankruptcy, she said, "was like something fell out of the sky. No warning." Bethlehem's final CEO, Robert S. "Steve" Miller, was hired in 2001 to salvage the company, not to shut it down—or so employees were led to believe. But one month after he took over, the company was in Chapter 11.

Most of the workers I've talked to lay the blame on Bethlehem management. "In the first fifteen or twenty years after World War II, when they were making money hand over fist, they ran the place into the ground," John Bosse said. By the early seventies, he told me, "the handwriting was on the wall. People knew we were down the tubes. But we never thought, none of us, that we would lose the benefits we walked out with. We were always under the impression that what you went out the door with, you were gonna keep."

Or as Melvin Schmeiser acidly joked in his 2003 testimony before the U.S. Senate Special Committee on Aging: "I refer to this as my Chicken Little story. I was told that the sky would have to fall before you lost your pension. Well, it fell."

I gave things up to get those benefits. And they took them
away like they never existed. How the hell they can get away
with it, I don't understand.

— DONALD LINDEMANN

Despite the company's troubles, it was all but inconceivable to many in
the community—both active employees and retirees—that Bethlehem
Steel would ever go under. Eddie Bartee Sr., who retired in 1996, said
that "we had been hearing about companies shutting down all over the
country. But it can't happen to Beth Steel. That was the mentality."

One of the steel companies that went bust before Bethlehem was
LTV (formerly Republic Steel) in Cleveland, which filed for bankruptcy in December 2000. As workers prepared to bank the furnaces—
equivalent to pulling the plug on a patient for whom all hope is lost—a
savior appeared. The Wall Street financier Wilbur Ross, an early player
in the private equity sweepstakes, had made millions buying, restruc-
turing, and then selling off ailing telecommunications firms felled by
the dot-com bust. In February 2002, he created a new company, International Steel Group (ISG), and offered to purchase LTV for the
rock-bottom price of $300 million. There was only one catch. He
would not assume the company's health care obligations to its retirees.

The USW—which had a contractual right to approve or deny the
sale of unionized mills—was faced with Sophie's choice: Which of
your children do you doom and which do you save? If they accepted
Ross's offer, active employees would keep their jobs, but the retirees
would lose the benefits the union had negotiated for them throughout
the years.

"The union was desperate. The city of Cleveland was desperate.
There were around five thousand jobs involved, in all the company's
plants," said Mark Reutter, a former *Sun* reporter who has posted regular updates on financial wheeling and dealing in the steel industry on
his Web site MakingSteel.com. "Wilbur Ross walks in as a savior, but
between the lines, he negotiated an extremely tough contract where
the retiree health costs would be eliminated by the LTV estate as a

precondition of him buying the plant. So in a moment of desperation that was a long time coming, and with the union in particular being very unprepared, they accepted it."

Two years later, this scenario was repeated when Steve Miller was unable to find a buyer for Bethlehem. At first it looked as though he had worked out a deal with U.S. Steel. But having managed their pension and health care obligations quite a bit more prudently than had Bethlehem's board, U.S. Steel execs weren't willing to take on their former rival's burden of debt. Miller then tried to get the U.S. government to assume the health insurance promises to retirees. No dice. The federal government didn't want to set such a dangerous precedent. Once again, ISG offered to clean up the mess—at a price. In January 2003, Ross bid $1.4 billion for all of Bethlehem's assets. In March, a bankruptcy judge in New York approved Bethlehem's request to dump retiree benefits. In May, ISG took over all of Bethlehem's properties, including Sparrows Point.

"Wilbur Ross is a brilliant man," said Reutter. "He's very clever, a good negotiator. One of his most excellent moves is that he did not try to eliminate the union. He did not try to make it a non-union shop. In fact, he came in with a peace plan. Miller and some of the other folks at Bethlehem and LTV had a real anti-union flavor. So the USW, which hadn't been able to organize any major mills in years, suddenly had this guy ready to play ball with them. But at an extraordinary cost."

When Bethlehem entered bankruptcy in October 2001, Reutter pointed out, it was losing money and didn't have much cash on hand, but it was flush with orders from long-standing customers like General Motors, General Electric, and Whirlpool. "Even when Sparrows Point was at its lowest point, it was still churning out a million and a half tons of steel a day," he said. Moreover, a few days before the company filed for Chapter 11, Miller had secured a $400 million loan from General Electric.

"If this company is terminally ill, why would savvy bankers like Jack Welch and company give them all this money?" he asked. "Well, for two reasons. First, by stepping in at that point, they become privileged secured debtors, superseding employees, stockholders, and business creditors. They are guaranteed their money back. Moreover, they can start accumulating fees for advising."

Often the very same managers who steered the company into bankruptcy stay on board to help "restructure"—and in the case of Bethlehem, they put out the word that pensions and benefits owed to retirees were the primary culprit in the company's misfortunes. "Their main complaint was that legacy costs were killing the company," said Reutter—even though the low cost of steel (below $300 a ton) at the time was also putting a huge strain on the resources of poorly managed companies like Bethlehem. But the board needed a scapegoat (in the biblical sense), a sacrificial victim that could be driven out into the desert with the sins of the community heaped on its back. The retirees—voteless in their union and of no further use to the company—became the offering.

Pete Selhorst compared Miller and others who argued that Bethlehem couldn't survive saddled with its legacy costs to blockbusters. "You know how they do it in real estate? They scare you that your neighborhood is integrating or something and that the property values are going down? Well, this was done on an industrywide scale. So they had those people out doing their work, and they are really good, Harvard Business School and all that." The media picked up on the legacy cost narrative, and it soon became the conventional wisdom, applied not only to Bethlehem but to other companies hoping to dump retirees like an aging wife.

Steelworkers themselves weren't aware of the behind-the-scenes deal making that led to the jettisoning of retiree benefits, Selhorst told me. "We didn't know what their overall plan was, and we didn't know that we had schemers in there. Back then there wasn't as much publicity, or maybe we weren't as aware as we are now because we are listening for these things. It just seemed like Bethlehem was on the front edge of this thing."

Before ISG took over LTV and Bethlehem, the pension plans of both companies were assumed by the Pension Benefit Guaranty Corporation, a federally backed agency that insures corporate pension plans. The PBGC works like any other insurance plan: companies pay premiums in case disaster strikes and they find themselves unable to back up their pension promises to employees following bankruptcy. Bethlehem was by far the biggest plan that the PBGC had ever swallowed; in 2003 the program posted an $11.2 billion deficit despite its paring down of many formerly generous Bethlehem pensions.

Len Shindel pointed out that the PBGC took over the Bethlehem plan just before the last big wave of Bethlehem employees would have been eligible for thirty-year retirements. "I think they saw it coming. The clock was ticking. There were a lot of people hired at Burns Harbor and Sparrows Point the same year I was, 1973. It was inevitable that they were going to take over before thousands of us qualified for the thirty-year retirement and they were gonna have this big slug of liability. And like it or not, they had the right to do it to protect the PBGC."

Retirees sixty-five and older receive essentially the same monthly check from PBGC as they had from Bethlehem. But those who retired early, seduced by the sweet deals Bethlehem had offered over the years to trim its workforce, found themselves in deep trouble. "Those guys got slammed," said Shindel, "if their pension was calculated on a lot of overtime and they retired young." The PBGC applied its own barebones formulas, which cut deeply into the monthly sums on which many former employees had based their decision to retire. Bethlehem pension checks of close to $3,000 a month were cut in half.

"Mine went from $2,850 down to $1,570," Melvin Schmeiser said. "My husband was getting close to $3,000 a month. Now he gets $1,500," Darlene Redemann told me. "I lost $750 a month when the PBGC took over," Tom Capecci said—but he counts himself lucky. "The mechanical guys worked overtime up the kazoo to get a good pension, and most of them went from $3,000 to $1,400 a month."

The PBGC calculates pension benefits on two criteria alone: age and plant service. "What you have to understand is that [PBGC] is like an insurance policy," Melvin Schmeiser explained. "If you're seventy-seven, we expect that we're only gonna pay you this much for a couple of years. But if you're forty-eight years old, we're gonna cut [your Bethlehem pension] because we'll have to pay you longer. They have a limit on what they'll pay, depending on how old you are. So the day it went into effect, $1,570 was the limit for what they would pay for my age at the time." The PBGC does not include overtime, incentives, or $400 monthly "kickers" in their accounting—all of these pension fatteners became irrelevant.

Not only were the supplements Bethlehem had promised to workers who retired early cut from their PBGC checks, but workers who had received them learned that they were expected to *pay back* the difference between what they had received during the months between the bankruptcy, when they were still receiving checks from Bethlehem, and the date PBGC took over the plan.

"I retired in 2001 and went on a Bethlehem pension. By the time they calculated everything up, it was a little over a year. So they are saying I owe them a year's back pay under the difference between what they calculated and what they were paying me back under the Bethlehem plan," Bill Lloyd explained. "They said they're being nice about it and they're not gonna charge me interest. But they will take 10 percent of my check every month."

Eddie Bartee Sr., who is still active in union affairs, estimates that approximately a third of Sparrows Point retirees experienced significant pension cuts. "When the PBGC came in, it didn't really affect anyone from 1997 on back. But they took away all the raises that were given after '96," he said.

The loss of pension money had a severe impact on one slice of the retiree population, but the loss of company-subsidized health insurance was a punch in the gut to all retirees and their dependents. Bethlehem may have woefully underfunded its pension plan, but it made no provisions at all for the $3.1 billion in health and life insurance benefits the company owed its former employees. This, more than anything, infuriates many retirees. "They signed contracts. They put the stamp on them," said Donald Lindemann. "If I signed a contract for my house and then said I couldn't make my payment this month, they'd take the house away. But these people took away what they promised for over thirty, forty years?"

For many years, "management considered its benefit promises as benign compared to wage increases," *Fortune* explained. Current expenses were "pay as you go," and the cost of future benefits owed to retirees was never factored into the books at all. Bethlehem, like many other companies, neglected to set up a trust fund for these expenses. Again, it's not as though the company's accountants and executives were unaware that they were accumulating a substantial debt to retirees. Issue after issue of the *Bethlehem Review* throughout the nineties contains articles about the rising cost of health care. Many of these articles took the form of calls for health care reform.

A 1992 article noted that "in the past three years, Bethlehem's health care spending amounted to $162 million in 1989, $205 million in 1990 and $222 million in 1991. For every ton of steel that Bethlehem produces, health care accounts for six percent of the total production costs—or $25 per ton." Throughout the nineties, the company and the union worked together to rein in costs. Eddie Bartee Sr. served on a health care cost containment committee, working alongside representatives from Bethlehem plants in Burns Harbor, Bethlehem, and Lackawanna. "We were able to negotiate some things to help reduce costs and to keep people from taking advantage of loopholes in the program," he told me. But they were fighting a losing battle as health care costs skyrocketed.

In retrospect, the decision by both employers and unions to back employer-funded health care, rather than national health care, in the postwar period now seems a terrible miscalculation, one that has severely hampered the ability of American businesses to remain competitive with overseas companies in nations with national health care plans.

"The union movement in a number of countries went in the direction of defining health care as a right not tied to employment," the historian Roderick Ryon told me. "But in this country they went in the direction of building up health care benefits for union members in the unionized industries, which made sense in a period of high employment and ascending wages. But the problem comes when the jobs go. That's why we have forty-seven million people today with no health benefits. Because a decision was made back in the postwar period to go with union-company negotiated contracts as opposed to, say, Canada, which said we'll have progressive taxation to provide national health insurance."

Nationally, nearly 120,000 Bethlehem retirees and dependents scrambled to find affordable health insurance in the wake of the bankruptcy, and meetings were held at various locations around Baltimore to inform Sparrows Point retirees and their survivors about the effect of the bankruptcy on their pensions and benefits. Rose Marie Weller attended one of the sessions at her local seniors' center. The room exploded, she said, when the counselor announced "that all the life and health insurance was gone and that we wouldn't get any pensions until the government took over. You should have heard the people in the audience. One man said a few words I won't repeat. One woman was crying."

Len Shindel helped staff a USW benefits hotline in the aftermath of the agreement. "People would call and say, 'What are we gonna do?'" he said. "It was a nightmare. We were just doing stopgap stuff, putting them in touch with state health insurance programs, AARP, and other agencies. In some cases people went on public assistance. We were just trying to have a place they could call so that if they got sick, they'd have something."

Donald Lindemann told me that he and his wife went from paying $120 a month to more than $550 a month for health insurance. Mary Lorenzo, who retired in 2001, said that her monthly bill for individual health insurance went from $89 to $534. Younger retirees were hit doubly hard, Ed Gorman pointed out. Not only were their pensions halved, he said, but because "many of them weren't sixty-two years old, they don't have Medicare. They had to opt for COBRA, which was around $625 a month."

Later, some took advantage of a special tax credit program that kicked in after the PBGC took over the Bethlehem pension fund. Under this IRS program, retirees between fifty-five and sixty-five receiving PBGC pensions can deduct two-thirds of their health insurance expenses. Each month they send a check to the IRS for the remainder. But the only people who were eligible for this program were those who had somehow managed to keep up with their COBRA premiums when Bethlehem stopped making payments on the company health plan.

"We were laying out big chunks of money every month while they were figuring it out," Alice Schmeiser told me. "I went through a whole bank account of $14,000 over that year period while they were figuring out who was going to be accepted. And if people didn't have that kind of money, they weren't even eligible, because you had to stay in, you had to stay current. A lot of people couldn't make it." Even under the IRS plan, the Schmeisers went from paying $150 per month for health insurance when Melvin Schmeiser retired in 2001 to $600. "We pay it every month," he said. "And it can't be a day late because they'll drop you in a heartbeat."

Struggling to find affordable health care, elderly Bethlehem retirees all but gave up the fight to replace their lost life insurance policies. "Technically, Bethlehem Steel was self-insured and they paid Met Life a fee for taking care of the paperwork. That's something that a lot of people never knew," John Bosse told me. "Because I was salaried and made a good living, I had a $75,000 life insurance policy that never cost me a dime. When they took it away, and Met Life contacted us about picking it up, instead of basing our rate on what our age was when the company took out the policy, they based it on our age now. I was sixty-eight years old. They told me that if I wanted to keep that policy, it would cost me $500 a month."

It's a story I heard over and over again from older retirees. "I had a $75,000 life insurance policy, and that's gone," Ray Rudacille told me in 2004. "It's more than I can afford to replace. At my age, I'm a pretty high risk." No question about that—two months after our talk, he was diagnosed with mesothelioma, and little more than a year later, he was gone. In the time it took me to write this book, a number of my sources were diagnosed with various types of cancer, and some have died, no doubt due to occupational exposure to toxic chemicals.

Melvin Schmeiser, who was so jovial and so kind the day we met to talk about his experiences on the Point, died of pancreatic cancer on April 27, 2008, at the age of sixty-one. His obituary noted his thirty-five years of service to Bethlehem Steel. World War II and Korea veteran Bob Strasbaugh had died a month earlier, at eighty-two, after living with asbestosis for twenty-five years. "They had a heck of a life insurance policy on him, which meant that we didn't have to carry that ourselves," said Nonnie. "And after we lost it, he was too old and unhealthy to get it."

Now that their life insurance is gone, many retirees worry about what will happen to their wives if they die first. Quite a few "wives of steel" of the postwar era never worked themselves and so do not receive pensions of their own. "My sister gets a $100-a-month pension," Donna Young said. "And she's not the only one. There are an awful lot of people who have little or no health insurance unless they are on Medicare. There are many older people who are suffering."

Rose Marie Weller, whose husband died at sixty-one while he was still working, told me that she lives on her Social Security and a $200 monthly Bethlehem pension. "But last month my house taxes came, and this month it's car insurance. Next month it will be something else." She was paying $279 a month to AARP for her health insurance (without a prescription plan) until Medicare Part D went into effect in 2006. "Now I pay $100-something a month, plus $69 a month for the prescription plan," she said. "Plus $30 for every prescription."

Len Shindel regrets that the Steelworkers did not use the bankruptcy as an opportunity to agitate for a change that would benefit not just steel retirees but all those facing job losses and insecurity stemming from a globalized economy very different from the one in which the Steelworkers and other industrial unions wrung a measure of prosperity and security for their workers.

"Looking back, it would have been good if, when ninety thousand retirees had lost their benefits, we had bused them into D.C. with their walkers and their oxygen tanks and used the opportunity to show the need for national health care," he said. "But union officers got buried under bankruptcy law and forgot the need for grassroots activism." The outcome, he said, "was as good as it was gonna get under an ugly health care system and a system that is ugly to working people."

I've asked a number of current and former union officers from Sparrows Point if they agreed with the Steelworkers' decision to accept ISG's offer even though it meant the loss of retiree benefits. Did the union do right? "It wasn't fair by any means," Eddie Bartee Sr. replied, "but if you want to be realistic and use common sense, the answer is different." The union "had its back against the wall," his friend Ed Gorman told me. "They did everything they could." Len Shindel thinks that "the benefits were gone anyway. There is no way that any owner would be able to generate profits while paying the retiree benefits."

Only Tom Capecci, president of the 2610 retirees' group, had a different outlook. "The retirees got dumped. They don't get nothing from nobody. I feel bad when I go to Costco and see some old woman getting a $250 prescription and know that she's got a choice between $250 of groceries and her prescription. My wife still works, and I'm on her health insurance plan—otherwise, it would take my whole pension to buy medical for us."

The men who negotiated the sale of Bethlehem to ISG made out pretty well. Steve Miller earned $900,000 in 2002 while the company was operating under Chapter 11 bankruptcy protection. He and fourteen other top executives negotiated lump-sum payments of two times their annual base salaries, a lump-sum payment of benefits, and an additional payment to cover any tax liability they might incur as a result of payments they receive under the agreements. Dwayne Dunham, CEO for only sixteen months before turning the company over to Miller, was given a $2.5 million severance package. The math just doesn't add up to the retirees. "If they are in bankruptcy, how can they do that?" asked Capecci.

My father's cousin Donald Lindemann, who at seventy-four works part-time as a security guard at M&T Bank Stadium while his wife works part-time at the former Sparrows Point Country Club because "it makes life a little better," told me that he would "love to run into one of those big millionaires because I'd tell them what I think. They didn't leave us nothing. I'm very bitter about it."

• SCRAP •

The summer after the 2004 presidential election, as I contemplated writing this book, I drove down my old street of redbrick row houses, a few miles west of the Sparrows Point works. Things looked much the same as they did when I was growing up. Kids were riding their bikes on the sidewalks, and old people were sitting on their porches to escape the heat. The bowling alley at the top of my street had been converted to a church, not quite mega but aspiring, with an X-Press-O Café Christian Fellowship ("Music, Fun, Food for the Whole Family") to tempt the wayward faithful inside. The parking lot of the Duda-Ruck Funeral Home across the street was packed as always, its six viewing rooms still full after half a century of burying our dead—undertaking being one industry immune from the effects of globalization.

As I drove across Peninsula Highway, the quickest route to the steelworks from my old neighborhood, I felt happy to find so much unchanged. Maybe it's not so bad, I thought. But once I crossed the bridge and drove up the back road of the mill skirting the harbor, I began to feel uneasy. For one thing, I wasn't supposed to be there, as the many NO TRESPASSING signs informed me. For another, this was no longer Bethlehem Steel, as I couldn't help but notice when I drove past a sign reading COLD MILL COMPLEX, BETHLEHEM STEEL CORPORATION in which the word "Bethlehem" had been painted over, but with the missing logo and letters still visible beneath the paint.

Most of the huge mill buildings I remembered from childhood had been torn down. Rusted trains sat motionless on tracks. An eerie hissing escaped from a baroque tangle of pipes overhead, the only sign that something was still being manufactured on-site, something that required gas to be piped in through copper tubes. Signs pointing to the many parking lots of the plant—A, B, C, D, E, F, and G—remained, a poignant reminder of the multitudes of workers who once poured onto those lots each day.

I drove away from the decimated works spooked. For someone who remembers the place as it once was, seeing the Point in that state was like seeing your father's corpse tossed on a scrap heap. The feeling is common among those contemplating the gutting of American manufacturing and the effect of job loss on blue-collar communities. To be born working class once meant a lifetime of economic struggle and uncertainty, with little opportunity to earn a living wage, to purchase a home, to send your children to college, to retire with dignity. For a time—all too brief, it now seems—that changed. I have asked people who worked at Sparrows Point at its peak what they prized most about the job, and all have mentioned its security.

"The best thing was that I was able to maintain a decent standard of living," said Eddie Bartee Sr. "The kids went to school, and those that wanted to go to college went. I don't live in no $500,000 house, but I'm very comfortable here. I eat what I want. I dress well. I got a nice car and a few dollars in the bank. I don't own a jet, but if I want to go to France or Germany, there is enough money to do that. So I'm blessed."

Wimpy Doyle's three children all went to college (where two studied to be social workers). "They didn't go into the mills, for which I'm thankful," he said. "A lot of your life was the turn—seven three-to-elevens, seven eleven-to-sevens, and six daylights, with every fourth weekend off. I didn't want that for them." But for himself, he said, "it was steady employment, good pay, good benefits, job satisfaction. And the guys were mostly good."

As for the company that employed them and its relationship with the union, "you fought 'em but they didn't give you a bad time about it," said Joe Kotelchuck. "The negotiations were fair." Charlie Brown, whom I met at a Steel Bowl reunion, told me, "My father always said that we owed everything we had to Bethlehem Steel."

That kind of job security, and the way of life it supported, have mostly disappeared today. The history of Sparrows Point and its people is but one chapter in a much broader narrative that has played out in industrial communities across the United States. "Workers here benefited for a hundred years from the global economy. Now they are victims of the global economy, as many American workers are," said the labor studies professor Bill Barry.

The past few years on Sparrows Point mostly support that observation—but not entirely. The retirees got dumped, no question, and Dundalk as a whole is economically stressed. But workers who survived the transition from Bethlehem to ISG say they initially welcomed the change of management. "It became a completely employee-driven and -controlled workforce," Mary Ellen Beechner told me, "where the people on the shop floor make the decisions."

The Steelworkers union did its part to make the new company more competitive, agreeing to a 30 percent cut in the workforce and radical reductions in the number of job classifications and pay scales. "We used to have thirty-two job classes," Redemann said. "With ISG we only had five." ISG also evened out the hourly rate between top and bottom jobs in the mill. "A roller's wages used to be half as much more than the other guys'," Redemann said. "Now it's only a $2 difference between the roller and the helper."

The perpetual conflict between union and management had seemingly been replaced by a more enlightened philosophy in which company, union, and workers sought the common good. "There are no more white hats," the ironworker John Moyer told me in 2004. "Everybody is in this together." Cliff Bawton, the proprietor of

Friendly's Tavern who had been listening to steelworkers complain about Bethlehem for years, said that "most people now seem pretty happy."

Part of the reason for that happiness was because under ISG, Sparrows Point steelworkers were making serious money. Freed of the burden of its pension and retiree benefits and from the shackles of restrictive union work rules, ISG quickly turned a profit, reporting a net income of $24.9 million in the fourth quarter of 2003. A spike in global demand for steel combined with a 30 percent tariff on steel imposed by then president George W. Bush helped fuel a big return on an initial public offering of company stock in December 2003—$493 million.

As steel prices leaped from $391 a ton in 2003 to $700 a ton in 2004, ISG used some of its cash to buy bankrupt Weirton Steel for $255 million, transforming the infant company cobbled together from a bunch of dying mills into the number one integrated steel producer in the nation. And the two thousand or so steelworkers remaining on Sparrows Point reaped the benefits of that near-miraculous transformation.

"When we were interviewed for ISG, we were told that our salaries would be a slight increase from what they were at Bethlehem but that we would get 20 to 40 percent on top of that as bonus," Beechner said. "We all looked at one another and were like, 'Right,' because we had been promised so many things through the years. But doggone it if I didn't get a $35,000 bonus my first full year of working for ISG."

Beechner is a salaried health and safety engineer, but hourly employees too profited, earning 20, 30, 40 percent extra. "Ross threw a lot of money at us to keep us from leaving," said Gary Valentine, a thirty-year veteran. "The younger guys especially." Workers called it the $100,000 club.

Wilbur Ross was hailed in the business press as the man who had single-handedly saved the American steel industry, and ISG was touted as a model for a new kind of American manufacturing—one that would "compete globally, by keeping production costs down, which it has done in part by paring corporate staff and management jobs and by reaching collective bargaining agreements that allow it to cut job classifications." Everybody (except the retirees) seemed to love ISG. "They were a great company to work for," said Redemann. "Then they flipped."

In October 2004, ISG's board agreed to sell the two-year-old company to the Indian steel magnate Lakshmi Mittal, reaping its investors $4.5 billion. Wilbur Ross alone received an estimated $267 million in cash and stock options from the sale; four other ISG execs split approximately $60 million. Like Ross, Mittal was a bargain shopper, combing through an international rack of rejects to find hidden treasures: sick steel companies that could be bought for a song, stripped, and retooled for profitability. With its purchase of ISG, Mittal Steel LTV became the largest steel company in the world, with annual shipments of 52 million metric tons and $32 billion in sales a year. *Business Week* called Lakshmi Mittal the raja of steel.

Folks in Baltimore's steelmaking neighborhoods were not impressed. Many were baffled that the United States government would permit a foreign company to take over a big chunk of the American steel industry. After decades of hearing Bethlehem and other domestic steelmakers blame foreign steel for their declining profitability, and watching local manufacturing jobs disappear as longtime employers of all kinds closed up shop to move overseas, now the government was going to allow a foreigner to take over the Point?

"How do you stand up in Washington year after year in the Stand Up for Steel campaign and then go and sell to a foreigner? We're missing something here," railed Redemann. "How does the government allow all these big foreign tycoons to take over the American economy and destroy it? NAFTA was bad enough. But what the United States is doing now, I just don't get it."

Mittal quickly slapped up shiny new corporate signage on the Point—something ISG had never done—but soon after the company announced its merger with the Belgian steel giant Arcelor in June 2006, the U.S. Justice Department filed an antitrust suit against the company. In February 2007 the Justice Department notified Arcelor-

Mittal that it had to sell Sparrows Point within ninety days. Shrugs and black humor greeted news of the announcement on the Point. "Some of the guys have been joking that Wal-Mart Steel is next," a line operator named Dave Matheny told me.

For a time it seemed the works might fall back into American hands. James and Craig Bouchard, sons of a former Inland Steel executive, partnered with a Brazilian iron ore and metal producer and a Ukrainian steel company to form a shell company called E2 Acquisition Corporation. They submitted a winning bid of $1.4 billion, and in September 2007, Craig Bouchard came to Sparrows Point to assure workers and the union that he and his coinvestors planned to run the mill at full capacity, to hire and train new workers, and to invest in new facilities. In a nod to the works' storied history, he announced that they would rename the facility Maryland Steel Sparrows Point.

Workers adopted a watch-and-wait attitude. "As one of the older employees down here, I'm a little skeptical about their plans," Gary Valentine told me. Smart man. On December 17, 2007, ArcelorMittal announced the termination of the purchase agreement with E2 due to the inability of the Bouchards and their coinvestors to secure financing.

Three months later, on March 21, 2008, the Russian steelmaker OAO Severstal announced that it was buying Sparrows Point for $810 million—half its actual value, according to *Forbes* magazine. The company's CEO, Gregory Mason, said that Severstal had no plans to cut employment, wages, or benefits and that it would invest up to half a billion dollars over the next five years to bring the facility up to full capacity. But by September 2008, "challenging market conditions" forced the company into layoffs at not only Sparrows Point but Severstal North America's three other mills.

During its brief tenure, Severstal has become Bethlehem 2.0, fighting with state regulators about leakage of benzene and other toxins into Baltimore harbor, forcing senior employees to retire and replacing them with contract employees, and failing to properly maintain equipment. In September 2009, flames from the recently renovated Big L blast furnace shot one hundred feet into the air—a consequence, workers say, of the company's use of low-cost raw materials to feed the furnace. They are producing more steel per person than ever, and their union has long since adapted to a new reality where a bare-knuckle fight against the company might lead to a shutdown. "In the old days, for the Steelworkers it used to be 'Us against the company, mano a mano. Who's tougher? We'll strike you for longer than you can strike us,'" said Bill Barry. "But now the work just leaves. It's like trying to hold water."

I attended a Labor Day parade and rally that Barry organized in 2008. In some ways it was a sad gathering. Forty or so people showed up to march from the CCBC campus to Heritage Park in Dundalk. Most were over sixty. Led by a jazz combo from Musicians Local 40-543 playing "When the Saints Go Marching In," the small but surprisingly fierce contingent strolled into the park, stood in a circle, and testified to what the union movement meant to them.

Doug Harding, a member of the American Federation of State, County and Municipal Employees, pointed out that today's corporate chiefs "want to get rid of people like us because they want to strip away everything working people fought for from the '30s onward—the pay, the health care, the retirement benefits. They want to drive us back to where we were eighty years ago. They are big organizations, and they have government running interference for them on every level."

"Too old to work, too young to die," said an old-timer whose name I did not catch, quoting Walter Reuther, the first president of the United Auto Workers. "Reuther said that at the bargaining table when he was fighting for pensions. Well, what you gain at the bargaining table, you can lose at the ballot box." The mood of the speakers was somber, reflecting the general sense that corporate power was operating with no checks whatsoever—and that working people seemed too apathetic or individualistic to rise up and defend themselves.

Yet little more than two months after that Labor Day rally, Barack Obama won the presidency in a grassroots campaign driven by economic pain and an overwhelming desire for change. I spent the weeks before the election interviewing folks in Dundalk and Sparrows Point, trying to get a sense of whether white working-class supporters of

Hillary Clinton would be willing to vote for Obama. I knew that many would not. My mother was so angry at what she saw as the anti-Hillary bias of the media that she started making campaign calls for John McCain. Like a lot of women from working-class backgrounds, she loved McCain's pick of Sarah Palin. A Reagan Democrat, she defines herself at seventy-five as a conservative, though her recent voting record (Clinton, Gore, Kerry, McCain) doesn't really support the label.

My brother, who voted for Bush in 2000 (but not in 2004), backed Obama, but he was the only white man among the truck drivers he works with to do so—and he put up with a lot of teasing and harassment from his co-workers. Most are Republicans who take their political cues from Fox News and talk radio, and they weren't buying my brother's argument that Obama was for the working man.

But at the Battle Grove Democratic Club, where over a thousand people had turned up to see Bill Clinton stump for his wife during the primary battle, I heard a different story from the Democratic faithful when I visited in October 2008. "The party is more united than it has been for a while," said fifty-seven-year-old Garry Mangan, president of the club, as we sat chatting with his wife and sister. Mangan, who worked at Sparrows Point from 1969 to 1973 before becoming a plumber, said that between the war and the economy, people were disgusted and ready for a change. "The color of the skin has nothing to do with it," he said. "People are looking beyond that to improve their standard of living."

Dale Volz, a self-described retired public servant and real estate agent who said that he had supported Obama from the start, wasn't sure if the candidate would be able to reverse a forty-year trend in which a plurality of votes in the southeastern part of the county had gone to Republican candidates in every presidential election since 1968 (save for Bill Clinton's second term). "I love these people," he said. "To know them is to love them but not always to agree with them." Amen to that.

A few weeks later, I finally got a chance to sit down with LeRoy McLelland, the tin mill worker who had launched a lawsuit challenging the Department of Justice consent decrees back in 1977. He told me bluntly that many of his Essex neighbors would not vote for

Obama, "to be honest, because he's black." But as a die-hard Democrat, he himself would vote for Obama, though it was clear that he didn't quite trust him. With billions being spent on bailouts for banks and insurance companies while "here's the steel industry, on its knees, being bought out by foreign countries," he was in no mood to reverse his lifelong voting record as a union Democrat. "I'm a Democrat," he said. "Never voted for a Republican, and I think it goes back to when I started to vote. In my mind, the Republicans were for the rich and the Democrats were for the working class."

LeRoy and I talked frankly about race, and he told me that many of the whites he knows have never really adjusted to the rapid progress African Americans have made as a group over the past thirty years. "They feel the fact that the blacks have got so far with recognition, things they were not able to do in the past. I think that's still embedded in a lot of people." He pointed out that all of Baltimore's top elected officials are African American, as are many heads of agencies. Our conversation helped me to understand that one reason why some whites without a college education harbor such deep racial hostility may be because they have watched their fortunes fall as (in their view) those of African Americans have risen.

After our conversation, I e-mailed LeRoy a link to footage of a fiery speech that Richard Trumka, the secretary-treasurer of the AFL-CIO, delivered to the Steelworkers in July 2008. Trumka confronted the race issue head-on, arguing that "we in the labor movement know better than anyone else how racism is used to divide workers, and when it does, we all wind up losing." There was no good reason for any union member to vote against Obama, he said, and only one bad reason: racism. After watching the video, McLelland wrote back that Trumka's speech "should be played in every union hall in America."

Barack Obama won the election in part by appealing to Americans to put old divisions and grudges behind them and to unite for the common good. The message hit home for some in Dundalk. I looked at the raw data from the election and found that though John McCain won more votes in Dundalk, it was not a rout—8,322 votes were cast for Obama, versus 9,783 for McCain. In some precincts, the gap was as narrow as 11 votes. Precinct 13, in Turner Station, delivered the most lopsided count—1,135 for Obama and 16 for McCain. The biggest spread at any other Dundalk precinct was 776 votes for Obama versus 1,199 for McCain, in Precinct 4. Though there's no way to know for certain, I would not be surprised to discover that many of the Dundalk residents who voted for Obama are from union families. Unions remain "the most integrated institutions in American society," as Trumka pointed out, and union members well understand that "we are strongest when we are united."

No doubt that partly explains why, way back in 1947, the first Republican Congress elected since 1934 passed (over President Harry Truman's veto) the Taft-Hartley Act to counter the CIO's plan to unionize the South. Taft-Hartley outlawed mass picketing, sit-down strikes, and sympathetic boycotts. It made it possible for employers to once again threaten workers who promoted unionization, and it permitted the federal government to order striking workers to return to their jobs. In *Which Side Are You On?* the labor lawyer Tom Geoghegan said that when people ask him why labor no longer organizes the way it did in the thirties, "the answer is simple: everything we did then is now illegal."

By calling a halt to mass organizing after the war, Taft-Hartley prevented a critical mass of Southerners from developing the kind of worker unity across racial boundaries that slowly, albeit painfully, unfolded up north. A hybrid of North and South and—critically—a union workplace, Sparrows Point was a kind of experiment for how unionization might have played out in the South. As the Sparrows Point story shows, both the union movement and the industrial workplaces it sought to reform were tainted by racism and by the usual complement of human faults and failings. And yet the system worked. The labor movement did improve the material circumstances of life for millions of Americans, black and white, immigrant and native-born. Just as significant as the economic benefits was the state of mind that created and sustained the labor movement. Unions provided a vehicle for transforming "me" to "we." I don't know too many people these days who consider their co-workers "family," the word used more than any other to describe the relationship among employees, company, and union. "It was a protective family atmosphere," the former tin flopper Phyllis Moskowitz told me. "Everybody sort of stuck together."

And this wasn't true just for steelworkers or the World War II and Korea generations now passing. I recently chatted with a fortyish former autoworker named Gregory who had worked at the sprawling GM plant on Dundalk's borders. When the plant shut down in 2004, he took a buyout rather than transfer to another GM plant. He now works for the Baltimore City Health Department—unlike many of his co-workers, he saw the handwriting on the wall and went back to school to pick up a science degree while still at GM. Gregory said that he likes his new job, but as we spoke, it became clear that he misses the camaraderie of his old workplace. "We were like a village," he said, working together, playing together, and defending each other. "If someone stepped to one of us, he had to deal with all of us." Black or white, it didn't matter, he said. They were united as a group.

Like the steelworkers, Gregory and his co-workers spent a lot of time in the bars, restaurants, convenience stores, and other small businesses near the plant, meeting up at the Royal Farms in the morning for coffee, bowling together after their shifts, and closing down the nearby taverns, sticking around while the staff locked the doors and counted out the register after last call. "We kept those places going," he said. Now that the plant has closed, so too have some of the local businesses supported by its employees. Although Gregory made great money working for GM, it sounded to me like what he misses most is the same thing expressed by the steelworkers: something hard to describe but tied up with being part of a team—unity.

Seventy-five years ago, John L. Lewis said that the future of labor is the future of America. Looking back, it seems he was right. But where does that leave us now? In 2006, corporate profits in the United States increased 21.3 percent, accounting for the largest share of national income in forty years, according to the Commerce Department, and the share of national income going to wageworkers and salary workers fell to levels not seen since 1966, despite strong productivity gains. Between 1990 and 2005, the median wage of a full-time American worker increased 4.5 percent, while the wages of top earners rose 33 percent for those in the 98th percentile of earners and 82 percent for those in the 99.99th. It wasn't until the housing bubble burst and taxpayers were left holding the bag that many seemed to realize they'd been had—bought off by easy credit that disguised their shrinking purchasing power.

A couple of years ago, I asked Eddie Bartee Sr. about the criticism one often hears of unions, that steelworkers and autoworkers "got greedy" and demanded too much. Those who blame the unions, he replied, don't understand that "they were simply doing their job: to represent the employees and get the best benefits they could for them, and the best working conditions. That's what the union was all about." In 1955, when more than a third of working Americans belonged to a labor union, prosperity spread throughout the population; today, when fewer than 8 percent of workers in the private sector are unionized, it is concentrated in the hands of those at the top.

The manufacturing jobs of old are probably not coming back, but if workers in jobs impossible to send overseas—construction, health care, retail, food production—were to organize, labor's long decline could be reversed.

On average, unionized workers make 30 percent more than non-unionized workers in the same job—according to Department of Labor statistics, $863 versus $663 a week for the typical non-union worker. For those who believe that labor's power is spent, consider this: in Baltimore, the United Workers won a living wage for stadium cleaners in 2008 after a three-year struggle. Prior to the campaign, the cleaners were day laborers, employed by temp agencies that paid them a flat rate that averaged out to $4.50 an hour. Today they make $11.30 an hour working for a single employer who won the stadium contract. "Before we won that victory I was saying to myself, 'What made them think these people are going to get $11.30 an hour?' Because it just didn't seem like they was gonna let that happen," said Bernadette

Scudder, a former stadium worker who is now training to be a United Workers organizer. "It wouldn't have happened if the union hadn't stepped in."

That's exactly the type of scenario feared by those fighting any attempt to strengthen laws protecting employees seeking to organize unions. The proportion of American workers who say that they would choose to be in a union if they could has increased steadily over the past twenty years. But today, as in the early decades of the twentieth century, employees who try to form a union are threatened, intimidated, and very often fired. A recent study by Kate Bronfenbrenner, director of labor research at the Cornell School of Industrial and Labor Relations, found that employers threatened to shutter plants in 57 percent of NLRB elections between 1999 and 2003, fired workers for union activity in 34 percent of those certification campaigns, and threatened to cut wages and benefits in 47 percent of elections.

During the 2008 presidential campaign, labor's goal of passing legislation to more easily organize workplaces ran into heavy opposition from corporate interests. Business groups spent more than $20 million on television ads to defeat Democratic candidates backing proposed changes to labor laws. As this book goes to press, labor is gearing up for a fight over the Employee Free Choice Act, which would toughen penalties for companies that violate workers' rights. But with or without government support of the kind that made the great organizing drives of the 1930s possible, American workers themselves will have to step up to the challenge and fight for their own interests—as well as reject divisive propaganda masquerading as populist politics.

Over the past twenty years, a rogues' gallery of fake men and women of the people who have never themselves struggled to pay a gas or electric bill or to put a child through college or had to decide between groceries and prescriptions have sown conflict and division by persuading their white audiences that what is good for their neighbor—particularly if that neighbor is black, Latino, gay, liberal, or a recent immigrant—cannot possibly be good for them. It's an old trick, and it's sad that so many still fall for it even though our history teaches exactly the opposite. "Many of the things that we are seeing today, the divisions in the workforce—it's exactly what held organizing back one hundred years ago," said Bill Barry. "It was divide and conquer."

On November 4, 2008, a decisive majority of Americans cast their votes against division and for unity. Only time will tell if we as a nation can overcome the demons of our history for longer than one joyous day and find our way to a new future together. But over the past year I have pondered a remark made by one of my sources about his generation's response to the defining issue of their time—one that feels eerily similar to our own.

As I watched the enormous crowds pouring into the nation's capital, waving flags and smiling despite the bitter cold and an economy shedding jobs at a vicious clip, his words echoed in my mind. "They always said that they woke a sleeping giant," said Willy Cohill, recalling the way the nation united to fight fascism abroad. "They didn't realize what the American people could do. But we showed them."

Willy died on August 3, 2009. His last words to his younger brother were "Jim, I had a good run."

ACKNOWLEDGMENTS

Red Canoe, Pete and Nicole Selhorst's coffee shop in northeast Baltimore, became my second home during the writing of this book. Pete not only spoke to me at length about his own career at the Point but also provided introductions to other sources. Thanks for all the coffee, conversation, and wireless Internet!

Mark Reutter, author of the magisterial *Making Steel: Sparrows Point and the Rise and Ruin of American Industrial Might*, is the only person I know who is as obsessed with Sparrows Point and its people as I am. His sage advice and analysis, as well as his broad knowledge of the Point's history, were enormously helpful.

The staff at the Dundalk–Patapsco Neck Historical Society allowed me to spend many hours digging in their vast archives of documents and photos, and I always enjoyed the time I spent in their company—even if they did make me listen to *The Rush Limbaugh Show* while I was working.

Len Shindel and Alfred Wolfkill shared with me old documents very precious to them, which I took far too long to return. Many, many thanks to both of you.

Adam Stab reminded me that American history has two strands, black and white, and sharpened my understanding of the central role black steelworkers played on Sparrows Point.

Mark Bochetti and Norman Knoerlein read early drafts of the manuscript and pointed out its shortcomings. This is a stronger, more balanced book as a result.

Cal Walker, Ann Finkbeiner, Paula Fazio, Jean Rudacille, and Rafael Alvarez offered vital support as I revised the book. Many thanks for your generosity.

My writing group—John Barry, Betsy Boyd, Doug Basford, and Darcelle Bleau—provided great feedback and suggestions on the manuscript as well as delicious snacks.

Without material support provided by my agent, Flip Brophy, and my editor, Jeff Alexander, I could not have finished this book. Thank you both for keeping me going.

Finally, my thanks to the officers and members of Steelworkers Locals 2609 and 2610 for the conversation and wonderful lunches.

To all the retirees, active steelworkers, and family members who gave so generously of their time, their spirit, and their memories, this book belongs to you.

NOTES

PATRIOTS

4 *"You can look far and wide"*   John Waters and Simon Doonan, *Shock Value: A Tasteful Book About Bad Taste* (New York: Thunders Mouth Press, 1981), 76.

12 *according to the 2000 census*   http://censtats.census.gov/data/MD/1602423975 .pdf.

ROOTS

16 *In the early years of World War II*   This point has been disputed by a couple of sources who maintain that Bethlehem was always quite strict about the age requirement for employment. It may be that certain workers brought their underage sons into various mills with the approval of their foremen.

19 *blacks and whites "got along good"*   The steel towns of western Pennsylvania experienced a much higher degree of racial tension. "The influx of Black Southerners into the mill communities of Western Pennsylvania intensified the prejudices of many Whites. The initial presence of Black newcomers in Homestead during the war pushed White residents, particularly steelworkers, to the verge of race riots. Whites in Duquesne reacted very negatively to an expanding Black pres-

ence after 1916. . . . By 1923, the growth of the Black population in Johnstown created a tense racial atmosphere which culminated in a police riot against the city's recent Black migrants." Dennis C. Dickerson, *Out of the Crucible: Black Steelworkers in Western Pennsylvania, 1875–1980* (Albany: State University of New York Press, 1986), 62–64.

21   *the Baltimore Iron Works*   Neal A. Brooks and Eric G. Rockel, *A History of Baltimore County* (Towson, Md.: Friends of the Towson Library, 1979), 37.

21   *"35 or 40 young, healthy and stout"*   John Bezis-Selfa, "Forging a New Order: Slavery, Free Labor, and Sectional Differentiation in the Mid-Atlantic Charcoal Iron Industry, 1715–1840" (Ph.D. diss., University of Pennsylvania, 1995), 148.

21   *"cheaper, more reliable and pliable"*   Ibid., 124. See also Charles G. Steffen, *From Gentlemen to Townsmen: The Gentry of Baltimore County, Maryland, 1660–1776* (Lexington: University Press of Kentucky, 1993), 53.

22   *others set up incentive systems*   Bezis-Selfa, "Forging a New Order," 323. See also Charles B. Dew, "Disciplining Slave Ironworkers in the Antebellum South," in *A Question of Manhood: A Reader in Black Men's History and Masculinity*, vol. 1, eds. Darlene Clark Hines and Ernestine Jenkins (Bloomington: Indiana University Press, 1999), 205–27.

23   *Pennsylvania Steel Company sent surveyors*   For a detailed account of the founding of the Sparrows Point works and town, see Mark Reutter, *Making Steel: Sparrows Point and the Rise and Ruin of American Industrial Might* (Urbana: University of Illinois Press, 2004).

24   *African American men recruited from the South*   Ben Womer, "Thoughts as Town of Sparrows Point Falls," *Dundalk Times*, August 2, 1973. According to Womer, founder and first president of the Dundalk–Patapsco Neck Historical Society, "the first shovel of dirt turned over at Sparrows Point to start the building of the mills was turned over by a Negro." Southern black men laid the railroad track to and from the peninsula, he said. In February 1899, the Baltimore–Sparrows Point Railroad began service, making eight stops between the Point and Union Station in the city, a journey of approximately forty minutes. Trolley service started in 1903 and continued until 1958.

24   *"my father and grandfather"*   Margaret E. Lindemon, "Gems of Remembrance," Bethlehem Steel Papers, Dundalk–Patapsco Neck Historical Society.

25   *the Zion of company towns*   Frederick may have had another model in mind too. In the Wood files at the Hagley Museum and Library in Wilmington, Delaware, I came across a handwritten note dated April 5, 1899, attached to a news clipping. The note was from Maurice Wood of the London office of Pennsylvania Steel and read, "I am enclosing you a cutting from today's Times which I'm sure you'll find interesting." The article was titled "Industrial Labor in Russia," and it

addressed "questions related to the general well-being of the working classes, and particularly to the means by which a larger permanent staff of skilled workmen could be secured in manufacturing and mining industries." The piece noted that "nearly all the large manufacturers provide barracks for their people, in which lodging, light, and fire are furnished from one shilling to eightpence per month."

25 *"A part of the lifework"* Frederick W. Wood Papers, Hagley Museum and Library, Wilmington, Delaware.

26 *Meat from cattle, sheep, hogs* *Reflections: Sparrows Point, MD 1887–1975* (Dundalk, Md.: Dundalk–Patapsco Neck Historical Society, October 1976), 10.

26 *The company also provided land* "Church was a must for everyone on Sparrows Point. The father was excused if he was working the day shift, but everybody else was expected at church unless they had a very good reason for not being there. If you missed church, the parson would be at your door the next day to know why." Lois S. Myers, Bethlehem Steel Papers, Dundalk–Patapsco Neck Historical Society.

26 *two years later, one for black children* The Colored School at Sixth and J streets was a two-room building "without textbooks or other instructional materials" (Mario Jondo, "A Black Perspective: The History of Sparrows Point," *The Dundalk Eagle*, September 20, 1979). However, the teachers seem to have been of the highest quality. "We had tremendous teachers," Eddie Bartee Sr. recalled. "Those teachers *made* you learn."

27 *"what struck us more than anything"* *Reflections*, 24.

28 *"cut the malaria with a knife"* Ibid., 27.

28 *"Colored and foreign labor"* *Fourth Biennial Report of the Bureau of Statistics and Information of Maryland, 1890–1891*, Maryland Historical Society, Baltimore.

28 *"in shacks along the banks of the creek"* A woman named Elizabeth (Bank) Thomas told the local historical society that her father saw a sign in his hometown in Romania, an ad saying "Come to America, good wages, housing and free education for children" posted by Bethlehem Steel. He came (arriving during the great Baltimore fire of 1904) and worked for two years, then sent for his wife and three children. Four more children were born in the town of Sparrows Point. Bethlehem Steel Papers, Dundalk–Patapsco Neck Historical Society.

29 *management chose carefully* *Reflections*, 33. In 1892, the population of the town was approximately thirty-five hundred. There were six hundred houses and over four hundred pupils in the schools.

30 *Most families on the Point took in* Frederick W. Wood Papers, Hagley Museum and Library, Wilmington, Delaware; Myers, Bethlehem Steel Papers, Dundalk–Patapsco Neck Historical Society. According to Myers, houses were rented

"only if they [tenants] promised to rent their extra rooms to newcomers. Sometimes one house would care for three families. There was no water or electricity
in the houses at that time."

30 *many housewives on the Point were actually running* Karen Olson, *Wives of Steel:
Voices of Women from the Sparrows Point Steelmaking Communities* (University
Park: Pennsylvania State University Press, 2005), 54.

DIRT

33 *equipment from the Ashland Iron Works* For an account of early iron making
operations at the Point, see John B. Lovis, *The Blast Furnaces of Sparrows Point:
One Hundred Years of Ironmaking on Chesapeake Bay* (Easton, Pa.: Canal History
and Technology Press, 2005).

33 *"We allow no liquor to be sold"* Excerpt from *Fourth Biennial Report of the Bureau
of Statistics and Information of Maryland, 1890–1891,* Maryland Historical Society, Baltimore.

34 *"on the last train"* "The Cloud That Lies O'er Sparrows Point," *The Baltimore
Sunday Herald,* April 9, 1893. Single-page copy of original article, Bethlehem
Steel Papers, Dundalk–Patapsco Neck Historical Society.

34 *the arrest records of the Sparrows Point Police Department* These ledgers are
archived at the Historical Society of Baltimore County, Towson, Maryland.

34 *The daylight shift worked* Bethlehem Steel Papers, Dundalk–Patapsco Neck
Historical Society.

36 *a model for other communities* Compared with the conditions that black steelworkers and their families encountered in western Pennsylvania, this may be
true. "Overcrowded housing and the unsanitary and polluted atmosphere of
Pittsburgh and the milltowns made Black migrants extremely susceptible to serious, and sometimes fatal, illness. Between 1915 and 1930, the rate of death per
1,000 people for Blacks in Pittsburgh was between 19.1 and 33.8. For Whites in
the city, it was substantially lower, 12.0 to 26.3." Dennis C. Dickerson, *Out of the
Crucible: Black Steelworkers in Western Pennsylvania, 1875–1980* (Albany: State
University of New York Press, 1986), 58.

36 *January to June 30, 1910* Frederick W. Wood Papers, Hagley Museum and
Library, Wilmington, Delaware.

37 *Over that four-year period* Letter dated October 12, 1914, Wood Files, Hagley
Museum. Even today, working in a steel mill remains dangerous. In 2006, fourteen workers were killed in American steel mills. Many of the accidents involved

overhead cranes. See Myra Pinkham, "Breaking the Taboo," November 6, 2008, http://www.hoistmagazine.com.

37 *"You wouldn't believe"* An article in *The Union* published on March 26, 1892, noted that "46 deaths have occurred in the past two years, 19 from accidents and 27 children." Bethlehem Steel Papers, Dundalk–Patapsco Neck Historical Society.

38 *capsule descriptions of these fatal accidents* Sixteen pages listing the name, age, and job category of the deceased, the date and location of the accident, and a brief description of how the accident occurred and the nature of the deceased's injuries. Private correspondence of Joe Lawrence.

GUNS

52 *"Christ told him he would start in"* From 1902 to 1910, laborers made thirteen and a half cents an hour, according to payment vouchers in the Frederick W. Wood Papers, Hagley Museum and Library, Wilmington, Delaware. The union men meeting to discuss Sparrows Point in 1915 were clearly skilled craftsmen, based on the wages discussed and also on the fact that during this period, only skilled craftsmen were unionized.

52 *"or else he will not get men"* By the mid-1910s, approximately seven thousand men worked in the Sparrows Point mills and shipyard.

52 *expense statements and invoices* Frederick W. Wood Papers, Hagley Museum and Library, Wilmington, Delaware.

53 *goods at the company store* Not until the late 1920s was outside competition allowed on Sparrows Point. Caplan's department store was the first, followed by two grocery stores (Eddie's and Rosen's), a drugstore, a sweetshop, and a hardware store. Most of the merchants were Jewish, one of the few ethnic groups that did not have much of a presence on the Point until that time. "All of the merchants ran a tab and having worked for Saul Savetman and Fred Rosen, I know that often the tab was not paid. In loaning $1 or extending credit, it made no difference whether you were salaried or hourly, black or white. The key to having credit extended was that you dealt with them on a regular basis and that you rented a house from the company." Fred Dice, "Turning the Clock Back," *The Dundalk Eagle*, January 26, 1989.

53 *"Every detail of working the great plant"* Quoted in Katherine Stone, "The Origin of Job Structures in the Steel Industry" (paper delivered to the Conference on Labor Market Stratification, Harvard University, March 16–17, 1973).

54   *Frick's* ~~wwuie~~ Ibid., 66.

55   *foremen and supervisors in city factories*   Roderick Ryon, "Baltimore Workers and Industrial Decision-Making, 1890–1917," *The Journal of Southern History* 51, no. 4 (November 1985). "Workers struck when plant owners refused to yield on the supervisor issue, and no other labor matter, except wages, prompted as much unrest in the city. The city's size gave workers some control over their work by offering job-seekers a full range of industries and business firms within those industries to choose among, thereby prodding employers to listen to employees complaints" (568).

55   *In 1907 alone, sixty thousand people*   Annual Report of the Bureau of Statistics and Information of Maryland, Bureau of Industrial Statistics, Baltimore, Maryland, 1907.

56   *"life is largely colored by"*   C. Macfie Campbell, M.D., "The Sub-Normal Child: A Study of the Children in a Baltimore School District," *Mental Hygiene* 1, no. 1, (1917): January, 96–147.

56   *"The battlefield of the Somme"*   Mark Reutter, *Making Steel: Sparrows Point and the Rise and Ruin of American Industrial Might* (Urbana: University of Illinois Press, 2004), 121.

57   *"I consider the Bethlehem Gun Plant"*   Lance E. Metz, "A Short History of the Bethlehem Steel Corporation," in Andrew Garn, *Bethlehem Steel* (New York: Princeton Architectural Press, 1999), 20.

57   *"Bethlehem Steel was the first U.S. firm"*   Ibid., 32.

57   *he had coveted the great steelworks*   Reutter, *Making Steel,* 108.

58   *"I worked nights and many Sundays"*   Margaret E. Lindemon, "Gems of Remembrance," Bethlehem Steel Papers, Dundalk–Patapsco Neck Historical Society.

59   *"a Roland Park for the working man"*   "Dundalk Historic District," three-page typed history, Dundalk–Patapsco Neck Historical Society. "It is said that the town was born out of the necessity to provide for those who were working to fight the war against Kaiser Wilhelm. However when the war was over most of the families remained and their decendents are proud to call Dundalk home."

59   *lack of housing was severely hampering*   The report notes that "a conservative estimate of the number of industrial workers required for the operation of various plants now in operation, or about to start work, and located on the eastern side of the Patapsco River between Baltimore and Sparrows Point, is 30,000 men, which would mean a provision, through all agencies, of housing accommodations for some 150,000 people. At the present time, the housing facilities at Sparrows Point are entirely inadequate, so that in the case of this plant alone, which employs at present about 8,000 men, some 5,000 of them have to live in Baltimore city. . . . A majority of the men at the Sparrows Point plant are forced

to pay from 20 to 30 cents a day carfare, and to spend from an hour to two hours on crowded cars each day." Phillip S. Hiss, Dundalk Papers, Dundalk–Patapsco Neck Historical Society.

59 *"What was a bare field"* The Baltimore Evening Sun, July 11, 1918. Dundalk Files, Dundalk–Patapsco Neck Historical Society.

60 *"At no time shall the land"* Deeds, Dundalk–Patapsco Neck Historical Society.

60 *"Residents not only built"* Louis S. Diggs, *From the Meadows to the Point: The Histories of the African American Community in Sparrows Point* (self-published, 2003), 12–13.

62 *munitions workers at a Baltimore factory* Ryon, "Baltimore Workers," 576–77.

62 *"twin evils—schemes to lower pay"* Ibid., 576. "A worker prone to do too much was a social outcast, a 'hog,' 'chaser,' or 'rusher.' Union seniority rules kept employers from giving them preference over other workers."

63 *No such thing happened at Sparrows Point* Reutter, *Making Steel,* 140. Reutter notes that where Frederick Wood set employee compensation on a fixed basis (day rates for laborers, set tonnage rates for skilled workers), Schwab instituted an incentive program that rewarded skilled and semiskilled employees who took on extra work. Laborers were exempt, thus "Schwab's incentive system had the effect of widening the 'spread' between the lowest and best paying jobs at the plant."

63 *"The company was very successful"* Tom Capecci, "Brief History of USWA Local 2610," unpublished.

63 *In 1919 over four million workers* Robert H. Zieger and Gilbert J. Gall, *American Workers, American Unions: The Twentieth Century,* 3rd ed. (Baltimore: Johns Hopkins University Press, 2002), 37.

64 *"I am with you"* Ibid., 39.

64 *"an unacceptable substitute"* Reutter, *Making Steel,* 151.

64 *a year's worth of handwritten minutes* Bethlehem Steel Papers, Baltimore Museum of Industry.

66 *The strike itself sparked violent* Dennis C. Dickerson, *Out of the Crucible: Black Steelworkers in Western Pennsylvania, 1975–1980* (Albany: State University of New York Press, 1986), 88–89.

67 *a postwar depression that crushed* The Baltimore Sun, April 15, 1948. The same thing happened to black steelworkers in western Pennsylvania. "Immediately after the war, shifts to peacetime production put Black laborers out of work throughout the steel region. . . . During the recession of 1920–21 the number of Black laborers in Allegheny County fell from 16,726 to 10,010, a decrease of 40.2 percent. . . . During January 1921, within the space of twelve days, 2,100 Black men, many of them steelworkers, poured into the Provident Rescue Mis-

sion in Pittsburgh in search of employment referrals and material relief." Dickerson, *Out of the Crucible*, 93–94.

67   *"the community is practically bankrupt"*   One-page document (perhaps retyped from newspaper article?) dated July 3, 1921, Dundalk Files, Dundalk–Patapsco Neck Historical Society.

UNITY

69   *"I worked for the Baltimore County Health Department"*   *Reflections: Sparrows Point, MD 1887–1975* (Dundalk, Md.: Dundalk–Patapsco Neck Historical Society, October 1976), 36.

70   *"the silence of the mills"*   Lois S. Myers, Bethlehem Steel Papers, Dundalk–Patapsco Neck Historical Society.

71   *by 1933, over 20 percent*   Jo Ann E. Argersinger, *Toward a New Deal in Baltimore: People and Government in the Great Depression* (Chapel Hill: University of North Carolina Press, 1988), 30–32.

71   *"We've been nearly starving"*   Ibid., 115.

73   *The National Industrial Recovery Act*   Declared unconstitutional by the United States Supreme Court on May 27, 1935, and Section 7a was invalidated. However, on July 5 of that year, Congress passed the National Labor Relations Act. "Many employers, utterly convinced that the Court would strike the new legislation down, continued to fight the unions without restraint," say labor historians Robert H. Zieger and Gilbert J. Gall. However, "when Court approval finally came, the NLRB did indeed prove a vigorous supporter of union goals, and it played an important role in sustaining union gains in the later 1930s." Robert H. Zieger and Gilbert J. Gall, *American Workers, American Unions: The Twentieth Century*, 3rd ed. (Baltimore: Johns Hopkins University Press, 2002), 81.

73   *When Roosevelt's secretary of labor*   "Miss Perkins Visits Mills at Sparrows Point," *The Baltimore Sun*, July 29, 1933; Mark Reutter, *Making Steel: Sparrows Point and the Rise and Ruin of American Industrial Might* (Urbana: University of Illinois Press, 2004), 235.

75   *A flyer distributed by the Socialist Labor Party*   Bethlehem Steel Files, Baltimore Museum of Industry.

75   *"one of the epic confrontations"*   Zieger and Gall, *American Workers, American Unions*, 88.

76   *"Our first task was to banish"*   David Brody, "The Origins of Modern Steel Unionism," in *Forging a Union of Steel: Philip Murray, SWOC, and the United*

Steelworkers, eds. Paul F. Clark, Peter Gottlieb, and Donald Kennedy (Ithaca, N.Y.: ILR Press, 1987), 21–32.

76   *"Company police at Sparrows Point"*   Reutter, *Making Steel*, 260.

77   *It would take an outsider*   "It is important to remember how weakly steel was organized on the eve of the war. Of the major steel producers only U.S. Steel and Jones & Laughlin had signed contracts with SWOC during the 1936–37 labor surge. The other major steel producers remained aggressively anti-union." Mark McCullough, "Consolidating Industrial Citizenship: The USWA at War and Peace, 1939–46," in *Forging a Union of Steel*, 46.

77   *"The greatest enemy of our nation"*   The Reverend John F. Cronin was a Catholic priest and professor of economics at St. Mary's Seminary who actively supported the labor movement. This quote is taken from *Steel Labor* (vol. 6, no. 9, September 25, 1941), which urged steelworkers to vote for SWOC in the coming NLRB election.

78   *A flyer distributed by SWOC*   Bethlehem Steel Files, Baltimore Museum of Industry.

78   *himself a devout Catholic*   Philip Murray was greatly influenced by the social teachings of the church, especially the concept of a just industrial order in Pope Leo XIII's 1891 encyclical *Rerum Novarum*. Melvin Dubofsky, "Labor's Odd Couple: Philip Murray and John L. Lewis," in *Forging a Union of Steel*, 20–21. Murray knew firsthand the power of mine owners and steel companies. He began working at the age of ten in the non-union mines of western Pennsylvania, where "he quickly learned how helpless the individual miner was compared to management. The victim of job inequities and a failed strike, Murray concluded that only a union could protect miners against victimization."

78   *"You need a labor union"*   Cronin, *Steel Labor*, September 25, 1941. For more on Cronin and his support of labor (and fight against communists in Baltimore labor unions), see Kenneth D. Durr, *Behind the Backlash: White Working-Class Politics in Baltimore, 1940–1980* (Chapel Hill: University of North Carolina Press, 2003), 34–41.

81   *"No industry with steel's open shop history"*   David Brody, "The Origins of Modern Steel Unionism," in *Forging a Union of Steel*, 25.

81   *recovery was well under way*   The Baltimore Sun, September 17, 1939.

82   *passing out union cards*   Roderick N. Ryon, "An Ambiguous Legacy: Baltimore Blacks and the CIO, 1936–1941," *Journal of Negro History*, vol. 65, no. 1 (winter 1980): 18–33.

83   *"a dozen or so blacks and ten or twelve whites"*   Ibid.

83   *"Had their vote been against us"*   The Baltimore Afro-American, September 27, 1941.

83 *During* 1941, *over 2.3 million industrial workers* Zieger and Gall, *American Workers, American Unions*, 106.

83 *In most of these strikes* SWOC won 220 out of 393 NLRB elections between 1937 and 1942. In the next two years it won another 462 victories in 535 new elections. Membership in SWOC rose from between 40,000 and 50,000 in October 1936 to 535,000 about a year later, when the total number of workers within the union's jurisdiction was about 800,000. By 1942, the union claimed 660,052 members, though it was the exclusive bargaining agent for only 190,000. Not until the end of World War II did dues-paying membership reach 800,000. In 1946, the union had 853,308 members, of whom 712,308 were paying dues. Lloyd Ulman, *The Government of the Steel Workers' Union* (Berkeley: University of California Press, 1962), 6.

83 *"union contracts that carefully governed"* Zieger and Gall, *American Workers, American Unions*, 111.

LIBERTY

86 *From 1942 to 1944, the blast furnaces* John B. Lovis, *The Blast Furnaces of Sparrows Point: One Hundred Years of Ironmaking on Chesapeake Bay* (Easton, Pa.: Canal History and Technology Press, 2005), 30.

87 *"turned businessmen, insurance, automobile"* *The Baltimore Sun*, May 28, 1943.

87 *sustaining attack by aircraft* Earl A. Shelsby Jr., "Last of First Liberty Ship," *The Baltimore Sun*, October 26, 1958.

88 *"Every state is represented"* *The Baltimore Sun*, April 5, 1944.

89 *"People come from everywhere"* During the war, a quarter of a million out-of-state workers poured into the Baltimore metropolitan area, and approximately 45 percent of them settled there permanently. "45% of Out of State Workers Remain," *The Baltimore Sun*, September 1, 1946.

The influx of new workers created a housing and sanitation crisis. "Due to the migration in the defense industries the housing situation in Eastern Baltimore and Baltimore county is very acute. In the Dundalk area, approximately one thousand additional families have moved in that area. The sewage system has never been enlarged to take care of these families. At the present time, a small pumping system pumps the outfall into a cesspool approximately 16 ft. in diameter and 12 ft. deep which is much too small. This cesspool is open on top; when the wind is blowing from the cesspool towards the homes, the stench is so strong that it is almost impossible to endure it. The drain from many of the homes runs into the alleys and streets and turns them into sewers." Frank J. Bender, Maryland regional director, CIO, *Problems Created by Migration to Baltimore from the Labor Viewpoint*, report prepared for the House Committee Investigating National Defense Migration, Bethlehem Steel Papers, Enoch Pratt Free Library, Baltimore.

89   *on June 10, 1943*   My grandmother used the 1941 date book as a kind of all-purpose almanac and address book for years, recording not only the births of all of her grandchildren but also recipes, telephone numbers, and other important information.

90   *greatly increased racial tensions*   Roderick N. Ryon, "When Baltimore's War Effort Tripped over Race," *The Baltimore Sun*, August 11, 1983. See also Kenneth D. Durr, *Behind the Backlash: White Working-Class Politics in Baltimore, 1940–1980* (Chapel Hill: University of North Carolina Press, 2003), 26–27.

93   *CIO unions aggressively recruited*   Roderick N. Ryon, "An Ambiguous Legacy: Baltimore Blacks and the CIO, 1936–1941," *Journal of Negro History*, vol. 65, no. 1 (winter 1980): 18–33.

95   *"Our ultimate aim"*   Preamble to the charter of United Steelworkers of America Local 2609, Kotelchuck Papers, Baltimore Museum of Industry.

95   *laborers at Sparrows Point*   Data from wage tables in original United Steelworkers of America contracts, Kotelchuck Papers, Baltimore Museum of Industry.

95   *The United Steelworkers of America voted to strike*   "Steel Mills Here Stop Production," *The Baltimore Sun*, January 22, 1946. "Spokesmen for the Sparrows Point steel mill, largest tidewater plant in the world, said buildings were shut down at midnight and that there is no production at all underway now."

96   *The contract ratified by Bethlehem Steel*   Explaining the reasons for the 1946 strike, the *New York Times* labor reporter Abe Raskin pointed out that "the expectation was that there would be tremendous unemployment after the war and a tremendous loss of purchasing power. The trade union movement viewed itself as having two big challenges: to prove that it was not just a puppet of the War Labor Board that would collapse if it had to stand on its own, and two, to maintain the purchasing power of its members." "Comments," in *Forging a Union of Steel: Philip Murray, SWOC, and the United Steelworkers*, eds. Paul F. Clark, Peter Gottlieb, and Donald Kennedy (Ithaca, N.Y.: ILR Press, 1987), 116.

96   *eliminating wage inequities*   "The earnings of steelworkers varied enormously depending on their skills, the city in which they lived, and even the corporation for which they worked." Wages were much lower in the South, and variation across occupations in the same mill sometimes approached 400 percent differentials between the highest- and lowest-paid workers. "One of the union's greatest accomplishments in this period was to narrow this internal gap, which was so

large as to be divisive." Mark McCullough, "Consolidating Industrial Citizenship: The USWA at War and Peace, 1939–46," in *Forging a Union of Steel*,
65–66.

BOOM

98   *POW bracelets*   In the last years of the Vietnam War, some students at my
Catholic elementary/middle school in Dundalk wore nickel-plated bracelets
printed with the name, rank, and date of loss or captured or missing American
soldiers. Many years later, my brother and I looked up the names of our soldiers
at the Vietnam Veterans Memorial in Washington, D.C. One of our soldiers was
listed as missing, the other as dead. That was the extent of our involvement with
Vietnam; I was twelve when Saigon fell, and I didn't know anyone who either
fought or protested the war. But Dundalk remains a place where some homes fly
the iconic black and white flag depicting the bowed head of a POW encircled by
the legend REMEMBER. A trailer displaying photos of every one of the 1046 Mary-
landers lost in the war is an enduring presence at the Dundalk Fourth of July
parade and Heritage Fair, where the Vietnam Veterans of America do a brisk
business selling T-shirts that proclaim MY DAD [OR GRANDDAD] IS A VIETNAM VET-
ERAN AND I'M DAMN PROUD OF HIM.

99   *Take the penguins*   "What's Up with the Eastpoint Penguins," *The Dundalk
Eagle*, November 21, 2006. As Harry Young pointed out, "Dundalk was a hell of
a place to grow up, but you had to live here to understand it."

100   *"The need for skilled workers"*   Carroll E. Williams, *The Baltimore Sun*, May 9,
1951. "Demand for workers is especially concentrated in shipyards, steel mills,
foundries, heavy and light."

100   *"If you want a good man"*   Rea Murdock, "Jobs Plentiful, Workers Scarce," *The
Baltimore News-American*, September 25, 1966.

106   *chief forelady, Elizabeth Alexander*   For more on Alexander and the tin floppers,
see Mark Reutter, *Making Steel: Sparrows Point and the Rise and Ruin of American
Industrial Might* (Urbana: University of Illinois Press, 2004), 362–78. Also "Elizabeth Alexander: Dundalk's Lady of Steel," *The Dundalk Eagle*, September 25,
1986. Alexander started working at Sparrows Point in 1925. During World
War II, she supervised over one thousand women; after the war, the number
decreased to five hundred. "Mrs. Alexander broke up knife fights, counseled
drinking employees, organized banquets and plays and bought the women uniforms." She retired after forty years of service.

107   *"asked me if I minded"*   "Both steel companies and the USW adopted the rheto-

ric of racial fairness and equal employment opportunity; they pointed to a hand-
ful of blacks who held responsible positions in the mills and in company and
union offices. Black steelworkers in the rank and file knew a different reality."
Dennis C. Dickerson, *Out of the Crucible: Black Steelworkers in Western Pennsylvania 1875–1980* (Albany: State University of New York Press, 1986), 212.

110   *just about everyone in Baltimore*   In 1958, approximately forty-one thousand people in the Baltimore metropolitan area were directly employed by Bethlehem,
either at Sparrows Point or in one of Bethlehem's other facilities in the area. By
1968, that number had declined to thirty-six thousand, including the Baltimore
district sales office, Buffalo Tank Division, and three shipbuilding and ship
repair shops.

112   *Strikes and layoffs hit them hard*   USW called nationwide strikes in 1946, 1949,
1952, 1955, 1956, and 1959. The longest of these, lasting 116 days, was in 1959.
"The average Baltimore steelworker lost as much as $2000 in wages during the
116-day strike. . . . It will take between 4½ and 5 years before the workers will
recoup all of the wages lost during the July 15–November 6 walkout." To settle
the strike, the company agreed to pay the full cost of group life insurance and
Blue Cross Blue Shield coverage, which had previously been paid on a fifty-fifty
basis. "The men struck to protect their hard-fought gains in working conditions,
seniority and incentives. They weren't about to let them go down the drain, and
their union with it, no matter what the cost," said Edwin Abbott, a USW district
representative. *The Baltimore Sun*, January 18, 1960.

113   *In the immediate aftermath of World War II*   Robert H. Zieger and Gilbert J.
Gall, *American Workers, American Unions: The Twentieth Century*, 3rd ed. (Baltimore: Johns Hopkins University Press, 2002), 144.

115   *African American men from Baltimore*   From 1940 to 1950, the percentage of
African American men working as steelworkers in Maryland rose from 16.3 per-
cent to 27.5 percent of the workforce. Only 16.7 percent were in skilled posi-
tions, however, versus 42 percent of whites. Mark McCullough, "Consolidating
Industrial Citizenship: The USWA at War and Peace, 1939–46," in *Forging a
Union of Steel: Philip Murray, SWOC, and the United Steelworkers*, eds. Paul F.
Clark, Peter Gottlieb, and Donald Kennedy (Ithaca, N.Y.: ILR Press, 1987),
58–59.

118   *to get a black elected*   The absence of black officers in Steelworkers locals and in
the International (headquarters in Pittsburgh) was an ongoing problem.
"Despite the presence of 225,000 Blacks in the 1,000,000 member union, non-
Whites held a little more than twenty positions out of 800 in the early 1960s."
Dickerson, *Out of the Crucible*, 224.

123   *"Long hours and changing shifts"*   Karen Olson, *Wives of Steel: Voices of Women*

from the Sparrows Point Steelmaking Communities (University Park: Pennsylvania State University Press, 2005), 80.

SMOKE

126   *On a sunny May morning*   "2 Killed in Explosion at Bethlehem Plant; 22 Others Are Injured," *The Baltimore Sun*, May 4, 1968.

127   *a devil's gift*   As early as 1959, Bethlehem Steel was ordered by the State of Maryland to draft a plan "in the immediate future" to stop water pollution in and around Sparrows Point. "The commission felt that the time had come for a firm plan and positive action by Bethlehem, including a specific proposal for the treatment of contaminated waste water discharge and the correction of water pollution conditions now existing adjacent to the Sparrows Point plant. . . . Preliminary estimates indicate that a large expenditure of money will be required." "Bethlehem Steel Is Asked for Anti-pollution Action," *The Baltimore Sun*, June 26, 1959.

127   *Steelworkers' salaries kept cash registers*   According to the American Iron and Steel Institute, for every one job in the steel industry, seven additional jobs are created in other economic sectors, such as raw materials, transportation, and services. *Steel and the National Defense*, American Iron and Steel Institute, Specialty Steel Industry of North America, Steel Manufacturers Association, and United Steelworkers, January 2007, www.steel.org.

127   *progress always has a price*   Articles in *The Baltimore Sun* throughout the 1970s report on a seemingly never-ending string of fines against Bethlehem for pollution and health and safety violations. For example: "Study Finds 25 Steelworkers at Bethlehem Exposed to Lead," July 29, 1974; "Bethlehem Failed to Report 65 Violations of the Water Pollution Standards During the First 6 Months of the Year," September 24, 1975; "State Water Officials Ask Court Action as Bethlehem Misses Clean-up Deadline," July 2, 1977; "Bethlehem Gas Victim Had Been Ill," October 25, 1978; "Bethlehem Cited, Fined by the U.S. for 10 Violations," December 14, 1978; "Bethlehem Appeals Smoke Fine," January 4, 1979; "9th Death in 13 Months Spurs Bethlehem Steel Probe," April 13, 1979.

130   *Prior to the Great Depression, nearly nine thousand people*   Jeanne B. Sargent, "Slow Death of a Company Town," *Baltimore* magazine, August 1973.

131   *many families resisted moving*   Ibid. "An elderly widow paying $35 for a six room house cannot comprehend having to move to a six room walkup somewhere else at $125 a month."

131 *"It was hard to watch"* Gwendolyn Zimmerman, "Sparrows Point," *The Dundalk Eagle*, July 15, 1999.

134 *The first lawsuit charging* Robert Benjamin, "Ex-workers Sue Bethlehem over Asbestos Diseases," *The Baltimore Sun*, August 23, 1981.

134 *Two years later* Allegra Bennett, "Bethlehem Workers Sue over Asbestos," *The Baltimore Sun*, July 14, 1983.

136 *The son of a Highlandtown tavern owner* Peter G. Angelos was born in Pittsburgh on July 4, 1929. His father was an immigrant steelworker there and struggled during the Depression. The family moved to Baltimore when Peter was eleven, and his father opened a bar and restaurant popular with steelworkers. Angelos built his law practice in the 1960s representing labor unions. He had an office in USW 2610 on Dundalk Avenue The asbestos settlement netted him a reported $250 million.

137 *But the big money dried up* By the early nineties more than half of the largest asbestos manufacturers in the country had filed for bankruptcy. Asbestos litigation was the longest, most expensive mass tort in U.S. history, with more than six thousand defendants and six hundred thousand claimants. The total cost of litigation is over $200 billion. Stephen J. Carroll, Deborah R. Hensler, Jennifer Gross, et al., "Asbestos Litigation," RAND Corporation Monograph, 2005.

138 *A series of reports published* Joseph F. Collins and Carol K. Redmond, "The Use of Retirees to Evaluate Occupational Hazards," *Journal of Occupational Medicine* 20, no. 4 (April 1978): 2601–2606; Sati Mazumundar, Trudy Lerer, and Carol K. Redmond, "Long-term Mortality Study of Steelworkers," *Journal of Occupational Medicine* 17, no. 12 (December 1975): 751–55; J. William Lloyd, Frank E. Lundin, Jr., Carol K. Redmond, and Patricia B. Geiser, "Long-term Mortality Study of Steelworkers IV: Mortality by Work Area," *Journal of Occupational Medicine* 12, no. 5 (May 1970): 151–57; Sati Mazumundar, Trudy Lerer, and Carol K. Redmond, "Long-term Mortality Study of Steelworkers IX: Mortality Patterns Among Sheet and Tin Mill Workers," *Journal of Occupational Medicine* 17, no. 12 (December 1975): 751–55.

138 *deaths among its shipyard and steel plant workers* Thomas B. Edsall, "Bethlehem Cancer Study Results Queried," *The Baltimore Sun*, May 11, 1978.

139 *NIOSH analysts found numerous* Ibid.

140 *"Pollution is a dirty word. So is unemployment"* *Bethlehem Review*, April 1977.

140 *"Bethlehem's Sparrows Point complex"* Mark Bowden, "Inside Sparrows Point," *The Baltimore News-American*, May 1979.

140 *a private 3000 acre* Over the years, acreage was added by acquiring privately

owned tracts of land (1917) and by filling in waterways and building out from the shoreline.

140   *"one of the four or five worst"*   Frederic B. Hill, "Bethlehem Steel Ranked in Top Five Air, Water Polluters," *The Baltimore Sun*, May 22, 1973.

141   *Bethlehem had worked out a deal*   Michael K. Burns, "Point's Pollutant Limit Eased," *The Baltimore Sun*, December 16, 1973.

141   *This permit approved*   Edsall, "Bethlehem Cancer Study."

141   *"The county office of Permits and Licenses"*   Richard Ben Cramer, "County Inspects Bethlehem Infrequently with Kid Gloves," *The Baltimore Sun*, November 18, 1973.

142   *the Council on Economic Priorities termed*   Allegra Bennett, "Sparrows Point Ranked High in Cutting Pollution," *The Baltimore Sun*, October 3, 1977.

142   *Two men died of*   David Ahearn, "9th Death in 13 Months Spurs Bethlehem Steel Probe," *The Baltimore News-American*, April 13, 1979. "Since March 1978, 9 employees have died of carbon monoxide poisoning, falling through temporary flooring, heat stroke, machinery accidents, drowning, and being scalded with hot water."

142   *one of the men who was killed*   "Robert J. Carter had worked as a blastman for only two weeks and had received inadequate training, according to three veteran blastmen. Several days before he died he was exposed to the gas in a separate incident that required medical treatment." Steven N. Luxenburg and Mark Reutter, "Beth Gas Victim Had Been Ill," *The Baltimore Sun*, October 25, 1978. Carter was a father of four.

143   *aging equipment*   The company's view is explicitly stated in a *Beth Review* article: "We believe that old facilities with a limited life should be permitted to operate under less stringent regulations for a limited period if air quality standards can be met in the area in which the facilities are located." *Bethlehem Review*, April 1977.

143   *"The job ahead is a horribly costly one"*   "The environmentalists do not consider the cost of their demands against possible benefits to be obtained." James M. Reeves, "A Customer Looks at Steel's Problems," *Bethlehem Review*, 1978 (2).

144   *"pollution is not all man-made"*   *Bethlehem Review*, April 1977.

JUSTICE

146   *After being expelled*   Kenneth Lavon Johnson, "A Stand for Justice," Opinion-Commentary, *The Baltimore Sun*, May 13, 2004. This article discusses Johnson's participation in the 1960 lunch-counter action in Baton Rouge, Louisiana, his

subsequent expulsion from Southern University School of Law, and the 1961 Supreme Court decision on the case. The article was published after Southern awarded honorary doctor of law degrees to the expelled students. "Being expelled was one of the best things that ever happened to me," Johnson wrote. "I got to go to Howard and be taught by the masters of constitutional–civil rights law, which indelibly influenced my career."

147 *using the unit seniority system*   The system operated throughout the industry, not just on Sparrows Point. "Although membership in the Steelworkers union brought Blacks the safeguard of seniority, that occupational protection was limited. They had, in most cases, departmental seniority. Since Black steelworkers usually labored in segregated departments, their seniority became useless if they wished transfers to better-paying departments." Dennis C. Dickerson, *Out of the Crucible: Black Steelworkers in Western Pennsylvania, 1875–1980* (Albany: State University of New York Press, 1986), 244.

149 *CORE officially became involved*   Francis Brown told Shindel that he "was talking in the [Sparrows Point] locker room and an employee by the name of Francis Bernard Jones said: 'You have plenty of mouth but not action. I just sat down in the lunchroom. They will not serve blacks. I'm going back tomorrow. Are you going with me?' I said: 'Yes.'" Calling Jones "the steelworkers' Rosa Parks," Brown said that he and Jones went to the union hall to talk to the president of their local, who "told us that if we continued that kind of action, they would take no responsibility for our jobs. We got really angry," Brown said, "and headed straight down to the Congress of Racial Equality on Gay and Eden St." Len Shindel, "They Acted Like Men and Were Treated Like Men," Opinion-Commentary, *The Baltimore Sun*, February 17, 1992.

150 *"Once CORE came in"*   Francis Brown founded the Pharaoh's Social Club on Collington Avenue. Pharaoh's became a meeting place not just for steelworkers but for other Baltimoreans active in the civil rights struggle. Many steelworkers repaid CORE's assistance by joining the organization and supporting its activities. Ibid.

150 *One memorable day*   I have not been able to establish the exact date of the protest at Bethlehem Steel headquarters. Douglas recalled it as May 1968, whereas in Burleigh and Ageloff's account, the protest happened in late 1966. But their stories match in all other respects, down to the doors being locked against the protesters.

152 *more than $50 million worth of federal contracts*   "[Department of Defense] sanctions if invoked could include the suspensions or termination of Defense contracts." "Bethlehem Bias Ruling in April," *The Baltimore Evening Sun*, March 8, 1967. Pete Selhorst recalled manufacturing munitions on the Point at the time.

"During the war at Vietnam, the product would say 'bomb fins.' We would be making the coils. We knew what it was going to be used for. We knew where everything was going."

152 *The ruling that followed the investigation* William F. Schmick III, "Steel Plant Segregation Ban Ordered," *The Baltimore Sun*, February 3, 1967. See also Dickerson, *Out of the Crucible*, 243. "In 1967 the Office of Contract Compliance accused the Sparrows Point plant of Bethlehem Steel of discrimination against Black workers. A federal district court decision in 1973 mandated plant seniority which permitted Black workers to transfer to jobs anywhere within the facility without loss of seniority." Three years earlier, similar rulings at Bethlehem's Lackawanna plant and U.S. Steel's Birmingham facilities mandated replacement of unit seniority with plant seniority.

153 *Douglas and his group continued* Letter from W. G. Smith, general manager, Bethlehem Steel Corp., to Lee Douglas and Benjamin Hamlin, June 3, 1968. Private correspondence, courtesy of Lee Douglas.

153 *opportunities for promotion and leadership* Antero Pietela, "Steelworkers Bias Group: Struggle Continues," *The Baltimore Sun*, April 23, 1974.

154 *"The tone of civil rights"* "The Johnson Administration in the 1960s, like the Roosevelt Administration in the 1940s, was especially sympathetic to the aspirations of black steelworkers. Strengthened by the Civil Rights Act of 1964 and Executive Order 11246 of 1965 which authorized the secretary of labor to supervise and coordinate nondiscriminatory employment activities of contractors using federal funds, the Johnson Administration prodded steel companies and the steelworkers union to equalize educational opportunities for Black employees. Federal laws, especially Title VII of the 1964 Civil Rights Act, provided the Justice Department during the Johnson and Nixon presidencies with enough legal ammunition to sue steel firms and local steel unions for their alleged discriminatory treatment of Black laborers." Dickerson, *Out of the Crucible*, 243–44.

154 *"anarchy, rioting, and even civil"* Kenneth D. Durr, *Behind the Backlash: White Working-Class Politics in Baltimore, 1940–1980* (Chapel Hill: University of North Carolina Press, 2003), 145.

155 *In Turner Station, older men* "In 1968 when the riots were going on in Baltimore City, and people were running amok in the city, there was a group of fathers and men walking through Turner Station, saying to the youth that you won't go into the city in the riots. They stood in the streets and stopped the young people from Turner Station from going into Baltimore to participate in the riots. This said to me that this is the strength of the community. It says that even if the entire world goes crazy, you will be righteous. This type of strength

has a profound effect on the youth of the community." "Remembrance of Mr. Dunbar Brooks," in Louis S. Diggs, *From the Meadows to the Point: The Histories of the African American Community in Sparrows Point* (self-published, 2003), 151.

156   *steelworkers were paid approximately*   Herbert Hill, "Race and the Steelworkers Union: White Privilege and Black Struggles," *New Politics* 8, no. 4 (winter, 2002): 174–207.

158   *"filthy hazardous working conditions"*   Original document, courtesy of Len Shindel.

159   *"the militant leadership of"*   Original document, courtesy of Len Shindel.

The wildcat strike in the coke ovens meets the definition of rank-and-file insurgency, a trend visible not only in Baltimore but also in USW locals around the country at the time. "In the first half of the 1970s, steelworker disenchantment over wages, working conditions, and union leader responsiveness to the membership continued to increase." Philip W. Nyden, *Steelworkers Rank-and-File: The Political Economy of a Union Reform Movement* (New York: Praeger, 1984), 4.

On Sparrows Point, the insurgency group produced a newsletter, *Steel Unity*. A 1974 issue (fragment, undated) directly addressed the question of the group's allegiances: "A lot of people have asked if Steel Unity is a communist group. No, it is not. It is open to anyone who is willing to fight against the company and for the working class. Most of the people who work with us are not communists. Some of us are."

160   *with plant service the key factor*   The consent decree arguably headed off what might have become an even more volatile situation at Sparrows Point. The January 1973 order by the secretary of labor wiping out unit seniority had awarded "superseniority" to 5,405 employees, "who could request transfers within 90 days. At that point, as one black worker remembered it, 'all hell broke loose.'" Not all of those awarded and benefiting from superseniority were black; a demonstration outside the Steelworkers hall that November demanding that the International pursue grievances filed in the wake of the decree included some white union members. The consent decree signed in April of the next year ended superseniority and bumping. Durr, *Behind the Backlash*, 185–86.

RECKONING

173   *rivals and brothers*   Peter Selhorst, who was a member of both locals at various times, said that "2609 had much clearer political leadership, and for better or worse, it seemed like a little more democratic process. It was run by a caucus and

was a more interesting local to be in, in terms of being politically active and holding a lot of meetings and discussions. In 2610 they wouldn't let the people they didn't like talk."

174   *insatiable hunger for "fringe benefits"*   A 1971 *Bethlehem Review* article described vacations, payments under savings and vacation plans, holidays, life insurance and death benefits, sickness and accident disability benefits, hospital and physician services, pensions, Social Security benefits, and federal and state employment compensation as "payments for time *not worked*"—compared with wages and salaries "paid for *time worked*" (emphasis in original). Noting that total wages and salaries in 1971 came to $955,168,000 and benefits to $363,416,000, the article stated that "that kind of money can hardly be called a 'fringe.' . . . On the average, about $3000 was paid out, or set aside, during 1971 for each Bethlehem employee for those benefits."

175   *From 1945 to 1978*   Clarence D. Long, "Sparrows Point and the Export of Jobs," Opinion-Commentary, *The Baltimore Sun*, September 22, 1978. "At Bethlehem Steel's Sparrows Point plant, annual steel production has declined by nearly 3 million tons since 1970 and 4500 workers there have been fired, laid off or have had their hours reduced because of import competition," Long wrote. "In the U.S. as a whole, steel imports rose between 1976 and 1977 by 35%, to an all-time record of 19 million tons. Some steel plants in Ohio, Pennsylvania, and New York have closed even though U.S. demand for steel in 1977 was the third highest of any year in history."

175   *the 116-day strike of 1959*   The largest single strike in U.S. history, involving 519,000 steelworkers and 250,000 workers in other industries. John P. Hoerr, *And the Wolf Finally Came: The Decline of the American Steel Industry* (Pittsburgh: University of Pittsburgh Press, 1988), 101.

176   *Bethlehem management waited far too long*   For a discussion of Bethlehem's decision not to adopt continuous casting in the early sixties despite a successful pilot program, see John Strohmeyer, *Crisis in Bethlehem: Big Steel's Struggle to Survive* (Pittsburgh: University of Pittsburgh Press, 1986), 60–62. Bethlehem's failure to adopt continuous casting early on was shared by other big American integrated steel producers. "By 1981, only 21.1 percent of the steel tonnage in the United States was made by continuous casting, while Japan was using the more efficient process to produce 70.7 percent of its output. The European countries were manufacturing 45.1 percent by continuous casting; and even Canada, with 32.2 percent, had a better output than the United States."

178   *"We were making evolutionary changes"*   Ibid., 62.

178   *"Bethlehem Steel just wasn't interested"*   Ibid., 59.

179   *"you had a lot of featherbedding"*   A problem shared with other plants. "We exag-

gerated the labor force to make sure there was always somebody there to fill a job to keep the operations going. And we exaggerated the maintenance forces to make sure there was always somebody there to fix the machines." Ibid., 68.

181   *Increased automation*   "Investment in automation will mean unemployment for thousands of steelworkers at Sparrows Point. Bethlehem Steel Corporation privately plans to cut the workforce to 9,000 from the present 18,000. . . . Other steel mills and auto plants are not hiring; they are laying off too. These workers have nowhere to go." Alan Fisher, "Workers Pay the Price but Are Denied the Fruits," *The Baltimore Sun*, September 30, 1981.

181   *"you don't do my work"*   Not just an informal agreement but part of the union contract. Clause 2B (or the past practices clause), written into the 1956 contract, stipulated that established labor practices cannot be changed unless there is a change in underlying conditions, barring companies from combining jobs to reduce the number of workers needed to complete a task. Companies tried to modify this clause in 1959 and lost the fight. Just as delayed modernization was the primary failing of the companies, the refusal to compromise on the issue of past practices was the most damaging mistake made by the union in terms of keeping American steelmakers competitive.

182   *slapped BUY AMERICAN stickers*   In 1978, eight states enacted laws or adopted regulations extending preference in public works projects to steel produced or fabricated in the United States. The Congressional Steel Caucus unsuccessfully lobbied for national legislation in the Ninety-sixth Congress. The 19.3 million tons of foreign-made steel sold in the United States in 1977 "stole American steelworker jobs. They stole American steel companies' chance to make that steel and to make a profit doing it." *Bethlehem Review*, 1978 (4).

183   *"A return of 4.7 percent"*   *Bethlehem Review*, December 1972.

185   *"was not a good year"*   *Bethlehem Review*, March 1973. "Though the general market for steel picked up in the latter part of the year, the demand for structural steel shapes, plates, reinforcing bars, and other steels used by the construction and machine-tool building industries lagged well behind the general economy. Bethlehem's product mix is weighted in favor of these construction steels, so we did not benefit as much as some other companies from the general upswing."

185   *At the close of the year*   *Bethlehem Review*, December 1973.

185   *"dismally low production"*   *Bethlehem Review*, March 1976. "Depressed orders for steel were also reflected in the number of employees on the job. During 1975, the average monthly number of employees working at all Bethlehem operations fell to 113,000, down from 122,000 the year before."

185   *"Are buyers willing to pay"*   "Our Side of the Price Increase," *Bethlehem Review*, December 1976.

186   *Foreign steelmakers were the major target*   "Europeans have an advantage of about $20 a ton and the Japanese about $40 a ton," stated a *Bethlehem Review* article describing voluntary import agreements adopted by Japanese, British, and other European steelmakers in 1972. "We better be better." *Bethlehem Review,* June 1972. By 1978, when a record 21.1 million tons of foreign imports were shipped, "about 33 percent (seven million tons) of the imported steel came here from the small, developing countries of the world and Canada." *Bethlehem Review,* 1979 (1).

186   *"Why can foreign steel be shipped"*   *Bethlehem Review,* June 1977.

186   *"Simply because our foreign competitors"*   In an interview with *U.S. News and World Report,* Lewis Foy sought to explain why Bethlehem had sustained third-quarter losses of nearly half a billion dollars in 1977. Apart from the high cost of energy and environmental cleanup, he said, "the import situation has taken all of the integrity out of the market. All of the foreign countries that built steel mills since World War II find themselves with tremendous excess capacity. The majority of these facilities are either government owned or government subsidized in some way."

     Quotas on foreign steel would not solve the problem, he said. "Quotas are hard to police. That is why we are taking a firm but basically simple position: that the Government enforce the 1974 Trade Act, which says that commodities cannot be dumped in the U.S. at a price that is either below the home-market price or below the foreigners' cost of production." Interview reprinted in *Bethlehem Review,* 1977 (4).

187   *"soft, pompous, dull"*   Msgr. Charles Owen Rice, "United Steelworkers in Struggle," *The Pittsburgh Press,* August 13, 1976.

187   *Ed Sadlowski was a populist*   "A veteran of 20 years and a few days in the USW and steeped in the history of the labor movement, Sadlowski makes his major appeals to those seeking a return to the basic principles of trade unionism and to those wanting new leadership." Ira Fine, "Sadlowski Dawning on USW," *The Pittsburgh Press,* September 19, 1976.

187   *"no man will have to be subjected"*   E. Kelley, "Interview with Ed Sadlowski," *Penthouse,* January 1977.

188   *prohibited a nationwide steel strike*   The ENA also contained the first local right-to-strike clause. "While there would be no industrywide strike, the ENA expressly granted local unions the right to strike individual plants over strictly local matters. These included such issues as wash-up and relief time on the job, the condition of locker rooms and parking lots, and other items that had long been festering in the plants. The locals had never had authority to strike over

these matters. Over the next several years, many locals would discover that this new-found strike ability was far more limited than it first appeared. But it helped win approval of the ENA." Hoerr, *And the Wolf*, 112.

188 "*the most incredible money-making machine*" Ibid., 113.

188 "*COLA alone contributed*" Ibid., 114.

189 "*Management gave up too much*" Ibid., 115. Philip Nyden notes that "the ENA was touted as a way of stopping the encroachment of imports onto the American market, and thereby a method for saving American steelworkers' jobs. The argument was that foreign steel producers were likely to get a foothold in the American market during a strike-produced shortage. The growth of imports after the 1959 strike was cited as evidence." The ENA functioned as both "a political pacifier and a red herring." Philip W. Nyden, *Steelworkers Rank-and-File: The Political Economy of a Union Reform Movement* (New York: Praeger, 1984), 62.

189 *Sadlowski's Time for a Change slate* "Sadlowski received 43.1% of the 578,142 votes cast. The Fight Back candidates won majorities in ten of the twenty-five districts. Given the campaign's focus on basic steelworkers in the industrial belt running from the Northeast through the Midwest, it was not surprising that all of the districts won by Sadlowski were in this area. He received the larger share of votes surrounding large industrial cities containing large basic steel plants— Baltimore, Pittsburgh, Youngstown, Cleveland, Detroit, Chicago, and Milwaukee." Ibid., 89.

190 *the "giveback" contracts of 1983 and 1986* For a discussion of the economic and political climate that led to concessions, see Hoerr, *And the Wolf*, 59–70 and 333–60. At the September 1982 Steelworkers convention in Atlantic City, "McBride made no attempt . . . to mask his belief that the union must reduce labor costs in the steel industry. 'Our successes,' he said at a news conference on September 21, referring to USW contracts, 'have created some problems. [The steel companies are] not playing any games. They're in serious trouble'" (337). The rank and file rejected this interpretation, Hoerr notes. "One of the more militant local presidents, David Sullivan, president of Local 6787 at Bethlehem's Burns Harbor plant, made this point. Steel's financial troubles, he said, came about because of Reaganomics, changes in the world economy, and the tight monetary policy of 'greedy bankers' and the Federal Reserve. Concessions had not saved jobs in other industries. Instead, they had undermined the general principles of unionism" (353).

This perspective was shared by many on Sparrows Point. "I remember the international union coming in and saying, 'Lookit, we need to take concessions, and we need to set up committees where we start to work better,' and they were just thrown out," Len Shindel told me. "They were thrown out here. They were thrown out in Burns Harbor. Looking back, they had some validity to what they were saying, but they came off as such stooges for the company that people just rejected them. These were guys who were getting ready to retire, so at that point they were in their sixties, in the eighties, and we were just not listening to them. In retrospect, if it had been done differently, if people had felt like they could have set up joint committees and retained some strength, as we tried to do later, there might have been better outcomes."

191   *"When business picks up"* "Trimmed Down as a Way of Life," *Bethlehem Review*, 1983 (3).

191   *Despite the deep cuts* "1985: Another Year of Losses," *Bethlehem Review*, 1986 (1). This was the issue of the *Review* that announced Trautlein's departure as CEO. He was succeeded by Walt Williams, a 1951 graduate of Bethlehem's Loop Course who had spent three decades with the company. Williams "was a straight-talking, roll-up-your-sleeves engineer who spent virtually all of his career in operations or shipbuilding" and stressed labor-management cooperation and more fluid communication as the key to restoring profitability. "While we cannot directly control market forces or government policies, there is much more we can do internally, working with each other, to greatly improve our quality, service and on-time deliveries," he said in an interview. "In the eyes of workers, he was the anti-Trautlein." "Forging America: The Story of Bethlehem Steel," *The Morning Call, Allentown, Pennsylvania*, December 2003, special issue, 103.

192   *an 11 percent pay raise* Mark Reutter, *Making Steel: Sparrows Point and the Rise and Ruin of American Industrial Might* (Urbana: University of Illinois Press, 2004), 437.

195   *"Do your own job"* Original flyer, Job Protection Committee, courtesy of Len Shindel.

196   *membership at Local 2610 plummeted* Tom Capecci, "A Brief History of Local 2610," unpublished.

200   *Drug abuse and alcoholism became* Bethlehem began its alcoholism program in 1965. A 1971 article in *Bethlehem Review* profiled Lawrence T. Smyth, M.D., medical director of the Johnstown plant before becoming medical director of the corporation, who was a recovering alcoholic himself. Smyth noted that treating alcoholism among the workforce required "a team approach" that included recovering alcoholics in the various plants "to give hope to the alcoholic." "Teamwork Is the Answer to Alcoholism," *Bethlehem Review*, June 1971.

201   *"It was a hushed"* "The Pete Ross Story: A Celebration of Life over Death," *Sparrows Point Spirit*, 1988 (4).

LEGACIES

203   *owes much of its distinctive character*   The Morning Call, 39. "The Bethlehem beam, as it was sometimes called, used a wider flange to provide strength so that architects and builders could reach into the heavens. Builders could move columns farther apart, allowing them to use less steel and build higher without rivets or angles."

204   *the Port Authority of New York and New Jersey filed*   "The court suit never came to trial, but Bethlehem lost what it thought would be a whopping contract. . . . Bethlehem could not recover the estimated $500,000 spent on engineering and estimating work that went into preparing the bid. Further, its engineers had substantial input into the design of the twin towers, now a Manhattan landmark, but did not receive a smidgen of credit. Robert Linn, the Port Authority's deputy director for physical facilities, concedes that many of the new design concepts were tested with Bethlehem experts before being adopted." John Strohmeyer, *Crisis in Bethlehem: Big Steel's Struggle to Survive* (Pittsburgh: University of Pittsburgh Press, 1986), 114–15.

204   *The economic upheaval that followed*   "Bethlehem Steel Corp. filed for Chapter 11 bankruptcy court protection from creditors Monday, saying that cost-cutting efforts could not make up for the impact of cheap steel imports coupled with a slowing U.S. economy. The company said its annual revenue has fallen by $1.3 billion since 1998 due to the impact of imports and reduced demand for steel products, and that the Sept. 11 terrorist attack has worsened its short-term outlook due to the expected drop in demand for autos, appliances, and new homes." Chris Isidore, "Bethlehem Steel in Chapter 11," CNN Money, October 15, 2001, http://money.cnn./com/.

204   *a few years' reprieve*   "Bethlehem's fleeting resurgence also was the result of a strong national economy and the misfortunes of its competitors. . . . What government trade quotas and tariffs couldn't do, a strong economy and weak dollar did almost overnight. Imports that made up 26 percent of the steel consumption throughout the mid-1980s plummeted to under 18 percent in the late 1980s and early '90s. Steel prices spiked by 10 percent, and Bethlehem was profitable once again. Between 1987 and 1990 the company recorded $380 million in profits, including a record $403 million in 1988." *The Morning Call*, 103.

204   *Their efforts restored the Point*   "One plant dramatically improved its operational performance in 1987, and it was Sparrows Point. The plant turned around by focusing on producing higher product quality, lowering costs and enjoying higher volume and price realization. A total team effort was evident with this improved performance, and the plant's results climbed steadily during the

year, resulting in a tremendous comeback to a near break-even financial performance and positioning it for continued improvement in 1988." *Bethlehem Review*, 1988 (1).

"At Sparrows Point, the plant had the highest level of shipments since 1979, and returned to profitability, which was also last recorded in 1979. The plant benefited from increased volume, improved realized prices for its product lines and top-level production by its continuous slab caster." *Bethlehem Review*, 1989 (1).

205   *"Every time it closed a plant"*   Carol J. Loomis, "The Sinking of Bethlehem Steel," *Fortune*, April 5, 2004, 182.

209   *the company had deposited*   *Bethlehem Review*, 1988 (2).

209   *"thus moving themselves largely out"*   Loomis, "Sinking of Bethlehem," 187. Though workers may not have been aware of this maneuver, other front-office financial bonanzas created great anger and resentment. For example, soon after asking for further concessions from steelworkers in 1993, Bethlehem's CEO, Curtis Barnette (who succeeded the retiring Williams in 1992), and four other top executives split a $1.3 million bonus. "Barnette also took a 30 percent raise, increasing his salary to $500,000 a year. The timing assured that relations with the work force would not be easily repaired." *The Morning Call*, 106.

210   *"I refer to this"*   U.S. Senate, *America's Pensions: The Next Savings and Loan Crisis, Hearing Before the Special Committee on Aging*, 108th Cong., 1st sess., October 14, 2003, serial no. 108–24 (Washington, D.C.: U.S. Government Printing Office), 137.

212   *Miller then tried to get*   Actually, the USW had fought for years to win protection of retiree benefits through federal legislation. Although a bipartisan bill— the Steel Industry Legacy Relief Act of 2002—had more than 225 cosponsors from both parties, enough for a majority in the House of Representatives, it was blocked by Republican leadership (with the support of the Bush administration), which refused to bring it to the floor for a vote.

212   *When Bethlehem entered bankruptcy*   "The company said it has arranged $450 million of financing from GE Capital, subject to bankruptcy court approval. Miller said the company's previous plan to arrange for $750 million in financing was no longer realistic in the current economic environment. But he said the $450 million of new financing is sufficient because none of it has to be used to refinance old debt, as much of the $750 million would have been. 'The $450 million is more than the $750 million by this math,' he said." Isidore, "Bethlehem Steel in Chapter 11."

213   *became the offering*   Via a February 6, 2003, letter to the Section 1114 Bank-

ruptcy Code Committee, proposing the termination of retiree benefits. On February 4, Beth Steel's executive committee and financial advisers had agreed to recommend the sale of Bethlehem's assets to ISG. The Bethlehem board voted to approve the sale on February 8. "As part of the agreement to sell Bethlehem's assets to ISG, neither party will assume retiree or health benefits or life insurance obligations, which averaged more than $19 million a month in 2002." USW president Leo Girard initially called the move "a morally callous act"— before agreeing to it. "For a bankrupt company that is doling out millions in golden parachutes to top executives to say that it must cost off the health care benefits of people who have worked a lifetime in the mills is a disgrace." "Bethlehem Seeks Health, Insurance Plan Termination," *Business Journal*, February 10, 2003, http://www.businessjournal.com/.

216 *"management considered its benefit promises"* Though by 1994, the company's health plan made up 6 percent of Bethlehem's total costs. "While wages had increased 38 percent since 1980, the company's health care costs increased 285 percent." Carol J. Loomis, "The Sinking of Bethlehem Steel," *Fortune*, April 5, 2004.

Bethlehem CEO Hank Burnette had been a strong supporter of the Clinton plan to provide universal health coverage. "Our nation's health care system is the most expensive in the world, and without change, it will cripple our ability to compete in the global market." *The Morning Call*, 107.

217 *a special tax credit program* A 65 percent tax credit for retirees aged fifty-five to sixty-four whose pensions are paid by the PBGC. Enrollment is not automatic but is reviewed on a case-by-case basis.

218 *Struggling to find affordable health care* Bethlehem filed its motion to eliminate retiree health care and life insurance benefits on February 6. Payment of benefits terminated on March 31, 2003.

220 *The men who negotiated the sale* Gus G. Sentementes, "Beth Steel CEO Got No Bonus," *The Baltimore Sun*, April 1, 2003. The article noted that Miller and Bethlehem's other chief executives "were denied bonuses and stock options as the company posted a $739 million loss while operating under Chapter 11 bankruptcy protection" but that Miller had received a salary of $75,000 per month since joining the company in September 2001.

Beth Steel's senior vice president and chief financial officer, Leonard M. Anthony, was paid $320,000 in 2002, a 55 percent increase over his 2001 salary.

Lawyers, accountants, and consultants involved in the bankruptcy also profited handsomely. "In total, law firms, accountants and advisers applied for $35 million in legal fees and about $1.8 million in expenses for Bethlehem's bankruptcy. Those fees, of course, take precedence over those from unsecured creditors." Dan Shope, "Some Made Millions from Steel Troubles," *The Morning Call*, December 21, 2003.

<h1 style="text-align:center">SCRAP</h1>

224   *"a completely employee-driven"*   Mary Ellen Beechner pointed out that ISG's management philosophy was similar to that of Nucor, a highly successful minimill. A new type of steel mill, the minimill is a fraction of the size of huge old integrated steelworks like Sparrows Point and produces steel from scrap, not ore. Nucor tore off big chunks of Bethlehem Steel's customer base in the nineties. After buying LTV and Bethlehem, ISG brought in former Nucor employees to run the mills, including Rodney Mott, former vice president and general manager of Nucor, who became president of the new company. Mark Reutter, *Making Steel: Sparrows Point and the Rise and Ruin of American Industrial Might* (Urbana: University of Illinois Press, 2004), 449–50. See also *The Morning Call*, 105.

225   *Friendly's Tavern*   By 2007, the tavern had closed.

225   *Sparrows Point steelworkers were making*   Under ISG, the workforce shrank from 3,500 to 2,600. Management was trimmed by 42 percent, and 850 workers accepted early retirement and buyout packages. Between 2003 and 2006, productivity at the Point rose 15 percent. "Feeling Pressure for Profits," *The Baltimore Sun*, May 14, 2006. "Our people are making more money than they ever did," said ex–general manager John Lefler. "Sure there are less of them, but they're doing well." Lorraine Mirabella, "International Steel Earned $24 Million in 4th: Bethlehem's Buyer Posts First Results as a Public Firm," *The Baltimore Sun*, February 27, 2004. See also "ISG Profits," Yahoo Finance, Thursday, February 26, 2004, http://biz.yahoo.com/prnews/040226/clth01z1.html.

225   *Wilbur Ross was hailed*   Matthew Benjamin, "The Commodity King," *U.S. News and World Report*, January 31, 2005. See also Daniel Gross, "The Bottom-Feeder King," *New York* magazine, November 8, 2004. "So long as companies fail—and the government stands as a pension backer of last resort—this genteel phoenix will keep on buying damaged goods that the market has given up on." For a more critical perspective on Ross, see Mark Reutter, "Looking at the Social Costs of the Bethlehem Steel Reorganization," speech delivered to the Great Lakes chapters of the Turnaround Management Association, May 18, 2006, http://www.makingsteel.com/.

226 *reaping its investors $4.5 billion*   Nicholas Stein, "Wilbur Ross Takes a Honey-moon," *Fortune*, November 29, 2004; Steven Pearlstein, "Ross Profits from Shunned Steel Assets," *Washington Post*, October 27, 2004. "According to TheDeal.com, the sale of ISG for cash and stock worth $4.5 billion will net Ross a 12-fold gain on the original $100 million investment from his private equity fund. Other early-stage equity investors, including Washington's own Howard Hughes Medical Institute, will enjoy a sevenfold gain on their initial $343 million stake. And those who bought shares for $28 at last year's IPO can satisfy themselves with a 50 percent return in less than a year."

226 *the largest steel company in the world*   Stanley Reed, "The Raja of Steel," *Business-Week*, December 20, 2004, http://www.businessweek.com/. See also Stanley Reed, "Mittal and Son," *BusinessWeek*, April 16, 2007, 45–52.

226 *merger with the Belgian steel giant*   "Mittal Launches $22.8 Billion Offer for Arce-lor," *The New York Times*, January 27, 2006; "Mittal Steel Executive Finds Support for Takeover Bid," *The New York Times*, February 21, 2006; Paul Maidment, "Lak-shmi Mittal's $19 Billion Year," *Forbes*, March 10, 2005, http://www.forbes.com/.

226 *the Justice Department notified*   "Justice Dept Requires Mittal Steel to Divest Sparrows Point Steel Mill," Justice Department press release, February 20, 2007. "The Department of Justice announced today that it will require Mittal Steel Company N.V. to divest its Sparrows Point facility located near Baltimore MD to remedy the competitive harm arising from Mittal's recent $33 billion acquisition of Arcelor S.A. The Department said the acquisition as originally proposed would have substantially lessened competition in the market for tin mill products in the eastern United States."

227 *"I'm a little skeptical"*   In July 2006, the L furnace broke down, halting produc-tion and forcing a monthlong layoff. The six-foot-tall L furnace was last relined in 1999 at a cost of more than $100 million; a number of sources have told me that the furnace needs relining again soon if the new owners expect to continue manufacturing iron on-site.

227 *half its actual value*   Lionel Laurent, "ArcelorMittal Deal a Steal for Severstal," *Forbes*, March 21, 2008.

228 *"like trying to hold water"*   David Welch, "Go Bankrupt, Then Go Overseas," *BusinessWeek*, April 24, 2006, http://www.businessweek.com/. "Miller [Bethle-hem's last CEO, now at Delphi] doesn't talk much publicly about his goals for fear of further inflaming an already outraged UAW, but the gist of Delphi's plan is apparent in its bankruptcy filings. . . . Its reorganization plan would ditch everything in the U.S. except safety technology, radios, information and enter-tainment systems, electronics, wiring, and engine controls. . . . To pull off a

downsizing of that scale, Delphi would close or sell 21 of 29 plants it has identi-fied as noncore businesses, according to the filings. An additional 12 plants are not named in the reorganization plan, but a company spokesman says some of those will go, too."

228   *corporate power was operating with no checks*   Between 1979 and 2005, the top 5 percent of American families saw their real incomes increase 81 percent. Over the same period, the lowest-income fifth saw their real incomes decline 1 per-cent. In 1979, the average income of the top 5 percent of families was 11.4 times as large as the average income of the bottom 20 percent. In 2005, the ratio was 20.9 times. See http://www.demos.org/inequality/numbers.cfm for more data and graphs.

230   *a fiery speech that Richard Trumka*   AFL-CIO's Richard Trumka on Racism and Obama, http://www.youtube.com/watch?v=7QIGJTHdH50.

230   *I looked at the raw data*   http://resources.baltimorecountymd.gov/Documents/Elections/pollingplaces1107.pdf and http://www.elections.state.md.us/elections/2008/election_data/Baltimore_By_Precinct_2008_General.csv.

231   *the Taft-Hartley Act*   The passage of the Taft-Hartley Act "was the culmination of the larger postwar political effort to sever the ties tentatively established dur-ing the New Deal between labor unions and the government." Philip Murray denounced the act in scathing terms: "The Taft-Hartley bill was conceived in sin; its promoters were diabolical men who, seething with hatred, contrived this ugly measure for the purpose of imposing their wrath upon the millions of workers." Ronald W. Schatz, "Battling over Government's Role," in *Forging a Union of Steel: Philip Murray, SWOC, and the United Steelworkers*, ed. Paul F. Clark, Peter Gottlieb, and Donald Kennedy (Ithaca, N.Y.: ILR Press, 1987), 92–94.

231   *why labor no longer organizes*   Thomas Geoghegan, *Which Side Are You On?: Try-ing to Be for Labor When It's Flat on Its Back* (New York: Farrar, Straus and Giroux, 1991), 52.

232   *corporate profits*   Rex Nutting, "Profits Surge to 40-Year High," MarketWatch, March 30, 2006, http://www.marketwatch.com/.

233   *the median wage of a full-time American worker*   According to the Economic Pol-icy Institute, as union membership declines, from roughly one-quarter of the workforce in the late 1970s to barely one-eighth in 2004, wages fall "not only because some workers no longer receive the higher union wage rate, but also because there is less pressure on non-union employers to raise wages." In 2003, "the average blue-collar union job paid $30.76 an hour in wages and benefits, compared with $18.11 for the nonunion job." One consequence: "47 percent of the real national income growth has gone to corporate profits, and only 15 per-

cent to wages and salaries" and recovery from the 2001 recession "is the first post–World War II recovery in which corporate profits grabbed a bigger share of the growth than workers' pay and benefits." David S. Broder, "The Price of Labor's Decline," *The Washington Post*, September 9, 2004.

233 *the United Workers won a living wage*   "Living Wage Victory at Camden Yards," http://www.unitedworkers.org.

234 *The proportion of American workers*   Richard B. Freeman, "Do Workers Still Want Unions? More Than Ever," EPI Briefing Paper #182, February 22, 2007, Economic Policy Institute, Washington, D.C.

234 *employees who try to form a union*   Kate Bronfenbrenner, "No Holds Barred: The Intensification of Employer Opposition to Organizing," EPI Briefing Paper #235, May 20, 2009, Economic Policy Institute, Washington, D.C.

SOURCES

ARCHIVES

Baltimore Museum of Industry
Dundalk–Patapsco Neck Historical Society
Enoch Pratt Free Library
Hagley Museum and Library
Historical Society of Baltimore County
Maryland Historical Society

PRIVATE COLLECTIONS

Joe Lawrence
Melvin Schmeiser
Len Shindel
Albert Wolfkill

BOOKS

Argersinger, Jo Ann E. *Toward a New Deal in Baltimore: People and Government in the Great Depression.* Chapel Hill: University of North Carolina Press, 1988.

Bezis-Selfa, John. "Forging a New Order: Slavery, Free Labor, and Sectional Differentiation in the Mid-Atlantic Charcoal Iron Industry, 1715–1840." Ph.D. diss., University of Pennsylvania, 1995.

Brody, David. *Steelworkers in America: The Nonunion Era.* Cambridge, Mass.: Harvard University Press, 1960.

Brooks, Neal A., and Eric G. Rockel. *A History of Baltimore County.* Towson, Md.: Friends of the Towson Library, 1979.

Clark, Paul F., Peter Gottlieb, and Donald Kennedy, eds. *Forging a Union of Steel: Philip Murray, SWOC, and the United Steelworkers.* Ithaca, N.Y.: ILR Press, 1987.

Dickerson, Dennis C. *Out of the Crucible: Black Steelworkers in Western Pennsylvania, 1875–1980.* Albany: State University of New York Press, 1986.

Diggs, Louis S. *From the Meadows to the Point: The Histories of the African American Community in Sparrows Point.* Self-published, 2003.

Durr, Kenneth D. *Behind the Backlash: White Working-Class Politics in Baltimore, 1940–1980.* Chapel Hill: University of North Carolina Press, 2003.

Geoghegan, Thomas. *Which Side Are You On?: Trying to Be for Labor When It's Flat on Its Back.* New York: Farrar, Straus and Giroux, 1991.

Helton, Gary. *Dundalk, Maryland.* Charleston, S.C.: Arcadia Publishing, 2006.

Herling, John. *Right to Challenge: People and Power in the Steelworkers Union.* New York: Harper and Row, 1972.

Hoerr, John P. *And the Wolf Finally Came: The Decline of the American Steel Industry.* Pittsburgh: University of Pittsburgh Press, 1988.

Lovis, John B. *The Blast Furnaces of Sparrows Point: One Hundred Years of Ironmaking on Chesapeake Bay.* Easton, Pa.: Canal History and Technology Press, 2005.

Metz, Lance E. "A Short History of the Bethlehem Steel Corporation." In Andrew Garn, *Bethlehem Steel.* New York: Princeton Architectural Press, 1999.

Metzgar, Jack. *Striking Steel: Solidarity Remembered.* Philadelphia: Temple University Press, 2000.

Nyden, Philip W. *Steelworkers Rank-and-File: The Political Economy of a Union Reform Movement.* New York: Praeger, 1984.

Olson, Karen. *Wives of Steel: Voices of Women from the Sparrows Point Steelmaking Communities.* University Park: Pennsylvania State University Press, 2005.

Rabinbach, Anson. *The Human Motor: Energy, Fatigue, and the Origins of Modernity.* Berkeley: University of California Press, 1992.

Reutter, Mark. *Making Steel: Sparrows Point and the Rise and Ruin of American Industrial Might*. Urbana: University of Illinois Press, 2004.

Steffen, Charles G. *From Gentlemen to Townsmen: The Gentry of Baltimore County, Maryland, 1660–1776*. Lexington: University Press of Kentucky, 1993.

Strohmeyer, John. *Crisis in Bethlehem: Big Steel's Struggle to Survive*. Pittsburgh: University of Pittsburgh Press, 1986.

Zieger, Robert H., and Gilbert J. Gall. *American Workers, American Unions: The Twentieth Century*. 3rd ed. Baltimore: Johns Hopkins University Press, 2002.

ORAL HISTORY

Lawrence Ageloff

Manuel Alvarez

Bill Barry

Eddie Bartee Sr.

Mary Ellen Beechner

Deidra Bishop

John Burleigh

Roosevelt Caldwell

Thomas Capecci

William Cohill

Neil Crowder

Blaine DeWitt

Lee Douglas Jr.

Wendell Doyle

Ed Gorman

Kenneth L. Johnson

Knoerlein family

Joseph Kotelchuck

Eugene "Tank" Levy

Donald Lindemann

Cliff Lockman

Mary Lorenzo

Judy Martin

Austin McLelland

LeRoy McLelland Sr.

Wayne Morris

Phyllis Moskowitz
John Moyer
Julie Poholorec
Darlene Redemann
Mark Reutter
Jean A. Rudacille
Jeffrey R. Rudacille
Raymond V. Rudacille
Roderick Ryon
Melvin and Alice Schmeiser
Jessie Schultz
Peter Selhorst
Len Shindel
Gresham Hertt Somerville
Robert and Nonnie Strasbaugh
Gary Valentine
Rose Marie Weller
Harry and Donna Young

Individuals quoted but not listed above were encountered at retirees' meetings of
Locals 2609 and 2610, the Our Lady of Fatima Social Club, the bungalows reunion,
the Steel Bowl reunion, the Dundalk Fourth of July celebration, or were interviewed
on the telephone.

INDEX

A NOTE ABOUT THE AUTHOR

Deborah Rudacille earned a Master of Arts degree from the Writing Seminars at Johns Hopkins University in 1998. Since then, she has published two nonfiction books, *The Scalpel and the Butterfly: The War Between Animal Research and Animal Protection* (Farrar, Straus and Giroux, 2000) and *The Riddle of Gender: Science, Activism, and Transgender Rights* (Pantheon, 2005). She has lived in Baltimore all of her life.

A NOTE ON THE TYPE

This book was set in Janson, a typeface long thought to have been made by the Dutchman Anton Janson, who was a practicing type-founder in Leipzig during the years 1668–1687. However, it has been conclusively demonstrated that these types are actually the work of Nicholas Kis (1650–1702), a Hungarian, who most proba-bly learned his trade from the master Dutch typefounder Dirk Voskens. The type is an excellent example of the influential and sturdy Dutch types that prevailed in England up to the time William Caslon (1692–1766) developed his own incomparable designs from them.

Composed by Creative Graphics,
Allentown, Pennsylvania

Printed and bound by Berryville Graphics,
Berryville, Virginia

Designed by Soonyoung Kwon